This Calls for a Drink!

THE BEST WINES & BEERS TO PAIR WITH EVERY SITUATION

By Diane McMartin

Workman Publishing
New York

Illustrations by Jen Kruch
Cover design by Jean-Marc Troadec
Oscar statuette on page 157 © A.M.P.A.S.(R)

Library of Congress Cataloging-in-Publication Data is available.

ISBN 978-0-7611-8484-3

Workman books are available at special discounts when purchased in bulk for premiums and sales promotions as well as for fund-raising or educational use. Special editions or book excerpts can also be created to specification. For details, contact the Special Sales Director at the address below, or send an email to specialmarkets@workman.com.

Workman Publishing Co., Inc.
225 Varick Street
New York, NY 10014
workman.com

WORKMAN is a registered trademark of Workman Publishing Co., Inc.

Printed in China
First printing June 2016

10 9 8 7 6 5 4 3 2 1

Contents

Introduction. v

The Basics. 1
Learn to Taste Wine and Beer without Losing Your Mind • Buying Wine
and Beer • Wine Labels Demystified • Glassware, Tools, and Other
Potential Rip-Offs

Dating, Mating, Rejection, and Heartbreak 31
Breakups • Online Dating • One-Night Stands • Family Matters •
Social Media Stalking • Your New Crush

Just Us Girls 63
A Trashy Girls' Night • Secret Single Behavior • Time-Consuming
Beauty Rituals

Growing Up and Getting Older 77
Your "Big" Birthday • Discovering Signs of Aging • Class Reunions •
Graduation • Thwarted Childhood Fantasies

The Holidays 103
Avoiding Mall Vertigo: Choosing Wine and Beer as Gifts • Hosting
Thanksgiving • Halloween • Your New Year's Resolution Diet •
Minor Holidays

Home and Hosting. 129
Roommates • Stuck Inside: Hurricanes, Tornadoes, and Other Climate
Change–Induced Severe Weather • Your New Home • Theme Parties •
Pretending to Be a Grown-Up (Dinner Parties)

Movies and Television **151**
Classic-Movie Night • Dress Snarking: Sparkling Cocktails for Awards-Show Season • Your Next Netflix Binge

Music **165**
Your Favorite Music • Music Festivals, or, Drowning Out the Stench of Patchouli and Weed

Reading **175**
Aspirational Magazines • Important Novels You Pretend to Have Read (or Can Barely Remember . . .)

Summer **187**
Embarrassing Yourself in the Great Outdoors • Other People's Vacations • Summer Trips • Your Overpriced Farmers' Market Bounty

Weddings **207**
Your Best Friend's Wedding • Your Proposal

Spawning **217**
Baby Showers • Learning the Ropes

Work **231**
Your "Just for Now" Job • Work Functions • Career Milestones

Glossary **246**

Online Resources **253**

Acknowledgments **256**

Index **257**

Introduction

When you're the person who knows about wine among your friends and family, you're asked a lot of questions: What should I order on a date? How do I choose wine for my wedding? What goes with meat loaf?

A couple of years ago, I arrived home to find my roommate sprawled on the couch looking miserable.

"What's wrong?" I asked.

"I got dumped. Again." I headed to the freezer to look for ice cream. "What wine goes with a bad breakup?" she moaned.

That day, the answer turned out to be cheap rosé, because that's what I had, but from then on, I began thinking about pairing wine and beer with situations and feelings, rather than just sauces and salads.

Food & Wine has you covered for that heritage pork roast with the price tag that made you wince at the register at Whole Foods, but what about the blind date you're dreading and anticipating in equal measure? And what should you sip while Google-stalking your high school crushes? You definitely need an adult beverage for that. Inspired by my roommate's dilemma, I started writing columns for *The Hairpin* that paired wine and other beverages with situations ranging from first dates to road trips, and readers responded to them in a way I never expected. I realized that people really need a way to talk about wine and beer that reflects how we live now. No one's coming home after a long day at work and making a complicated poached fish and beurre blanc and pairing it with the perfect Chablis. We're drinking while camping, or celebrating getting promoted with our friends, or solo-sipping on the couch while watching trashy television and eating greasy Thai food, or attempting home hair color in a really ugly bathrobe.

In this book, I hope to give you some inspiration and helpful information, but mostly I want to give you the freedom to have fun with what you're drinking. On a similar note, this is the kind of book you can dip into at any point, depending on your interests at that moment. No need to start right at the beginning and dutifully take notes—if you're drinking for fun and enjoyment, there's no need to be slavish about it. If you want a little information on how to taste beer and wine or what the heck kind of glassware to buy, start with "The Basics." But feel free to skip to the relevant chapters to figure out what to order on your date with that promising, but maybe slightly too bro-y guy from Tinder (page 38) or what to drink when you've finally finished your Ph.D. (page 94).

While these pairings are all meant to be fun and lighthearted—I mean, really, you don't need a drink for EVERY life situation; sometimes what you need is to drink some herbal tea, call your mom, and go to bed at a reasonable hour—I didn't want to leave you wondering what the hell hops actually *are*, or what wine critics are talking about when they call Chardonnay "buttery." So, I've included sidebars, along with a few longer essays, to help you navigate the often overwhelming world of wine and beer.

For each situation, I recommend a style of wine or beer, then one to three producers or brands that I consider good examples of that style. But here's a little advice about those specific examples: Don't get too hung up on them. Because the end of Prohibition left alcohol regulation up to the individual states, there is a *huge* amount of variation when it comes to what's available in each local market in this country. I recommend certain producers and brands that I love, but they may not be available where you are. We'll get more in-depth on buying wine and beer on page 6, but I actually don't recommend spending a lot of time hunting down a specific name I mention and ordering it blind from some store you find on the Internet that happens to carry it. Find a store that sells beer and/or wine where you feel comfortable, and if you can't find what I've recommended, ask if they can show you something similar. Say you're looking for the Guy Larmandier Blanc de Blancs Champagne that I recommend on page 81. A good retail assistant, even if she's never had that Champagne, will be able to pull the salient details from the name and description and find you a sparkler in a similar style. Who knows, it might be even better than what I recommended!

There is so much wine and beer out there, I can't even come close to tasting it all, and that's part of the fun. I hope these pairings make you laugh, inspire you to try something new, and maybe take the sting out of that breakup.

Cheers,
Diane McMartin

The Basics

Nothing should stand between you and your enjoyment of wine and beer, especially not intimidation created by flowery reviews and giant restaurant wine lists that look like doorstops. With that in mind, here are some tips to help you navigate tasting and buying wine and beer, a quick and dirty primer on reading wine labels, and a guide to buying glassware and other assorted gadgetry without bankrupting yourself.

Learn to Taste Wine, and Beer without, Losing Your Mind,

I n the already fraught world of beverages, tasting "properly" is probably the most fraught subject of all. The biggest thing that I try to drive home to my customers and students is that you are a much better taster than you think you are. Seriously, unless you're anosmic (my nightmare!), you've got the same basic equipment as top sommeliers and wine critics who make comparisons to things you've never heard of. My favorite are the writers who use British terms like "petrol," when they're from Wisconsin or something. Take off your monocle, buddy, you're not fooling anyone.

The main reason for all these outlandish descriptions is that people in the wine and beer trade are often trying to differentiate between a group of very similar beverages. In this kind of situation, your brain starts to filter out what's the same about them, and focus on what's different. What wouldn't even be noticeable to a novice becomes an incredibly evocative aroma of hot pavement on a summer day, or the flavor of fresh-baked cinnamon rolls. It's the same reason Sephora is able to carry about 10,000 shades of red lipstick and the sales assistants can give you a dissertation on the differences in undertone and texture in all of them—they stare at them all day, so of course they can! There is also some evidence that tasting analytically, the way beer and wine professionals do, actually changes the structure of your brain. When untrained tasters smell wine, the emotion- and memory-focused parts of their brains light up. Trained tasters tend to show activity in the analytical areas of the brain and more neural networks connecting those analytical areas with the emotional and memory-focused areas.

The more beer and wine you try, the more you'll taste the bright grapefruit flavors of American hops, or smell those tarry, leathery aromas in Nebbiolo, and you may even change your brain! Here are a few tips to get started.

Grab a decent glass.

No need to break the bank here, but using something a few steps up from those terrible thimble-like wineglasses you see at shitty Italian restaurants will go a long way toward your enjoyment of adult beverages. See page 20 for more information on glassware.

Look.

You can tell a lot about beer or wine from its color. For example, darker beer can indicate beer brewed with darker malt, and darker white wine can indicate advanced age or oak aging. And what about those "legs" that wine geeks are always banging on about? It relates to those tears that form on the side of your glass. The thicker and slower moving those tears are, the fuller-bodied the wine is likely to be. As you take the time to look at what you're drinking, you'll start to notice more and more nuances in wine's and beer's color and appearance, and learn what those differences mean to you.

Swirl.

Like the whole "legs" thing, swirling is another aspect of wine tasting that can get a little overwrought and pretentious. All you have to do is gently swirl your glass (you can use a table for support if you need to). You don't need to turn your wineglass into a fucking centrifuge. We're not trying to split the atom here. With carbonated beverages like sparkling wine and beer, you should be really gentle. All you're doing when swirling is getting some of those compounds that make these delicious fermented beverages smell like they do into the air, and thus, closer to your nose. As enticing as a glass filled with delicious beer and a foamy head pushing over the top is, when you're

You don't need to turn your wineglass into a fucking centrifuge. We're not trying to split the atom here.

tasting to learn a little bit more about what you're drinking, you'll get more out of that brew if you leave some room at the top of the glass.

Sniff.

I like to take a whiff of what I'm about to taste both before and after swirling. You'll notice that you pick up on different aspects that way. Really get your honker in there and breathe in. I find it helpful to divide aromas into 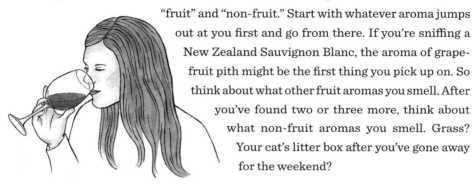 "fruit" and "non-fruit." Start with whatever aroma jumps out at you first and go from there. If you're sniffing a New Zealand Sauvignon Blanc, the aroma of grapefruit pith might be the first thing you pick up on. So think about what other fruit aromas you smell. After you've found two or three more, think about what non-fruit aromas you smell. Grass? Your cat's litter box after you've gone away for the weekend?

Taste.

Getting a little bit of air into your mouth as you're tasting will help you pick up on more nuances, for the same reason swirling does when you're smelling. You don't have to gargle like you're auditioning for a mouthwash commercial. When I teach classes, I make a big deal out of slurping loudly so that folks can hear me and they understand it's OK to make a bit of noise, but on your own or in a restaurant, you can just pull in a little bit of air and quietly slurp. Getting this air into your mouth helps aromas travel from the back of your throat up into the olfactory neurons, a process called retronasal stimulation. Bodies are weird, aren't they? Also, after you swallow (or spit, if you spend half your professional life spitting wine into gross communal spit buckets like I do), inhale a little bit and see what other flavors you pick up. You might be surprised!

See if those same fruit and non-fruit aromas are present, or if anything new pops up. Other things to think about when the wine or beer is actually in your mouth are how light or heavy it is; how tart, bitter, or sweet it is; and, if there are bubbles, what kind of texture those bubbles create in your mouth. Tannin is another element that isn't exactly a taste, but more of a drying sensation on your palate. Do you feel a chalky sensation, like you swallowed a piece of felt? That's tannin.

Wait for what lingers.

Finish is just a fancy way of saying "aftertaste." What flavors or sensations linger on your palate after you've swallowed? Do you taste a lingering sweetness? Does your mouth feel fresh and clean? Do you taste those blackberries and plums you picked up on while the wine was actually in your mouth? When those flavors hang around for a long time in a pleasant way, the wine in question is thought to have a long finish, which can be a sign of quality. But if you didn't like the wine in the first place, you might wish it didn't linger so long! I once read a hilarious review in which the writer referred to the finish as "mercifully short." Ha!

Share and remember.

I've read so many books and articles that recommend you carry around a little notebook and jot down notes about what you've tasted, but I think this is completely crap advice for most people. When I'm at a serious class or tasting, or when I'm tasting for work, I take notes, either on a laptop, in a notepad, or on index cards. But when I'm out with my friends or just hanging out at home with my roommates and our neurotic cats, and *especially* if I'm at a crowded walk-around tasting or at a winery or brewery, it's just not practical. If you like taking notes or your memory works best that way, by all means, rock out with your Moleskine, but I've found that most people, myself included, abandon this practice pretty quickly. What works a lot better is to just do what you're probably already doing with your smartphone— documenting your life—and snap a photo of things that you especially liked or thought were interesting. If you want to be able to try more things in that general category, try to get a good, clear shot of the label. It will help you remember what the beer or wine was called, obviously, and will be enormously helpful to the bartender or retail assistant you may be asking for a recommendation.

There are dozens of apps out there for wine and beer, and there will probably be dozens more by the time you read this. They're fun to play around with, but I find a lot of them are cumbersome to use. Instead, I keep drink photos on my computer, and upload those I've especially enjoyed or want to remember to Facebook or Instagram with my thoughts.

This brings me to my next point about learning to taste—you'll learn so much more if you share your thoughts and experiences with other people, whether it's on social media or in person. Other people often pick up on things that you've missed, and it just makes it more fun!

Buying Wine and Beer

Whether you're in a retail or restaurant setting, the best advice I can give is to ask for help. Once you've found a restaurant sommelier, bartender, or retail employee who seems actually interested in helping you, you've struck gold. We beverage weirdos are usually thrilled that someone is interested in what we do and wants more than just a recommendation for an oaky $20 Chardonnay to take to a dinner party. Don't get me wrong, those folks help us keep our jobs, so I'm happy to help them, but when I meet someone who wants to learn more? I usually get so excited that I end up practically inviting them over for dinner and they probably leave thinking I'm an awkward creeper. Anyway, here are some dos and don'ts for navigating stores and restaurants.

At the Store

Ask questions. Most of us are so wary of overly enthusiastic sales assistants who will try to push things we don't want on us that our first instinct is to say we don't need any help. I'm guilty of doing this myself! But if you push past that urge and engage with the sales assistant right off the bat, you'll have a much better experience and probably save time in the long run. Wondering why all the Pinot Noirs are so expensive? Are stouts really the best beer to have with oysters? Want to know what's the best Chardonnay to have with shrimp? Ask! And if you're new to the store, ask how the store is laid out. I make a point of going to wineshops and beer stores in every city I visit. My traveling companions love this fun compulsion of mine. From all these visits, I've learned that every store is laid out a little bit differently. If you're looking for Italian reds or Belgian tripels and you're not seeing them, ask for a tour of the store!

Form a relationship. Sure, bargain hunting is fun, but unless you're a true hobbyist and you know exactly what you're hunting for, you'll do much better in the long run if you form a relationship with the staff and have them recommend things to you. I love having an ongoing relationship with my customers and getting to know what they like and don't like. If something I know they'll love goes on sale, I make a point of showing it to them, and sometimes even write them a personal email to let them know. Sure, it's a sales technique, but it's one that benefits the customer. If you buddy up to your favorite staff member at your local wine/beer store, you may find the same thing happening to you.

If you're worried about being taken advantage of, well, keep in mind that wine and beer shops aren't exactly a haven for the true sharks of the sales world. People tend to get into the beverage and hospitality industry because they love it, not because they're great salespeople. Ninety-nine percent of people in the wine and beer industry aren't in it for the money. The top executives at huge wine companies like Constellation, and famous wine consultants like Michel Rolland, are getting rich. The rest of us are doing it because it's our passion.

Don't be afraid to give feedback! Let the employees at your local beverage emporium know what you liked and didn't like. We want to know, trust me! The more information you give the staff, the better they'll do at recommending things to you. Then, when you're looking for a special bottle for your anniversary dinner or what have you, you can be much more certain it'll be something you'll love, because that splurge bottle will be handpicked with your taste in mind. Recently, I had a customer email me asking me to put together a case of whites for him, and he mentioned that the last time I chose wine, he thought the whites were a little thin and watery. This is great to know! Now I have more information about him—I already knew he didn't like whites with too much oak influence, and now I know he likes a little more body, as well. He was much happier with the next group of wines I put together for him. When giving feedback, don't worry about using the right terminology, or butchering the pronunciation of a wine region—any information is good information.

At the Restaurant: Mastering the Wine List

Feel out the place. If you're in a big-name steakhouse or a hotel restaurant that's part of a major chain, now is not the time to get adventurous. This is the time to stick with a classic, full-bodied American red and follow the safe ordering steps covered in the "Weddings" chapter, on pages 208–209. If the restaurant has a quirky vibe and you see more on the wine list than big brands like Cakebread and Santa Margherita, branch out and try something you've never heard of.

Don't assume the least expensive wine is the best value. That's usually there for people who still want to order a bottle, but are intimidated by the list. The best values are often the wines that the sommelier loves and wishes people would order more. This is why talking to the staff is always such a good idea.

Ask to talk to the sommelier or beverage director and name a price point. If you have a budget, seriously, this is such a relief! And don't assume the sommelier will up-sell you to something ridiculous. Again, most people in the wine business are in it because they love it. Especially at a restaurant with an adventurous wine list, the wine director or sommelier is probably just a huge geek wearing a suit. Let him or her know what you like and what you're in the mood for, and see what happens. Don't worry that you're wasting their time because you're not in the market for $400 Champagne. When I worked in restaurants, I was always much more excited for the "average" customers who would say something like, "We're having XYZ and want to try something new—what's great for less than sixty dollars?" than the customers who rolled in with their giant watches and just ordered Krug and waved me away. Despite all the crazy stories you might have read in *Kitchen Confidential*, most folks in the hospitality industry are people pleasers. We want you to be happy and to help you have a great experience. The same goes for bartenders and staff in restaurants with a big beer program.

I've read dozens of books on wine and beer, taken classes, and made enough flashcards to stock my own Staples store. But I don't know everything, and thank goodness for that! When I go out, I try to take off my expert hat and ask the staff what they think is great. What's new on draft that I have to try? What bottle do people never order that you wish they would? I'm never sorry for having done this.

ʻWine Labels, ʻDemystified.

This is a subject that could easily become huge and unwieldy, so I'm going to keep things as quick and simple as possible. Wine labels can tell you a lot about both what's in the bottle, and what's important to the region in which that wine is made. Is the winery's name in huge, ornate letters? It's probably from a region like Bordeaux or the Napa Valley where the style of the producer has a huge influence over how the wine will taste. When you see the name of a place more prominently on the label, and the producer's name is a bit smaller or less conspicuous, that's a clue that in that wine region, terroir—the characteristics of specific plots of land—and weather are considered to be super important and have a big influence over how the wine will taste. These rules of thumb aren't universally true, of course, but take a closer look at wine labels and you'll start to notice these kinds of patterns.

We're focusing mostly on Europe here, because these tend to be the most confusing. In places like Australia, South Africa, and the United States, wines are labeled with the name of the grape, making it much easier for us hapless consumers. (Note: All wineries on labels in this section are fictitious.)

French wine labels

French labels are tough, because here in the United States, we're used to the name of the grape being on the bottle. Merlot, Pinot Noir, Chardonnay—these grape names are, to us, what the wine *is*. On a French label, none of that stuff is there. So, what the heck *is* it?

To the French, a wine is defined by where it's from. A wine *is* Côtes du Rhône or Bourgogne. Every French wine region has a different way of ranking quality, and a different point of view on making wine. What grape or grapes go into it are secondary to the place where they're grown. There's also the fact that every region has rules about what grapes you can grow where, so if you know what grapes they grow in Burgundy (Pinot Noir for reds or Chardonnay for whites) or Bordeaux (blends of Cabernet, Merlot, Malbec, Cabernet Franc, and/or Petit Verdot for reds, and blends of Sauvignon Blanc, Muscadelle, and/or Sémillon for whites), then you don't need it to be on the label. The French are coming around to the fact that many consumers outside of Europe relate to wine based on the grape variety, so in some cases it's becoming accepted to put the name of the grape variety on the label. But the French are very traditional and slow to change when it comes to their prized agricultural products like wine, mustard, butter, and the like, so this is going to be a slow, gradual change, and the naming conventions for top wines will likely stay place-based forever.

You can get a good idea of a region's point of view by what's most prominent on the label. In **Bordeaux**, for example, the name of the producer is usually front and center, because in Bordeaux the producer's style is considered to be most important, and producers are ranked in order of their reputation for quality. Let's dissect a label from Bordeaux a little more closely. So what does this label tell us?

1. **Producer:** Château Sophistiqué. See how ginormous Château Sophistiqué is on the label, looming over the name of the place? Let's say this fictional winery was part of the historic 1855 classification that ranked all the well-known Bordeaux wineries  according to reputation and quality. If that were the case, they'd really want to make sure you saw their famous name!

2. **Appellation (location):** Saint-Estèphe is a subregion of Bordeaux's Left Bank, an area known for reds that are mostly Cabernet Sauvignon. So, even if you didn't know anything about this wine, but you knew that

Saint-Estèphe was on the Left Bank, you'd know that the wine would likely be mostly Cabernet. You just wouldn't know exactly what percentage they're using and how much Merlot, Petit Verdot, or Cabernet Franc they're using as blending partners.

3. **Ranking:** Deuxième Cru Classé. In Bordeaux, where the style and reputation of the winery is paramount, even subregions have their own historic ranking systems. In the Médoc, where Saint-Estèphe is located, Premier Cru Classé, or First Growth, is the highest ranking and Deuxième Cru Classé, or Second Growth, is the second-highest.

In **Burgundy**, on the other hand, they're obsessed with ranking every teensy little patch of land, so what's most prominent on the label will be something place-related, either a village or a specific vineyard. On the label below, you can see that the name of the village, Gevrey-Chambertin, is in giant letters. Next is the name of the vineyard where the grapes were grown, "Les Champonnets," and its quality ranking, 1er Cru, which is *aaalmost* as good as Grand Cru, but not quite. The name of the producer is underneath all that. The winemaker knows that what will sell the wine is those famous village and vineyard names, not his own!

1. **Producer:** Domaine Jean Valjean et Fille. Notice there's no proprietary name like we often give wines in the United States, like Shafer One Point Five. In Burgundy, for the most part, they let the place name speak for itself.

2. **Appellation:** If it's red wine, and it's grown in Burgundy (you can see "Red Burgundy Wine" in small letters right above the producer's name), it's gotta be Pinot Noir. So, that's out of the way. Now, the label

is screaming "Gevrey-Chambertin" at us, right? Well, that's because within Burgundy, Gevrey-Chambertin is a village famous for its red wines. And it's telling us that it's not just from a specific village, but a specific vineyard, called Les Champonnets.

3. **Ranking:** This specific vineyard's quality ranking is Premier Cru, usually denoted 1er Cru on labels to save room. There are three vineyard quality rankings in Burgundy: *Lieu Dit* ("named place"—not officially ranked, but good enough to mention on the label), Premier Cru, and the highest, Grand Cru.

Even with these basics, you'll probably need help deciphering a label from Bordeaux or Burgundy. With both of these classic regions, my best advice is to ask questions, and start small. Ask for help from your local wineshop—describe the style of wine you like and choose a not-too-expensive option from whatever producer or subregion the sales assistant recommends. This is the easiest way to figure out if, say, you prefer a Cabernet-heavy Left Bank Bordeaux or a slightly softer Merlot-based Right Bank, or if you prefer a steely, crisp Chablis or a rich Meursault when it comes to white Burgundy.

In **Champagne**, labels get a little more complicated. The thing about Champagne is that, more so than other styles of wine, it's a "made" wine. It takes a lot of manipulation to trap those bubbles in the bottle, remove the sediment, and cork it properly (see pages 80–81). Add to this the fact that the Champenois are savvy marketers, and you have a recipe for a bevy of different terms that you see on bottles to justify their high price. Some of these terms have a concrete legal definition, and others are more like marketing terms—i.e., BS! Here are a few to look out for:

• **1er Cru and Grand Cru:** Just like Burgundy, Champagne has a ranking system that is tied to the quality reputation of different pieces of land. However, instead of ranking vineyards, in Champagne the villages are ranked. **1er Cru** (Premier Cru) means the grapes come from the second-best batch of villages, and **Grand Cru** means they come from the best.

Occasionally, these terms are used to indicate the grapes grown in the village: 1er Cru for Pinot Noir, say, and Grand Cru for Chardonnay. The French like to make things as complicated as possible.

- **Blanc de blancs** means "white from whites," and in Champagne speak, this means a white sparkling wine that's made from all-white grapes. Since the only white grape grown in any real quantity in Champagne is Chardonnay, this means a sparkling wine made from only Chardonnay grapes.

- **Blanc de noirs** means "white from blacks/darks," and it's a term used in sparkling winemaking to denote white wine made from red grapes. (Did you know that most red grapes are actually white inside?) By pressing the juice out of red grapes very quickly, you can make a white wine out of them. You can also just give the skins a little time with the juice and create a style of extremely light pink sparkling wine that in Champagne they call *Oeil de Perdrix*, which means "eye of partridge." Why is that an appealing descriptor? Well, the French also use "cabbage" as a term of endearment, so, you know, every culture is different.

- *Cuvée* is a term that doesn't have a great direct English translation. It means "selection," or a specific cask or group of casks of wine. In Champagne, however, it refers to the first pressing of the grapes, considered to be the highest-quality juice.

- *Tête de cuvée* doesn't have a strict legal definition, but it is used to describe the best, most expensive Champagne that a house makes. Let's take Veuve Clicquot as an example. That bottle with the distinctive yellow-orange label you see everywhere is the least expensive Champagne they make, and the one they make in the largest quantity. Their *tête de cuvée* is called La Grande Dame. It's a single-vintage Champagne that is made in smaller quantities, and is much more fussed-over and expensive.

- *RM* stands for *Récoltant-Manipulant*, which means that the people who grow the grapes also make the wine. It's like the Champagne version of being on an indie record label. These are also called "Grower Champagnes."

- **NM** stands for *Négociant-Manipulant*, which means that it's a Champagne house that buys grapes from multiple growers. NMs are the big guys like Mumm and Veuve Clicquot.

- **Clos** is a term you sometimes see on descriptions of specific vineyards, like Clos du Mesnil. It just means "enclosed," so it refers to the fact that the wine comes from a specific vineyard, or from a specific enclosure within a vineyard.

- **Brut Nature/Brut Zero/Brut Sauvage** are Champagnes that aren't given any *dosage* before they're corked. *Dosage* is a little bit of sugar or sweetened wine added to Champagne, meant to balance the high acidity that naturally occurs in grapes grown in cool climates. Champagnes that aren't given any of this balancing sweetness are something of a hot trend right now. Some no-*dosage* Champagnes are really wonderful (Cédric Bouchard's are fantastic, but not cheap, in the $100–$200 range). But often, these wines are just trendy bullshit that no one's really enjoying drinking—they just want to seem cool.

Italian wine labels

Italy: the bane of wine students everywhere. With hundreds of indigenous grape varieties and designated wine styles, it's tough to get a handle on. For the most part, Italian wines are named either for the place where they're grown, like you see in most of France, or for the grape and place of origin.

As with French labels, the location will provide plenty of clues about the wine. The two most famous Italian red wine regions are Tuscany, where the tart **Sangiovese** is the main grape, and the Piedmont, where the tannic **Nebbiolo** grape is king. If you see Tuscan areas like **Chianti**, **Montalcino**, or **Montepulciano** on the label, you can be sure that the wine is made from all or mostly Sangiovese. Likewise, if you see a label bearing the names of towns in the Piedmont like **Barolo** or **Barbaresco**, you can bet it's Nebbiolo-based.

Let's take a look at a Chianti label.

1. **Producer:** Castello dei Puccini

2. **Appellation:** Chianti, a town in Tuscany's center. Since it's Chianti, we know it's going to contain mostly Sangiovese.

3. **Quality Level:** Chianti Classico Riserva. This means that the wine has gone through two years of oak aging. Riserva is the highest and usually the most expensive of Chianti designations (you'll also see Chianti Classico, aged one year, and Chianti, which is aged from the harvest to March 1 of the following year).

Outside of Nebbiolo, other wines made in the Piedmont region are usually labeled with the grape they're made with and the place they're from. Some common grapes you'll see are the red grapes **Barbera** and **Dolcetto**, and the white grapes **Arneis** and **Chardonnay**. You'll often see these labels phrased as "[grape] d'[place]," like "Barbera d'Alba."

Spanish wine labels

Spain is a country where you see a big variation in how wines are labeled. Lower-priced wines, especially whites, are often labeled with the grape variety just like you see in the United States, so you'll see whites labeled Albariño or Verdejo (both crisp, fruity, dry styles), but you also see more traditional labeling where the wine is named for the place where it's made. Here are some of the more famous red wine regions and what the names mean.

Spain's most famous winemaking region is La Rioja, in the northern part of the country—so much so that people kind of forget about the other regions! If your idea of a great red wine is one that reminds you of something your grandfather would pull out of a musty cellar, and you love the smell of old bookstores, traditional **Rioja** is going to be your jam. Made from the Tempranillo grape and known for long aging in American oak barrels, Rioja comes in three tiers. Wines labeled **Crianza** will have the least amount of barrel and bottle aging (one year in barrel, one year in bottle); **Reserva** requires three years total, with a minimum of one year in casks; and wines labeled **Gran Reserva** need at least two years in oak and three years in the bottle to carry that designation.

Let's take a look at a Rioja label:

1. **Producer:** Viña Imitación

2. **Appellation and Style:** Rioja

3. **Quality Level:** Gran Reserva, meaning this wine has spent at least two years in oak and three years in the bottle.

4. **Ranking:** *Denominación de Origen Calificada* ("Qualified Denomination of Origin")

5. **Vintage:** *Cosecha* means "harvest," so the vintage is 2004.

If you love full-bodied reds, look for **Ribera del Duero** and **Toro** on Spanish wine labels. These are regions where the style of Tempranillo is bolder and richer, and will remind you more of full-bodied American Cabernets than the more traditional styles from Rioja.

If you're a fan of Châteauneuf-du-Pape or full-bodied red blends from the United States, then look for **Priorat**. The blends from this region in northern Spain usually contain quite a bit of Garnacha and Cariñena, often from older vines, and are blended with Syrah and sometimes small amounts of more famous grapes like Cabernet Sauvignon.

German wine labels

Germany is known mostly for **Riesling**, although Germans are enormously proud of their red wines made from Pinot Noir, which they call **Spätburgunder**. But Riesling is still king—by far the most famous white grape there—and there is a huge range of styles being produced and exported.

Although Germany's practices are changing, many labels still use the traditional quality designations, which indicate how ripe growers were able to get their grapes at harvest. In the past, the style of the resulting wine usually fell in line with the ripeness level—riper grapes were made into a sweeter style. Because of climate change and better farming, ripeness isn't as tough to achieve anymore, and now many German wine producers are focusing more on dry styles that showcase the differences in climate and soil conditions in their vineyards. But many wines are still made and labeled in the traditional style, so here they are in order of ripeness level:

- **Kabinett:** sweet/tart balance and light body.

- **Spätlese:** a little sweeter and richer, but usually lots of mouthwatering acidity on the finish.

- **Auslese:** Some wines made with this designation will taste rich and sweet, like what you imagine when you think of dessert wine, and some are made in a slightly lighter, more semisweet style.

- **Beerenauslese:** We are firmly in dessert wine territory now, with a dessert wine made from grapes that have been allowed to rot on the vine in a controlled way (referred to as "noble rot") that basically intensifies their sweetness and adds complexity.

- **Trockenbeerenauslese:** *Trocken* means "dry," but here it's referring to the grapes, not the wine! As in Beerenauslese, the grapes are allowed to rot, but they are left on the vines even longer, so that they shrivel and dry. These unctuous wines, which taste of honey and apricots, are very expensive and rare.

- **Eiswein** ("ice wine"): Super-syrupy, very expensive dessert wine made with nearly frozen grapes. These are so expensive and labor-intensive to produce that most wineries make them simply because they love them and it's tradition rather than as a way to make money. The conditions have to be just right for these wines, so they're not even made every year.

Some other terms to look for:

- **Trocken** and **Grosses Gewächs (GG):** If these terms appear on a label, that means the wine has been fermented all the way dry. Don't confuse plain old Trocken with Halbtrocken, which will be semisweet, or the aforementioned Trockenbeerenauslese.

- **Sekt:** Sparkling wine, usually made with Riesling or a blend of white grapes that includes Riesling.

Here's a German Riesling label:

1. **Producer:** Dr. Weißwein

2. **Grape:** Riesling

3. **Ripeness of Grapes/ Sweetness Level:** Kabinett (i.e., sweet/tart balance and light body)

4. **Vineyard and Region:** Vineyard of Wehlen within the Mosel region

Austrian wine labels

Poor Austria. Thanks to an unfortunate scandal in the 1980s involving a chemical uncomfortably close to antifreeze that was being used to doctor wine, folks were understandably scared of buying the stuff. Don't worry: This was all resolved decades ago. As a result, Austria has made a huge effort to repair its reputation as a quality wine-producing country, and in my opinion, they've succeeded!

Austrian wines are labeled with the grape they're made from, making them a little less intimidating for American consumers. **Grüner Veltliner** is the country's most famous grape. These wines are generally crisp, refreshing, and kind of like the perfect pair of jeans of the white wine world: They go with everything. Austria also makes killer **Riesling**, but unlike Germany, Austrian Rieslings are almost always dry. Other grapes you'll likely see are Pinot Blanc, Chardonnay, and Sauvignon Blanc.

Like Germany, Austria has a quality ranking system based on grape ripeness, but Austrian designations aren't tied to sweetness. There are two ripeness-based quality-ranking systems: one for the **Wachau**, Austria's most famous wine region, and one for the rest of the country. The designation that is most likely to actually make a difference to you in terms of how the wine tastes is the **Smaragd** designation used in wines from the Wachau. This is for the highest-quality Austrian whites, and you'll notice that these wines feel richer and fuller on your palate and are more complex. If you've tried a few Grüners and dry Rieslings and enjoyed them, it's worth splurging on something with the Smaragd designation.

Glassware, Tools, and Other Potential Rip-Offs

Wineglasses

Fancy brands like Riedel have, in a brilliant stroke of marketing, convinced everyone they need to spend 80 squillion dollars on ten different shapes of expensive glasses for every type of wine they drink. Then there's the "big glass" trend, where wineglasses the size of one's head have become socially acceptable. If you have small hands, these feel really, really silly. What is this, a fucking Renaissance Fair? You know the saying that you should never eat anything bigger than your head? That should apply to glassware as well.

What will really make a difference in your enjoyment of wine at home is just going from shitty to decent. Seriously, decent gets you 80 percent of the way there. So go from the kind of thimble-size glass you see at crappy Italian restaurants like you see on the left here, to the simple but reasonable alternative on the right.

Really, you can stop there. You don't need a different shape for every style of wine you drink. While it's true that if you took the exact same wine and tried it in ten different wineglasses, Pepsi Challenge–style, you'd notice that you perceive the wine differently, it's not a big enough difference to matter. You don't live in a wine classroom with filtered air and controlled conditions, or a Michelin-starred restaurant.

In fact, I really don't recommend the fancier Riedel lines like the Sommelier series. Don't get me wrong, they are gorgeous glasses, and just holding one makes me feel like, *Hmm, maybe this is what it would have been like if I went to law school and got a real grown-up-lady job,* but just look at those fuckers wrong and they shatter. Owning a set is like wearing a ball gown to your friend's apartment to watch *Game of Thrones* and eat Doritos. Too formal! Too much pressure!

So if you really don't need to match your glassware to exactly what wine you're drinking, and you don't need to spend a million dollars, how should you choose? Here's what really matters:

Your decor. Choose something that fits with your aesthetic. Schotts Zwiesel, a brand I wholeheartedly endorse, makes a zillion different styles and shapes. If you have a bachelor (or bachelorette) chic, stainless-steel-and-hard-edges thing going on in your place, one or two styles from the Pure line would be perfect. Or, if you're like my friend who refers to her apartment as the Princess

Penthouse (not actually a penthouse, it just happens to be on the top floor), something from the Diva line would be just the thing to match your girlie aesthetic. They have a slightly longer stem, so they won't fit in every dishwasher, but they're really pretty, so they're worth it.

Your budget. The best price-to-quality ratio in wineglasses is the aforementioned Schotts Zwiesel. They will run you about $10 per glass, they look nice, and they are usually durable enough to put in the dishwasher. Other places to look for decent wine and beer glasses that won't bankrupt you: IKEA (also a good source for modular wine racks), your local restaurant supply store, and Crate and Barrel.

Your size. It sounds silly, but this is something to consider if you are the main person using your glasses. If you played center on your college basketball team, a larger glass will feel more comfortable in your hand and won't make you feel like you look silly holding it. You don't want to have an *Of Mice and Men* moment holding a delicate little thimble. And if you have teeny, weird little paws for hands like I do and you can wear Capri pants as regular pants (true story), then you don't want a giant bowl big enough to fit an entire bottle of wine. Make sure the glass you're buying feels comfortable in your hand.

The size of your glasses. Yes, size matters. But like other things in life, only up to a point. You want something large enough to get the job done, but anything more just looks silly. Are we still talking about wineglasses? Anyway, you want a bowl large enough that you can fill it up halfway with a reasonable 4- to 5-ounce pour and still be able to swirl and really get your nose in there. Yes, it looks pretentious, but aroma really is about 75 percent of enjoying wine, and it's a huge part of enjoying beer as well.

> *You want something large enough to get the job done, but anything more just looks silly. Are we still talking about wineglasses?*

Sparkling wineglasses

Now, what about sparkling, you say? I say, use whatever! I use the same shape glass for everything, sparkling included. Sure, when you serve sparkling wine in a bigger glass, the bubbles will disappear a bit faster. But if you're nursing your fizz for that long, buy better shit! In all seriousness, if the shape you've chosen has a really wide bowl—say, it was labeled as a Burgundy bowl or a Pinot Noir glass—then you might want something to drink sparkling out of that's a bit narrower. My advice is to stay away from traditional Champagne flutes—they don't allow you to enjoy the aroma of your wine, they're a bitch to clean, and they never stay up in the damned dishwasher. Fancier lines like Riedel and Zalto make wider, tulip-shaped Champagne flutes, and these are a great choice if you have the budget. Zalto's glasses are very high-quality, but most of them are too big and unwieldy for me—the only shape that makes me sigh and consider pulling the trigger on buying a few is their Champagne glass.

Look at this bitch on the left here: So gorgeous, right? God, now I just want to stop writing and stretch out on the couch with the better part of a bottle of Guy Larmandier Blanc de Blancs in one of those fancy little shits, preferably while watching *Scandal* and fantasizing about being able to pull off all those gorgeous off-white and dove gray colors like Kerry Washington does. Anyway, back to glassware . . .

If you can't afford one of those, here's a more reasonable option for sparkling wine: Just buy the "white wine" glass from the line you chose. Something like the glass on the right is perfect for enjoying the aroma of your hipster-grower Champagne. Or the $6 Cava you threw into the basket at Trader Joe's and downed while watching *Broad City*. (Have it with those little hot dog in a blanket things and sweet hot mustard—it'll drown out the cheap Cava's less than fantastic finish and the whole package will be gone before you know it. Thank me later.)

A Word on Stemless Wineglasses

These were having an intense moment a couple of years back, and the fervor seems to be dying down a bit, thank goodness. Stems may be prone to snapping off in the dishwasher, but they are there for a reason. They keep your sweaty, grubby hands from warming the wine inside the bowl and from getting greasy fingerprints on the glass from all those potato chips you just ate. (Hey, no judgment—they are great with sparkling wine!) So, unless they're really durable or plastic and you're using them for parties, stemless glasses are kind of overrated.

Plastic "glasses"

There are a few nice plastic glasses on the market, but my favorite is **govino**. They are stemless, which is good for a party situation, and they come in regular wineglass and flute shapes. They also have a handy little divot for your thumb to go into—good for maintaining a grip while eating greasy appetizers. These usually retail for $3 each, and they are clear, lightweight, and pretty attractive. You can put them in the top rack of your dishwasher, and they are fairly easy to clean by hand, too. They're also great for picnics or for taking out on a boat if you're the kind of obnoxious person who owns a boat.

Beer glasses

Here's another dirty secret of mine. For certain beer styles that are lighter, or when I really want to enjoy the aroma, I just drink them out of wineglasses. I happen to really love saisons, lambics, and geuze, and I like to drink them out of an all-purpose wineglass like the one we discussed on page 21.

And yeah, if you're drinking something like a Yuengling or a Peroni that always tastes skunked anyway (seriously, these always smell like armpits to me! And yet I keep going back? Why?), go ahead and drink it out of the bottle, but if you actually want to enjoy your beer, pour it into a damn glass. And make sure it's clean and that you have FULLY rinsed off any soap, because soap residue and grease will keep that attractive head of foam from forming, and that makes for a wan, sad beer-drinking experience.

If you want to get the most of your brew, here are a few beer glasses you might want to keep on hand.

I like the stemmed **Tulip** or **Belgian Chalice**—anything with a more wineglass-like stem and bowl—for richer, more aromatic styles of beer, or for

styles that have lively acidity and carbonation reminiscent of Champagne. So, Belgian-style beers like dubbels and tripels, saisons, and lambics are a good choice for this stemmed glass style. It's also a good choice for strong, rich beers like Scotch ale, barleywine, Imperial IPAs, and double IPAs. Its smaller size and the presence of a stem says "stop and savor," rather than "gulp and go *aaaah*." The outward curve of the lip lets beer and foam enter your mouth at the same time, and the more generous bowl captures and enhances aromas. Also, that stem keeps your beer at the right temperature and your glass unmarred by your greasy hands!

If you drink a lot of pilsners and other lighter beers, the **Pilsner** glass is good to have on hand. Its long and narrow shape is elegant and keeps the refreshing fizz of these styles a little longer. Plus, the wide mouth allows the foam from these super-effervescent beers to spread out. Anything light, crisp, and quaffable is great for this type of glass. Session ales, pilsners, lagers, hefeweizens and other wheat beers, and kölsch are all good choices for this type of glass.

The **Nonick Imperial Pint** is a great all-purpose beer glass, and its slight bulge near the rim makes it easy to stack and a little more durable. Where this style of glass really shines, though, is with fuller, richer styles. It's perfect for stouts and other styles of beer that would be poured from a nitrogen tap, where you really want to enjoy that rich, creamy head. Traditional English ales, brown ales, and porters work well in this style of glass as well.

If you are a lover of super-hoppy IPAs and want to really enjoy those grassy, piney aromas to the fullest, consider splurging on a **Spiegelau IPA** glass. It may look funny, but it really does enhance the hop experience, especially if you don't fill it all the way to give your schnozz extra room to sniff.

Notice the ubiquitous shaker pint is not recommended. It really doesn't do anything for beer, and it's kind of boring. Keep it around for, you know, shaking cocktails.

If you're just going to buy one style of beer glass, I'd recommend a set of Nonick Imperial Pints. Then, for instances when you really want to get into the aroma of your brew, like the occasional delicate, fruity lambic, just fill your all-purpose wineglass and you're golden.

As long as your glasses are of decent quality and clean, don't sweat the details too much. The mere act of pouring your beer into a glass instead of drinking from the bottle will help you start enjoying the aroma more—even if it's just a water glass from IKEA!

Decanters

I've had it with decanters that take up the whole table. You know the ones you see at fancy restaurants where the body is so wide and flat you barely have room for your plate? Plus, these flying-saucer styles are always really difficult to pour from. I think decanting is overrated in general, but there are a few styles of wine and beer, and a few situations, that merit decanting.

When your wine is very tannic. Wines known for their aggressive tannins (that "Did I just swallow felt?" feeling you get with some red wines), like Barolo, benefit from sitting in a decanter for a few hours before you drink them. Exposure to air doesn't make the tannins go away; it just allows some of the fruit aromas and flavors to come out to play a little more, so that your perception of the tannin is blunted a bit by the increased presence of cherries, rose petals, and so on.

When your wine or beer contains sediment. Older wines and bottle-conditioned beers will have a layer of gunk at the bottom (yeast, in the case of the beer), and carefully decanting the wine or beer off of said gunk can make for a more relaxed pouring experience. You don't have to worry about getting the sediment mixed up in your drink and ending up with gritty, weird stuff in your glass. If you're decanting wine or beer for this reason, you'll need to be a little careful. Pour slowly, with a light source (no need to pull out a fancy candle, just use the flashlight function on your phone) near the neck, so that you can stop right when you see the wine or beer start to get cloudy. That's it! Sommeliers like to make it seem like this process is akin to performing neonatal surgery, and you certainly can make it more complicated, but there's really no need.

When your wine needs a little airing out. Modern winemaking techniques don't expose wine to much air as it's being made. One side effect of this is that it can cause wine to develop off odors. These range from that sulfur-y, struck-match smell to one that I can only describe as "farty." Sorry. These aromas are more common in wine bottled under screwcap, but they can happen with regular corks as well. Airing wine out by pouring it into another vessel and letting it sit for a bit can help these aromas blow off. For this type of decanting, you don't need to be as careful, so slosh that shit into your fancy decanter and revel in your rebelliousness!

That's basically it. Look for a style of decanter usually called "Bordeaux," for something with an elegant shape that won't take up the whole table.

Corkscrews

There are so many fancy corkscrews on the market, and most of them are useless. People in the wine industry tend to use some variation on the **double-hinged waiter's key** made by Pulltap's. They come in a million colors, and they are pretty inexpensive, which is good if you tend to constantly leave one in your pocket and have it confiscated by airport security.

No Respect: Screwcaps vs. Corks

One of the first types of alternative packaging that really started to take hold was screwcaps, and for years, they've been snubbed, especially by American consumers, who still tend to think of wine as something for a special occasion and not an everyday beverage. So, I'm here to tell you: Screwcaps are fine! In fact, they're better than fine. For most wine that you'll drink fairly soon, screwcaps are the better, less wasteful option, because you don't have to worry about losing product to cork taint (see page 60), leakage, and oxidation like you do with natural corks. However, there are a couple of small drawbacks to screwcap (called Stelvin) closures.

One is that we don't have as much data about how wine behaves over time when bottled under screwcap. The data we do have is pretty promising—wine seems to actually age more slowly under screwcap, which is a good thing if you ask me. But, if you're spending gobs of money on a Bordeaux you're going to put away for decades and you want it to develop those mature aromas, how long it takes for this to happen under screwcap isn't really well known or as easy to predict.

The other issue that is more likely to affect your drinking enjoyment is reduction. When wine is made and bottled in a reductive environment, that means it's not exposed to oxygen. As a result, it can develop strange aromas that range from sort of rubbery, like a new tire, to sort of, well, farty, like someone microwaved a huge bowl of brussels sprouts in the break room. God, Tina is just the *worst* sometimes, isn't she?

Often these reductive aromas can be resolved by exposing the wine to air—you can use a decanter for this, or just, you know, a pitcher or vessel of some kind. The wine has no idea if it's being housed in Riedel.

Sometimes reduction can't be "aired out" in this way, but even though this is still a kink to be worked out, screwcaps are still the way to go for 99 percent of wine. So don't fear the Stelvin! And if you get one whose seal doesn't seem to want to crack (this happens sometimes and you feel like an idiot, because who has trouble opening a screwcap?!), twist the bottom half of the enclosure instead of the top, and you'll be pouring in no time.

The **Ah-So** is good if you're opening a lot of bottles with older (like 15+ years) corks. But unless you've inherited someone's collection, how often are you doing that?

Wine preservation

Devices that pump inert gas over the empty space in a wine bottle, like Wikeeps, will help you get a few more days out of your wine, but they are not magic. And speaking of magic, there has been a *TON* of hoopla surrounding a device called the Coravin, which consists of a hypodermic needle that you can punch through the cork and use to pour wine from a bottle, supposedly without disturbing it. If you use it only a couple of times, and keep the wine in the refrigerator between uses, it works pretty well. But again, it is not magic. There's no guarantee that you can taste a bit of some bonkers expensive wine, and then open it again months later and have it taste exactly the same.

A lower-tech way to save half a bottle of wine, when maybe you've had two glasses and want to save the rest for later in the week, is to keep a clean half-bottle around. Decant your leftover wine into this half-bottle, stick a cork in it, and keep it in the fridge. The refrigerator will slow down the oxidation process, and because it's in a smaller vessel, it'll be exposed to less air. It's not a perfect solution, but it is practically free.

"Cellaring"

If you don't have the money to build a wine cellar or even to have a dedicated wine or beer fridge, here's what to avoid when choosing a place to stash your beer and wine: **light**, **heat**, and **vibration**. That's basically it! So try to find a closet or cabinet in a cool corner of your house away from radiators, the refrigerator, the microwave, etc. Light is especially lethal for beer, so keep that in mind. And with wine, while heat is not great, it's more important to keep your wine away from large swings in temperature. Basically, as long as you're not aging stuff for decades, and as long as your closet or cabinet doesn't get above the mid-70s Fahrenheit, you're probably OK.

Dating, Mating, Rejection, and Heartbreak

Wine and beer, our most ancient beverages, have been linked to love, romance, and marriage practically since the first grapes accidentally fermented and someone decided to take a chance and drink the resulting juice. They lubricate our first dates, loosen us up enough to take the plunge and have a one-night stand, toast our weddings, and soothe us after our breakups. Here are beers and wines to sip with the inevitable heartache, joy, excitement, and confusion that come with loving who you love, and wanting what you want.

Breakups

Breakups and alcohol are inextricably linked, so here are some ideas to get you through your next one. If you're going to be lying on the floor listening to *The Boatman's Call* and crying, you might as well drink something worthy of Nick Cave. And if you're reveling in your new-found freedom, you'll definitely want something to celebrate with. Because sometimes breakups are a goddamned relief, no? After you chuck someone who was really dulling your sparkle, those first few nights of crawling into your nice, clean, smooth sheets all alone can be an exquisitely wonderful feeling. Here's what to drink when you're newly single.

Let's say, hypothetically, that you were the jerk. You cheated, or you were emotionally unavailable and should probably spend your life alone rather than inflict yourself on any future unwitting partners. For this kind of breakup, consider what wine dorks call a "wine of contemplation." **Barolo Chinato**, a fortified red Italian wine that kind of tastes like cough syrup dipped in felt and dark fairy tales, is made for this type of moment. It's a little bitter and great with dark chocolate.

You're the dumper, and he or she was an asshat. Congratulations on dumping that asshole! To celebrate your moxie and clean start, it's gotta be Champagne—let's go one step further and make it a serious rosé Champagne. And unlike fortified wines, sparkling wine is never as good the next day, which means you'll have to invite a friend or two over to celebrate/commiserate with you, which is probably a good thing anyway. Or you could just have a really interesting night alone that involves way overspending on iTunes, singing along to weird songs you liked in high school, and writing long, rambling emails to your

A fortified red Italian wine that kind of tastes like cough syrup dipped in felt and dark fairy tales is made for this type of moment.

KNOW YOUR STYLES

Barolo Chinato (bah-RO-lo kee-NAH-toh)

REGION: Piedmont, Italy

GRAPE: Nebbiolo

DEFINING FLAVORS/AROMAS: Dark and liberally spiced, with plenty of Nebbiolo's signature assertive tannins. It's produced by steeping Barolo, an iconic red wine, in bark from the cinchona tree (known for producing quinine, the natural flavor in tonic water), along with herbs and spices such as cinnamon, coriander, mint, and vanilla. Combine these with the dark fruit flavors of Nebbiolo-based wine and you've got a truly unique experience—think cherry preserves, tar, mint leaves, and Christmas.

PERFECT FOR: Dark chocolate is wonderful with Barolo Chinato, but keep it simple. Now is the time for a few squares of expensive dark chocolate made by some hipsters who grind their own beans with homemade equipment in a church basement or something, not a rich, creamy dessert. It's also great by itself after a meal, when you want something to slowly sip while you wind down a night with friends and possibly a little too much food.

WHAT TO TRY: **Damilano**, a well-known Barolo producer, makes a delicious Barolo Chinato that is tough to find, but worth tracking down. Though it features the same bitter flavors that make Barolo Chinato what it is, it's a bit smoother going down and retains more fruit flavors from the original wine. More readily available, **Cocchi**'s Barolo Chinato is a bit more heavily spiced, with aromas of everything from honey to orange peel.

mother. Anyway, Champagne can be expensive (and the really good stuff is amazing, so it's a rabbit hole you might not want to go down!), so let's substitute with the **rosé sparkler** of your choice. Austria and Italy are both producing some good, interesting sparkling rosé these days.

Leo Hillinger's **Secco**, a Pinot Noir–based sparkler made by the chic, modern Austrian producer, is a delicious, festive crowd pleaser. With just a touch of sweetness and a beautiful pink color, its fruit flavors are like those tiny local strawberries that are in season for about a minute, and worth every penny you pay for them at the farmers' market. **Bründlmayer Sekt Brut Rosé**, also from Austria, is a little more Champagne-like in style and less fruity. More "sophisticated cocktail party" than "girls' night," it'll feel drier and less sweet on your palate. And finally, Italian producer **Lovisolo** makes a sparkling Nebbiolo that is as delicious as it is interesting. Although Nebbiolo is known for producing deep, tannic wines, this pink fizz shows a much more fun, fruity side of the grape, without losing that little bit of earthy, leathery, savory quality that Nebbiolo is known and loved for. Its tart cherry flavors are great with brunch food or potato chips.

If you've been blindsided by the awful "it's not me, it's you" type of conversation, you need something reaffirming and classic. Find a wine-shop where everyone looks either like a Brooklyn hipster or old enough to be your grandfather and ask for a **classic white Burgundy** (see pages 54–55 for details). Consume with butter slathered on a toasted baguette sprinkled with salt. Thank me later.

When you've been chucked for someone else, you need something cheering. Something a little bit sweet, like **Moscato d'Asti**, is just the ticket. It's like a Mimosa or Bellini, but you don't have to find peach puree. It's a fascinating sign of the times that the bottles being popped in rap songs today are much more likely to be Moscato d'Asti than a $300 bottle of Krug or Dom Pérignon. Almost every producer of more "serious" Nebbiolo-based wines in the Piedmont makes a Moscato d'Asti. Some are more delicious than others, but I've never tasted one that was more than $30 or failed to make me smile. Plus it's only 5 percent alcohol, so you can go a little crazy and down most of the bottle without becoming a complete hot mess and drunk dialing your ex.

If you had a mutual breakup resulting from a calm, measured conversation, congratulations! You're a mature adult. Now leave, you're making the rest of us feel self-conscious, with your kale smoothies and balanced checking account. It's time for you to choose your new house wine—something affordable, quaffable, and stylish that you can pull out whenever people come over in a casually sophisticated way. Try something just left of center that might become your new favorite, like northern Italy's **Dolcetto**, a fruity red that's great chilled with pizza, or **Jacquère**, an interesting white from France's Savoie region that's great for summer weather. **Pecchenino Dogliani San Luigi** is a version of Dolcetto that has the kind of fruit character I refer to as "pulpy," because it tastes almost like fruit puree in your mouth. Blackberry puree, to be exact. As for Jacquère, **Domaine Labbé Abymes** makes a crisp little number that is exactly the kind of refreshing, après-ski (after-skiing) wine you'd find in a chi-chi ski lodge in the Alps. Pretend that's where you are, instead of sitting on your couch eating a block of cheese with a stale baguette. It's lemony-tart, crisp, and the perfect style of white to keep on hand for unexpected guests.

KNOW YOUR STYLES

Moscato d'Asti (moe-SCAH-toe DAH-stee)

REGION: Piedmont, Italy

GRAPE: Muscat or Moscato

DEFINING FLAVORS/AROMAS: Semisweet, known for floral aromas and flavors of juicy peaches and apricots

PERFECT FOR: Light fruit desserts, brunch

WHAT TO TRY: **Oddero**, a small estate in the heart of the Barolo region, makes a super-fun, fruity Moscato that reminds me of those delicious candied apricots that you find around the holidays that taste intensely of dried fruit and leave your fingers all sticky. Yum.

La Spinetta is a prestige Italian producer (read: pricey Nebbiolo that dudes with expense accounts get excited about) that makes a lovely, fresh version of Moscato, a little less heady and aggressively fruity than some other producers I've tried. It's a good way to try an expensive label for less than $20.

Another Barolo producer, **Vietti**, makes a Moscato d'Asti that is considered to be the most classic—not too sweet, not too fizzy, not too any one thing. What wine geeks call balanced. Also: pretty label that makes it great for gifting!

˚Online Dating

Anyone who says they won't do online dating and thinks they'll still meet someone is either living in a dream world or still in college where you can just bump into someone at a party and have a girl-friend by the end of the weekend. Ah, those were the days. Now we're all so afraid of each other and convinced the world is full of perverts and/or people who will steal our identity that we have to hide behind our computer screen and ask a series of questions over email that we're convinced will let us know if the other person is a secret freak. Here's what to drink with what ends up in your inbox.

The quirky OkCupid guy. Every online dating site has its own, shall we say, unique personality. And when it comes to meeting someone on OkCupid, the odds are good, but the goods—whoo boy—can they be odd.

Out-nerd these nerds by being able to quote directly from everything in the Joss Whedon oeuvre, and suggest splitting a bottle of an interesting Italian white. Look for names like **Pecorino**, **Verdicchio**, **Fiano**, or **Greco di Tufo**. They tend to be inexpensive because they're usually made from grapes no one has heard of, and they are a characterful change of pace from the usual Pinot Grigio.

Ordering a bottle on a first date can be a too-bold move, but OkCupid guys are typically evolved enough (when they're not trying to wrangle you into some weird, polyamorous love triangle that is just an excuse to have a three-some) to not think you're naming your future children with them just because you suggested

Italian Whites Beyond Pinot Grigio

PECORINO

A native grape of Italy's Marche region, Pecorino is known for its ability to ripen fully, and thus create a nice, full mouthfeel in the finished wine (riper grapes = more sugar = more alcohol = richer mouthfeel and lack of that "thin, watery" feeling) while retaining the bright, lemony acidity that makes white wine refreshing to drink. Once thought to be extinct, it's making a comeback. **De Angelis** makes a great one (around $16) that feels nicely substantial on your palate, with its hints of pineapple and a finish that will leave your mouth watering.

VERDICCHIO

Another grape known for its refreshing acidity, it can be bland and watery when farmed poorly, but when treated right, it rewards with flavors of slightly underripe green apples and pears, lemon, and fresh almonds. Try the delicious, sophisticated, and refreshing **Le Vaglie**, a Verdicchio (about $20) from the producer **Santa Barbara**—perfect on a hot night, with flavors reminiscent of a fresh, crunchy pear.

FIANO

Fiano usually feels a little fuller-bodied than Verdicchio, and has interesting aromas and flavors that are more than merely fruity. There's a refreshingly herbal quality to many Fianos that reminds me of fresh fennel. **Terredora** makes one that's usually less than $25, and it features a citrusy pop of acidity on the finish that makes you want to come back for more.

GRECO DI TUFO

Greco di Tufo, to me, shares that fuller body with Fiano, but its aromas tend more toward ripe, juicy melon than fennel. **Pietracupa** makes a wonderful Greco di Tufo (about $30). This style is full-bodied without being oaky, and has a pleasing bitterness at the end that's a little like a slightly underripe pineapple that's a bit crunchy. It's perfect for grilled fish.

These all retail for $15 to $30, and are great with a wide variety of foods. So don't be afraid! Just say no to Santa Margherita Pinot Grigio, and say cheers to one of Italy's near-extinct, delicious whites. They've gone unappreciated and uncultivated for far too long, but if we buy them and support them, these heirloom tomatoes of the wine world will hopefully outlive the Olive Garden and everything on its wine list.

something "couple-y." Bottles are almost always better values on restaurant menus anyway, so throw caution to the wind, forget *The Rules*, and go for it. By the end of the date you may be able to look past the strange glasses on a chain (are you an 80-year-old woman from Boca Raton?) and the shirt that looks like someone abandoned it at a rave in 1994, and get your make-out on. And if not, at least you drank something decent. These interesting whites are becoming more and more available, but as you might expect, you're most likely to find them at restaurants and bars that focus on Italian food and drinks. Like those nerdy dudes, some of these heirloom Italian whites might seem weird at first, but hopefully they'll grow on you.

The Tinder bro. Tinder is a fascinating app because it more closely mirrors how we meet people in real life—scanning the crowd at a party or in line at Whole Foods until someone catches your eye. The space you're given for photos and a profile is so limited that what people choose to include becomes a Rorschach test. And what's with all the tigers? Has there been an increase in zoo-related injuries from men trying to impress women on the Internet by posing with exotic, dangerous animals? Tigers will fuck you up, guys! Didn't we learn anything from Siegfried and Roy?

> *Has there been an increase in zoo-related injuries from men trying to impress women on the Internet by posing with exotic, dangerous animals? Tigers will fuck you up, guys!*

The bro, who made sure to list his height (could we all get over this, please?), will probably expect you to order a Cosmo or something. As if! Surprise him and order a crisp, but not too hoppy **American pale ale**. A standard on the American craft beer scene, this style's hallmark is a balance between piney, citrusy American hops and caramelly maltiness. So that bracing bitterness that men seem to love as a sort of macho badge of honor is there, but it's tempered a little bit. Sort of like how you hope this guy maybe has a secret weakness for Emily Dickinson, or loves watching reruns of Jacques Pépin cooking shows late at night when no one's around.

What's the Deal with Hops?

Those intimidating beer nerds talk a lot about hops, don't they? IBUs, dry hopping, noble hops ... what are they talking about?

Hops are just the female flower of the hop plant, and they provide a pleasing bitterness, as well as other flavors, to beer. Bitterness and bubbles provide the "structure," or backbone, to beer's many other qualities and flavors, just as acidity and tannin do for wine.

So what makes these weird green flowers so bitter? Hops contain resins and oils that are made up of alpha and beta acids. During the brewing process, these oils contribute their bitter flavor to the beer. Many of these oils also have antibacterial properties, so back in the day when breweries weren't as squeaky clean as they are now, they helped keep that precious beer (hey, for much of modern history, it was one of the safest things to drink!) from spoiling.

The varieties of hops grown in the United States—usually in Washington

State and Oregon—have a very pronounced citrus and piney aroma and flavor, and are intensely bitter. Cascade, Centennial, and Columbus are three of the more successful varieties, but like wine grapes, there are dozens!

The **"noble hops"** of traditional beer-making countries like Germany and Austria tend to be more aromatic, but have a milder bitter flavor. These hops—like the kind you'd find in a traditional pilsner or Oktoberfest—are Hallertau, Tettnanger, Spalt, and Saaz.

IBU stands for International Bittering Units, which measure how much bitter flavor–inducing alpha acids have been absorbed from hops into the beer. Generally, mass-market beers like Budweiser have an IBU of around 10, and a more aggressively hopped craft beer is in the range of 60 (IPAs) to 100 (triple IPAs), with 100 being really, really bitter.

But like acidity, tannin, and alcohol, our *perception* of bitterness can't be measured in a handy scale, so trust your own palate and use IBUs as just one piece in the overall puzzle of figuring out what styles of beer you like.

As for **dry hopping**, this just refers to adding hops to the beer after fermentation. This produces a fresher, intensely hoppy aroma and flavor, but with less bitterness.

So don't let those beer geeks intimidate you anymore!

If Budweiser is what your dad drank after a long day of yard work, APAs are the lawnmower beer for the modern man. Clean-cut, classic, and not too complicated. **Sierra Nevada** is the gold standard—one sip of this ale, bursting with the fresh flavors and aromas of pine and grapefruit zest from American hops, and you'll taste why. **Drake's 1500** is another classic, available mostly on the West Coast. Dry-hopped to highlight American hops' bright, citrusy flavors, it's a bit more assertive than Sierra Nevada.

Trolling a new online dating site/app. It's called StingraY! Yes, you have to capitalize the Y, your friend tells you breathlessly. It's like Tinder, except when you reject a guy based solely on a profile photo, he gets a mild shock. Apparently this feature is available only on iPhone47, though—if you've got an Android your phone will just vibrate.

Good God, you think. *Am I meeting a guy, launching a spaceship, or partic-ipating in some kind of experiment secretly engineered by our alien overlords? I just want to find someone to keep me company at awkward family events and pick me up from surgery.* Look, your friend says. I just got "slimed" (that's what happens when a guy likes you) by Thad—he's an avid fisherman look-ing for his Ms. Pacman.

For that "I want off this crazy ride!" feeling, you want the beer equiva-lent of a hug. It's gotta be **chocolate stout**. Chocolate stouts get their name from the chocolaty-colored, dark malts used to brew them, and they are often poured from a nitrogen tap or bottled with a nitro canister. **Young's Double Chocolate Stout** is a British classic and has the most chocolaty, mild, creamy flavor. For something American, **Brooklyn Brewery Black Chocolate Stout** is pretty hard to beat, although at 10 percent ABV, it might beat you, so sip slowly! It's also a little darker and less sweet—think fancy dark chocolate more so than Cadbury mini egg.

Rejected from eHarmony. Congratulations, you're normal! Seriously though, being rejected from a dating site can make you feel a little bitter and, well, rejected. Everyone knows about Campari's bright orange color and exotically bitter bite, but for a bit of a change, seek out an **Italian bittersweet aromatized wine**. Like fortified wines, aromatized wines are "fortified" with some kind of spirit, but are also flavored with herbs, spices, roots, and other magical things harvested in the French and Italian countrysides. What makes the Italian bitter category a bit different is that they are usually doctored with gentian root or a similar botanical, which gives these drinks their trademark bitter bite and astringent, felt-dragging-across-the-tongue sensation. Similar to Campari, **Aperitivo Cappelletti** from Haus Alpenz, in its signature curvy bottle that looks kind of like a lava lamp, is a bit less sweet, mellower, and more, well, wine-like. Its orange flavor kind of reminds me of orange Dimetapp, but in a good, less sticky-sweet way. Topping off three-quarters of an ounce or so with sparkling white wine in a Champagne flute is fantastic, but you can get way more creative than that. If you like the idea of a Negroni, but they end up being a little too bitter for you, substituting Cappelletti is a great option for a smoother, milder cocktail.

For something a bit more adventurous, **Cocchi Vermouth di Torino** has an intriguing aroma and flavor profile—nuts, vanilla, cocoa, and citrus. This sounds like it would all be terrible together, but it's not, I promise. It's reminiscent of those fancy chocolate bars that have all kinds of nuts and dried fruit pressed into them. I like it on its own, chilled or over ice, but it's great in a Manhattan as well. Much better than listening to some straight-laced dude spout off on family values on the first date.

The Match.com investment banker. He's like the generic store-brand vanilla wafer of online dating. Whereas OkCupid can seem a little TOO crazy (are there any couples out there who AREN'T looking for a guest star for their threesome?!), Match.com is like going to a dinner party with your parents. But this guy seems all right. He seems to be able to banter with you. This bodes well! You'll likely be ordering by the glass wherever you two decide to meet, so it's more about what your order says about you.

These dates are always so awkward, and since no one wants to commit to a meal, you're often stuck drinking on an empty stomach. So a glass of something sparkling that's reasonably priced is a good option. It's usually a smaller pour than a glass of still wine, which helps with the empty-stomach problem, and ordering something like **Cava** or **Prosecco** is festive in a casual way. Champagne makes you seem a little too high-maintenance (plus ordering it by the glass is a huge rip-off), but inexpensive bubbly makes you sophisticated, but still normal enough to eventually bring home to Mom.

˙One-Night Stands˙

If you're sensible enough to have never had a one-night stand, what are you doing reading this ridiculous book? Stop making that pursed-lipped, judge-y face and go make some vegan chili and put it in Tupperware for your lunches this week, *mmkay*?

Now that it's just us floozies, we can move on to the important subject of what to pair with your questionable decision-making.

The summer intern. It seemed like the perfect plan. Everyone says not to shit where you eat, but what if you're only shitting where you eat for a limited amount of time, and then Chad will move on to whatever his real job is going to be, or, better yet, will go back home to Wisconsin and no one in your city will ever hear from him again? Wait, what's that, Chad? They offered you a full-time position? That's so . . . great! Yes, that means we can spend more time together!

To celebrate the new relationship you've suddenly, awkwardly found yourself in, or mourn your dashed hopes of extricating yourself from your fling with a minimum of fuss (the choice is yours—hey, he's pretty cute, so it might be worth a shot?), try a fun, frothy sparkler from the south of France called **Clairette de Die**. It's sort of a less mature version of Champagne—fizzier, fruitier, and cheaper (usually less than $30). **Carod** and **Jaillance** are two producers who make classic examples of this style that retail for between $16 and $20 and have really easy-to-like flavors of peaches, apricots, and orange blossoms. They're sweeter and simpler than Champagne, but fun in their own way. Kind of like poor Chad.

An ex. The appeal of sleeping with an ex is so clear it hardly needs to be explained. He knows where all your moles are. He's seen you with the stomach flu and first thing in the morning with drool crust on one side of your face, wearing nothing but a rumpled T-shirt, probably his, and probably for some sports team you know nothing about. So stop trying to seem sophisticated. Go to town, and then get some burgers and wash them down with that most embarrassing of popular varieties, **Merlot**. Yes, yes, some of the greatest French wines are made from

> *You're not looking for Cheval Blanc here, friends; you're looking for oaky, plush, old-school Merlot. And why is that such a terrible thing?*

the Merlot grape, that's the joke at the end of *Sideways*, blah blah blah. You're not looking for Cheval Blanc here, friends; you're looking for oaky, plush, old-school Merlot. And why is that such a terrible thing? Somewhere along the line we got the idea that if something isn't terrible and off-putting at first, if it's not an "acquired taste," then it must not be good.

As a style, Merlot's a bit tough to pin down, because its character can change quite a bit based on how it's made. Sometimes it's almost as structured and serious as Cabernet Sauvignon, and sometimes it's so soft and fruity, it's like grown-up Kool-Aid. The best ones are somewhere in the middle. Napa Valley winery **Joseph Carr** makes one that tastes of dark plums with a hint of chocolate and is right around $20. **Hedges House of Independent Producers Merlot** (about $13) has a little more tannin and lighter fruit flavors, so it's great for trashy-burger nights, but you wouldn't be embarrassed to bring it to a dinner party, either.

You'll start fresh in the morning. You'll dust off that online profile, you'll work out, you'll meet someone sensible with a real career. Just not until you . . . take care of this.

Stranger danger. If you're going to have sex with a stranger, at least let a friend know where you are, OK? OK. Now that we have that out of the way, let's move on to what to order while you're out with someone you want to take home. First of all, make sure your underwear game is on point. Tough when it's all in a rumpled, tangled ball in your laundry basket, but it's important for your confidence level. Now, like your perfume, you want a drink that's fun and trashy, but in a subtle way. So instead of wearing Pink Sugar or some horrible celebrity perfume that smells like someone threw up a fruit cock-tail, try a scent with a little more character, like Gucci's Rush, or Lolita Lempicka. Sexy, but with something interesting to say. As a more sophisti-cated alternative to a sticky-sweet cocktail, try a fruity, fun white like Italy's **Falanghina**. It smells like melons and tropical fruit, but will give you less of a headache than those sugary mixed drinks—trust me! **Cantine del Taburno**'s Falanghina is around $18 and a classic example of this style, while the version from **Terredora di Paolo** is around the same price, and a little more . . . elegant. Think pear and pineapple instead of tropical fruit. Like, you're rocking a little cleavage, but it's subtle cleavage. At least that's what you're telling yourself.

The anomaly. He's a bit older. He listens to jazz. He seems to actually have his shit together, unlike most of the adolescent man-children you're usually into. He not only made a reservation at a nice restaurant for your first date, but he asked you to meet him for a drink beforehand at a more casual bar he likes. He's mentioned

KNOW YOUR STYLES

Hefeweizen (hay-fuh-VIE-sen)

REGION: Munich, Germany

DEFINING FLAVORS/AROMAS: These hazy (thanks to their not being filtered), wheat-based beers give off a host of appealing aromas thanks to the yeast used to brew them. You'll smell everything from bananas to pineapple (the pineapple aroma reminds me of the flavor of the Mexican soda Jarritos) to cloves. The flavor is mild with very little bitterness, so if you're looking for a break from hop-heavy beers but still want something refreshing, hefeweizen is the ticket.

PERFECT FOR: Lighter dishes—this style of beer is great with a big salad as a meal, like a chicken Caesar. Traditionally, beers like this were drunk midmorning, but that's probably not a great idea in our modern era of constant texting and emailing.

WHAT TO TRY: If you want a truly authentic version of this style, classic German brewery **Ayinger Bräu-Weisse** is your best bet. Heavy on the smooth, banana-inflected elements of hefeweizen, it's the kind of beer you can imagine drinking in the afternoon. No judgment.

Tröegs, a brewery based in Pennsylvania, does a great version of this style that's a little heavier on those clove-y, peppery aromas and flavors and perfect with that takeout sushi you told yourself you wouldn't buy.

a play he wants to take you to. Jesus H. Christ, his socks probably match, too. He's probably got real, solid furniture that didn't have to be assembled.

For that pre-dinner drink, try a **hefeweizen**. It's got the not-too-heavy feel of a lager or pilsner, but is a little more interesting and flavorful. Having a go-to drink to order in any given situation instead of dithering over the menu might make you seem like you've got your shit together, too. There is a satisfying, creamy texture to the bubbles in a hefeweizen that really hits the spot. (If you work in the service industry, you're probably aware that it's a perfect post-shift drink—not boring, but not too challenging, either.) And don't ruin your hefeweizen's cloudy, dreamy flavors—reminiscent of Inca Kola and pineapples—by actually using that lemon wedge on the side. The funky haze and refreshing tang of this style does not need to be futzed with.

So order your hefeweizen and have a classy dinner with some grown-up conversation. Sure, you'll probably still bail in the morning and never call, but hey, you learned a few new things about Miles Davis, and that's something, right?

Family Matters,

A s if dating wasn't hard enough, once you've gotten over the initial hurdles and are in a "relationship," then you have to deal with your respective families. Your aunt who will try to give the two of you awkward and useless "gifts" like tacky Christmas ornaments. Your grandfather who will keep asking when you'll be ready to have kids, despite the fact that you've only known each other for five months. It's enough to make you think wistfully of sad stories you've heard about people being orphaned by war or tragic plane crashes. Well, maybe not quite, but it's at least enough to make you want a drink! Here's what to sip during those awkward silences.

Family reunion. Your family's reunions are mortifying enough, but now your boyfriend has insisted on coming with you. He'll even have his own T-shirt with the horrible pun on your last name. Make everyone happy and bring beer! Something in cans that's easy to carry and dispose of is always great at a picnic. Try an **American amber ale**, especially if the weather is a little cooler. It's got the assertive hop presence you'd expect from American craft beer, with a little more roasted, caramelly malt flavor, and a darker, you guessed it, amber color. **New Belgium Fat Tire** is on the lighter side for an amber ale, and its subtler, biscuity aromas make it refreshing and easy to drink. **Tröegs Nugget Nectar** packs more of a wallop, both hop and alcohol-wise. At over 90 IBUs and 7.5 percent ABV, you might want to stop at one, but you'll need it after the family hike, or the volleyball game when Uncle Mike got a little too competitive and spiked the ball right in your boyfriend's face.

When your families meet. If ever there was a situation that could drive a person to drink, your family meeting your significant other's family … whoo, boy! Maybe your parents voted for both Bushes both times and his folks are die-hard liberals. Or you're Jewish and he's Catholic (hey, they can at least bond over making their kids feel guilty!). Or your family is full of uptight Type A's and his family is always late and thinks having dinner at 10 p.m. is normal and appropriate.

What the Heck Is Amber Ale?

Amber ale is a bit of a catchall term for a style of beer that's darker than American pale ale, but lighter than brown ale, although there's a bit of overlap. When you break it down, American amber ales are really a stateside version of British pale ale. It's just that American consumers, when they see the word "pale" on a label or menu, expect a liquid as pale as a bleached blonde. In the 1980s, amber ale could mean a beer inspired by any number of British or European brewing traditions, from Irish red ales to Extra Special Bitters (see page 56). But eventually, a somewhat more uniform style was informally agreed upon.

Today, an American amber ale combines the intensely citrus and pine aromas and flavors of American hop varieties with the sweetness of caramel or crystal malts. The key difference between amber ales and those hop-heavy American pale ales and IPAs is that here the scale tilts more heavily toward malt. The combination of moderate hop bitterness with those toasted nut and toffee flavors can be immensely satisfying and reminiscent of a crisp fall day, with its cool, refreshing air, and the smells and sights of brown and orange leaves.

WHAT TO TRY

Bell's Amber Ale is the brewery's flagship beer for a reason. It's got a little more hop presence than some amber beers, but there's plenty of sweet, almost woody aromas and flavors as well. This style of beer is especially well suited to food, and Bell's Amber Ale just cries out for rich fall flavors like roast pork and sweet potatoes.

Anderson Valley Brewing Company Boont Amber Ale focuses more on those rich, caramelly malt flavors, and while the bitterness is there for balance, it's more in the background, providing a pleasingly bracing finish after all that malt sweetness.

For this kind of awkward family meal, you want to make sure at least what you're drinking isn't controversial. Try a **fruity, unoaked Chardonnay**. The spicy, vanilla-laced flavors of oak were very much in vogue for Chardonnay for most of the 1990s and early 2000s, but now many people have grown tired of this flavor profile, and are specifically asking for Chardonnays that aren't made this way. That rich, super-oaky profile has become rather divisive, just like your aunt Mary's politics. Thankfully, many California and other New World (non-European) wine regions have started labeling their unoaked Chardonnays as such. California's **Chamisal** is a richer, fruitier version of this style, while northern Italy's **Il Falchetto** is more crisp, clean, and citrusy. Both retail for under $20, good if you need to open a second bottle when they start to debate race relations in America's inner cities. Although you might need something stronger than wine for that.

Dinner with your significant other's parents is a situation where you want to bring a host gift that will really be appreciated. **Sparkling wine** is a great way to do this, because it can easily be enjoyed before or after a meal, but especially before. Bring it pre-chilled, and go with something a bit less expensive and more interesting than Champagne. When you bring people Champagne, it tends to disappear into a distant closet or wine rack for a "special occasion," never to be seen again, because an occasion that seems "special" enough never seems to come. Little do people know that non-vintage sparkling wine is best when it's drunk within a year of release. Don't hold on to that bottle of Veuve Clicquot for years! It'll taste terrible when you finally have it chilled once that mythical special occasion arises.

This is a great time to take a small chance at your local wine store. Because surely by now you've built a rapport with your favorite sales assistant (see page 7), you can ask what sparkling wine they think you should try that people don't buy as often as they should.

Most wine nerds love sparkling wine, the weirder the better, so you'll likely walk away with something that's way undervalued because of said obscurity, and you'll have a great little anecdote to share during those

A few sips of your left-of-center bubbly, and everyone will be leaning allll the way back and really getting to know one another.

awkward few moments of conversation when you're perched on the couch, in that overly formal, sitting-up-too straight way. You know, when like one-quarter of your butt is actually on the couch? As though any normal human sits like that. A few sips of your left-of-center bubbly, and everyone will be leaning *allll* the way back and really getting to know one another.

There's far more to sparkling wine than Champagne and Prosecco, and now is the perfect time to explore that. If you're stuck ordering online or browsing the aisles yourself, try **Franciacorta**, the Italian answer to Champagne. **Bellavista** is made from Chardonnay and Pinot Noir grapes, and has the same crisp, tart, bracing finish, but is less expensive ($35-ish) and more interesting than most true Champagnes.

Sleeping over at the parents' house. Nothing makes you feel like a real adult like sleeping on an air mattress, while your significant other bunks in his or her childhood bedroom, staring up at the Radiohead posters that are inexplicably still on the walls. Sneak into the kitchen and crack open one of the sweet, high-octane **Trappist ales** you were smart enough to bring. Toast your chaste evening with one of these monastery-brewed beers and sip as you quietly giggle at the photo albums you found in the living room.

Chimay's beers are pretty widely available. Their **tripel** is a gorgeous light caramel color and tastes like golden raisins and a little bit like an off-dry German Riesling! For a Trappist experience that's a little . . . lighter, try

Beer-Brewing Monks and Their Funky Yeasts: Trappist Ales

For a small country, Belgium has a wildly diverse beer culture, and perhaps no part of it is more famous than its Trappist ales.

Monastic orders have long produced food and beverages, both to sustain themselves and to sell to the larger community to support the order and their good works. The Trappists are the only Catholic order of monks who brew beer.

To be officially called a Trappist ale, a beer must come from one of the eight recognized Trappist breweries: Westmalle, Westvleteren, Chimay, Rochefort, Orval, and Achel in Belgium; Koningshoeven in the Netherlands; and Stift Engelszell in Austria. These days, most of these breweries are run by professional brewers, but the monks still supervise. Interestingly, many of these breweries make a much lighter-style beer for the monks themselves to consume, and sell only the richer, sweeter stuff.

So what is a Trappist ale, exactly? Each monastery's style varies a bit, due to local influences and traditions, but the beers share a few key traits. They tend to be top fermented, which accentuates rich, fruity, nutty flavors, and undergo a second fermentation in the bottle to create a trademark effervescence that is often compared to Champagne. Styles you'll see bear names like dubbel and tripel. These terms generally indicate that you're climbing the ladder in terms of richness in flavor and alcohol content—they refer to the original gravity of the malt and fermentable sugars. If you encounter a quadrupel, definitely don't make plans to, you know, operate a crane or make any important decisions. Koningshoeven's quadrupel clocks in at a healthy 10 percent ABV, and Rochefort's "10" hits 11.3 percent.

Beers merely brewed in the style of Trappist ales must call themselves "Abbey ales." So even if the beer you're looking at has a cute, old-fashioned picture of a monk on it, if it's called Abbey ale, it's not the real deal. Beers with this designation, like from the large brewery Leffe, may have monastic origins, or be named after monasteries, but the brewing is no longer supervised by actual monks. Beers in this category also tend to be filtered and more mass-produced.

Orval. The monastery's only exported brew is a golden ale simply called Orval, and its subtle hops combined with wild yeast fermentation give it a unique character that's sour, spicy, and refreshingly bitter all at once. There is a huge variation in style with Trappist ales (see box), but most of them are relatively high in alcohol, so you'll forget your awkward, slightly humiliating sleeping arrangements in no time.

Social Media Stalking

E veryone does it; no one admits it. You meet someone new, or remember someone from your past, and all of a sudden, you're in an Internet wormhole that threatens to swallow you completely. Maybe you're deep into a photo album and came dangerously close to publicizing your presence/shame with a "like" on a new boyfriend's vacation pic from 2005. Maybe you've learned the subtle art of signing *out* of LinkedIn before viewing your frenemy's job history so she'll never know you were there. Whatever your crazy sleuthing habits, enjoy a delicious beverage while indulging in socially deviant behavior.

The long-ago ex. Why is it that you have to Facebook-stalk that guy you made out with at Unitarian camp when you were 15? This kind of stalking is really interesting, because generally you don't have much emotional attachment to these people anymore, and at the time you knew them, you were barely a person, you were just an embryo with zits. So they could be anything now! A performance artist creating giant art installations in the desert, a manager at a water plant living in Albuquerque, or a computer programmer living in Seattle and having developed the same predilection for theater tech geeks as you, as though you're weirdly related. Facebook also provides maximum opportunity for voyeurism into a person's *whole* life (rather than, say, just their career like LinkedIn), so you can really get a sense of who this person is now—where they like to vacation, what they wear to a fall wedding,

whether or not they're still friends with the people you had in common when you knew each other. You're trying to imagine what their life is like now (and probably comparing it unfavorably to your own) and remembering what your life was like at the time you knew this person. Man, psychologists must really have a field day with social media.

This kind of delving into the past requires wine made in a place time forgot. **Carema**, an area in the northern part of Italy's Piedmont region, makes Nebbiolo-based wine that bears little relation to Barolo and Barbaresco, mostly because it's just not as . . . fussed over. Winemakers in this area are not interested in producing wines that are flashy because of their full body, super-assertive flavors, or use of expensive new oak. They're kind of like that friend from your past who you know, through the grapevine, is now wildly successful, but he's unstalkable. He still "doesn't believe in Facebook," and you're a little jealous of his ability to stay above all the social media craziness. Not jealous enough to delete your account, though. **Ferrando** makes a wonderful Carema called **Etichetta Bianca** that smells like truffles, hot pavement, and sour cherries, and is fabulous with anything braised. It's a little spendy at $50, but totally worth it.

Your new squeeze. Why would you need to stalk your current boy- or girl-friend? Well, at first maybe you're just looking at their old photos on Facebook. You really like this person, after all, so looking at their face/cute butt over and over—it's nice, right? But then you start delving deeper, going back further and further in time via their (very detailed!) photo albums, helpfully indexed by the date and location. Aww, look how young they looked at that dance. Wait, that's a fraternity formal. He was in a fraternity? This could change everything! Wait, is that a popped collar in that photo of him from high school? Douche alert! All of a sudden you've stalked them on the various online forums they belong to, and are reading their opinions on everything from electronics to slow cookers. What does it say that he made a flirty comment to someone who recommended he get a larger model? Jesus Christ, he wrote that in 2008, what does it matter now?!

You aren't going to find evidence of your significant other's secret freakiness by Googling.

Get a grip with a fresh, minerally **Chablis**. If you think you don't like Chardonnay, you need to try Chablis (and real Chablis that says it's from France on the bottle, not the scary stuff in the jug on the bottom shelf in the grocery store). The entry-level version from **Domaine Louis Michel & Fils** (about $25) feels full-bodied with citrus flavors reminiscent of preserved lemons, but will sort of race across your tongue in a way that's very pleasing and refreshing. **Domaine des Malandes Chablis** (around $20) is a softer take, less like a super-lemony laser beam, and more like a ripe Meyer lemon.

The acidity in Chablis is often described with words like *bracing, electric*—you get the drift. So what better way to jolt you out of the Internet wormhole you've gone down? Sit back, enjoy your wine, and delete your search history. Unless you're some kind of advanced-level hacker, you aren't going to find evidence of your significant other's secret freakiness by Googling.

Your childhood nemesis. This is some suspenseful shit. That bitch who beat you out for French club president could have gotten really fat and done absolutely nothing interesting, or she could be running around with YOUR dream job, swishing her shiny, shiny hair around. You find her on Instagram, and goddammit, she's perfect. That hair is still super-shiny. She seems to live on fruit salads and expensive-looking smoothies. Her nails are perfectly manicured. She seems to go to the beach all the time, yet is a successful lawyer? Why won't she stop being so perfect?! Remind yourself that you're great, no matter what she's doing or what her hair looks like, and get your hands on a **red Burgundy** (see page 54). The ones from **Domaine Jérôme Chézeaux**

What the Heck Is a Burgundy?

Burgundy is a small region in east-central France that wine geeks have been obsessing over for years. It all started back in the Middle Ages, with monks farming this difficult land for the church and the dukes of Burgundy. These monks were the OG wine geeks, and because of their meticulous recordkeeping, they figured out what grew best where. These records evolved into a complicated ranking system that's all about which tiny vineyard has a track record of producing better wine than another.

The only simple thing about Burgundy is the grape varieties. With a few obscure exceptions, white Burgundy will be made from Chardonnay, and red Burgundy from Pinot Noir. After that, it's all about specificity of place when it comes to how expensive (and, theoretically, how good) the wine is.

THE BURGUNDY HIERARCHY

Here's a breakdown of the rankings:

- **Bourgogne:** Wine just labeled "Bourgogne" can be made with grapes from anywhere in the designated Burgundy region.

- **Village:** Wines labeled with a village name (like Chassagne-Montrachet or Morey-Saint-Denis) have to be made with grapes from that village.

- **Vineyard:** Wines labeled with just a vineyard name are *lieu dit* or "named place" wines and have to be made with grapes from that single vineyard.

- **Vineyard + Premier Cru:** Wines made completely from grapes from a specific vineyard that is thought to be of especially good quality.

- **Vineyard + Grand Cru:** Wines made from a specific vineyard that's thought to be one of the absolute best when it comes to quality.

Think of these categories like a bull's-eye, with Bourgogne as the widest ring, and Grand Cru at the center. If that all sounds extremely confusing, it's because it is, even for people like me who work with wine for a living.

BUT WHAT'S THE DIFFERENCE, REALLY?

A lot is made of the differences between wines from one small subregion and another, and even one small vineyard and another. I'm not going to say that this isn't important.

There are noticeable differences that come from the location of these historic sites—what the soil is like, how much sun they get—that have an effect on the finished wine.

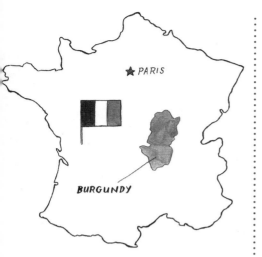

However, I have tasted a lot of Burgundy. Not crazy expensive, costs-as-much-as-a-car Burgundy, but the stuff that a normal person might conceivably buy for, say, a special dinner party, in the $20–$100 retail range. I've also watched a lot of my customers taste, buy, and experience these wines, and I think that the style of the producer has more of an influence on the finished wine in this price range. There are LOTS and lots of small growers and producers in this area, and they tend to be the best values, as opposed to the big brands you see in every grocery store, like Louis Jadot. These big brands aren't bad, per se, but I find wines that are more interesting and have more character for the same amount of money with smaller producers.

FINDING THE RIGHT BURGUNDY FOR YOU

Unfortunately, what's available in your local shop is going to vary wildly. This is why it's so important to have a relationship with your local wine store sales assistant, or with the online store you've chosen to make "yours" (see page 253 for information on buying wine online).

Ask a staff member in your store about their Burgundy selection, and ask them to pick a few bottles at the "Bourgogne" level from different producers. This will give you an idea of the style you like. When you go back and say, "I liked XYZ's Bourgogne Rouge because it was fuller-bodied, the rest felt too thin to me," the person helping you, if they know what they're doing, will be able to use that information to steer you toward more things you'll like.

When you figure out which producer's style you prefer, you'll feel more comfortable splurging on one of their village, Premier Cru, or Grand Cru wines for a special occasion.

are elegant, and feel like silk in your mouth—hardly any weight at all. Bet your nemesis drinks Mommy's Time Out Pinot Grigio or something boring and embarrassing, right?

Your ex's new girlfriend. Even if you were the one to end things with an ex, there's still a pang of regret about what might have been, and using social media to spy on his or her new boy- or girlfriend is one way to pick at that particular scab. Especially good for this kind of voyeurism is Instagram. Those filters just make everyone's life seem amazing and worthy of envy. Of course, no one posts an unfiltered photo of their ingrown toenail, only the foot containing that toenail wearing a new pair of shoes. Intellectually, we know this, and yet . . . there she is, looking perfect. She seems so much nicer and more social than you—look at her on that picnic with her friends! Look at her perfect, not-frizzy hair! Of course he'd rather be with her. Who wouldn't?

Fuel your shame spiral with a beer that has just what you're feeling in the name: Extra Special Bitter.

Fuel your shame spiral with a beer that has just what you're feeling in the name: **Extra Special Bitter** (ESB). This traditionally English style of ale basically tastes like a pub in the United Kingdom, with its slightly musty air, well-worn wooden bar, and gruff, older clientele. It's brown, it's a little funky, it smells kind of like honey whole wheat bread, and is in fact not that bitter at all compared to IPAs and APAs.

Fuller's is an English classic, with a fairly dark copper color and butterscotch flavor that might soothe your feelings of inadequacy. **Schlafly** makes a slightly hoppier, more "American" take on this style, with a lemony character and a bit more carbonation (ESBs tend to be less bubbly than most other beers). This gentle style of traditional beer is the alcoholic equivalent of an old-timer giving you an encouraging pep talk about how steady and dependable wins out in the end over flashy and Photoshopped. You'll have your moment in the sun, gloating about your life milestone on social media soon enough, so hang in there.

'Your New Crush.

Everyday life can get a little boring—work, bills, dodging your mother's phone calls. A good crush can lift you out of all that and make you realize all of the wonderful, giddy possibilities out there. Or at least make your morning commute a little more interesting. Either way, crushes are an excellent distraction. Here are some wines to drink with said distractions—or while thinking of them. Because sometimes the thinking is the best part . . .

The cute barista. How do their hairstyles come to exist? Do really cool people all just cut one another's hair? Because I think if I walked into a salon and tried to have the stylist give me some avant-garde, asymmetrical 'do, they would take one look at my clothes and just say, "Oh, honey, no." But your barista crush somehow manages to make this *hair* happen, and you can't stop staring at it. Even when you're in the mood for a big, sugary mocha with a mountain of whipped cream, you refrain and order a macchiato (a real one, for God's sake!) so as not to look like a gross person who doesn't appreciate real coffee. For this type of crush, it's important to get in touch with your inner hipster. It will give you confidence. Find a **sparkling Gamay** from the Loire Valley that's great with charcuterie someone made in his basement. Then go ahead: Order that mocha, ask out the damn barista, and share your cool, fizzy red. So what if you're not in a band?

Made by G from **Domaine des Nugues** is one of my favorites. It's fruity with a touch of sweetness, low in alcohol (about 9 percent), and the absolute perfect thing to drink with a sandwich or pizza laden with cured meats. **Maison P-U-R La**

Bulle also makes a good sparkling Gamay—it's like a fruit salad of cherries, strawberries, and raspberries you took to a picnic, so it's gotten all soft and juicy sitting out in the sun. The frothy bubbles pull it all together. And you can't beat the label: a lady bathing in a tub of sparkling red.

The high-school reconnection. So, what goes with laughing on the outside and cringing on the inside over the past? Or with wondering how much fatter/more wrinkled you are now than when you were practically an infant when an old flame asks you to meet up? Christ, I don't know. But if you're actually having dinner with someone you had a thing with in high school or college, it's time to show that you've arrived, that you're an adult, and Know Shit. For this kind of reuniting, which feels so . . . nerve-racking, you'll probably be at a restaurant. Order something impressive, but not too on the nose. Like, don't order a big, stonking Napa Cabernet. We're not businessmen with giant expense accounts and too-large cuff links circa 2003. Want to look serious, and like a grown-up who's arrived? It's **Barolo** time.

Bonus points for asking that it be decanted, which, given how young most Barolos on restaurant wine lists are, it will need. With its unique, orange-tinted color, serious tannins, and crazy, complex aromas that call to mind everything from asphalt to rose petals, it stands up to serious conversation and big, braised meat dishes.

And, don't worry: You look great.

The work crush. A reason to keep your eyebrows from heading too far into Frida territory if there ever was one. You need something to accompany savoring the delicious anticipation and parsing his or her every phrase with your friends. For this, I suggest the **Trashy Rosé Spritzer**.

Take a pint glass and add some ice. Fill the glass one-third to one-half with the cheap rosé of your choice. Dry is best. Spain is a good place to look for cheap rosé. I mean, try something from Provence if you want to get into the Peter Mayle of it all, but they're usually just pricey enough to make you feel bad about adulterating them. Anyway, add a dash of whatever juice you like, but keep it in the red or pink family—pomegranate, cranberry, you get the idea. Fill the glass the rest of the way with seltzer. If you really want to get crazy you can add a nice garnish, like a slice of blood orange, or one of those fancy, artisanal maraschino cherries that aren't an alien color. This is also a good time to use a fancy fruit liqueur, like Chambord, crème de cassis, or its slightly less sweet cousin, crème de mûre. Whichever you choose, just use a splash or two—it's strongly flavored, sweet stuff. The juice and seltzer will keep you hydrated for intense analysis.

KNOW YOUR STYLES

Barolo (bah-RO-lo)

REGION: Piedmont, Italy

GRAPE: Nebbiolo

DEFINING FLAVORS/AROMAS: The Nebbiolo grape is unique for its light color, in comparison to its heavy tannins, and famous for its complex aromas, which are also a hallmark of a less tannic grape, Pinot Noir. So if you like Pinot Noir, you may like a Nebbiolo-based wine like Barolo.

PERFECT FOR: Braised meat, mushrooms—anything with a lot of meaty, fatty umami action

WHAT TO TRY: **Brovia** is hands-down my favorite Barolo producer. I love their wines because they don't feel too heavy, and the fruit flavors are very clear and pure, like biting into that one perfect cherry in the entire overpriced bag.

They make single-vineyard wines that are pretty expensive and need some age to really be at their best, but their **Normale**, just labeled "Barolo," is delicious right when it's released, and is a bit less expensive at around $50.

Vietti's Barolos are expensive, but their **Perbacco** is a steal at around $30, and a Barolo in all but name. It's kind of their "second label" wine that they didn't feel was quite perfect enough to be called Barolo, but still delicious. Vietti's style is a little bigger and darker than Brovia's, so if you tend to like fuller-bodied wines, this is the producer to go for.

Oddero Barolo Normale (about $45) is a little heavier on the tobacco and tar aromas, and the tannins here are pretty serious, so definitely drink with some rich food!

On Drinking and Dining

When you're at a restaurant and the waiter pours you a sip of wine, what do you do? Most people just knock it back and nod, or perhaps stroke their chin knowingly as the waiter pours. But what's really supposed to be going on?

When you taste a wine at a restaurant, you're supposed to be checking to see if the wine is flawed in some way. Back in the day, the sommelier would do this for you, and the flawed bottle would never make it to your table. Nowadays, people feel funny about someone else tasting their wine, so this task has fallen to the person who ordered it. Here's what you're looking for when you sample it:

CORK TAINT

Cork taint is what happens when the cork is infected with a mold that taints the wine. This is what people are talking about when they say a wine is "corked." It has nothing to do with the cork breaking, or with bits of the cork getting into the wine. The easiest way I know to describe the smell of cork taint is that it's like a damp basement full of old cardboard boxes.

OXIDATION

Poor storage or a tiny hole in the cork will cause damaging air exposure. Did you ever leave your brown-bag lunch with apple slices in your locker over the weekend in high school? If you smell anything in wine that reminds you of that, be suspicious. Oxidation will also make white wines look darker and red wines look lighter or browner.

HEAT DAMAGE

Heat damage often occurs in tandem with oxidation, and its aromas are more like prune juice, or fruit compote—kind of an unpleasantly cooked, too-ripe aroma.

What do you do if you don't smell any of these suspicious aromas, but you just don't like the wine? Officially, you're still expected to pay for the bottle. In practice, it's more of a gray area because restaurants want you to be happy!

Both in restaurants and retail jobs I've had, the idea of someone having a wine I sold them that makes them grimace every time they take a sip really bums me out. Speak up! If it's moderately priced, the manager will likely decide to get you something else and not make you pay for the offending bottle. It gets trickier when it's a really expensive and/or older bottle. If you're going to splurge, do it at a restaurant with a serious wine program so that you can be confident the wine has been stored properly, and ask for advice from the sommelier.

The guy on the train. Have you ever extrapolated so much information from the couple of inches of sock between pant and shoe? Ooh, he's reading *The Economist*—he must be smart and informed! Or possibly weirdly conservative! But it'll all work out. **Pinot Bianco** from Alto Adige in northern Italy provides the perfect balance of substance and refreshment. The names and bottles will often look German (that long, skinny bottle shape), but don't let that short-circuit your brain into thinking that the wine will be sweet like so much German wine imported into the United States. Pinot Bianco will be crisp and dry, with just enough weight to sip alone, and by that I mean both without food and by yourself, because we don't live in a television show. Whose meet-cute story comes on a mass-transit car where everyone's bleary-eyed and caffeine-deprived?

> *Pinot Bianco will be crisp and dry, with just enough weight to sip alone, and by that I mean both without food and by yourself, because we don't live in a television show.*

Kellerei Kaltern, a cooperative winery in Alto Adige, makes wines that really over-deliver for the price. Their Pinot Bianco retails for $15–$20, but it drinks like a $25–$30 bottle. It has the nice, full body of a Chardonnay, and the crisp snap of a Sauvignon Blanc without the pungent citrus aromas.

Wines produced by **Manincor** are a bit more expensive than what you usually find in the Alto Adige region, but good heavens are they good. Elegant, finessed, just beautiful. Their Pinot Blanc (they use the French name instead of the Italian one, I guess because they're fancy like that) is the perfect thing to have with scallops or lobster if you're not going to swill it alone, and is about $20 or a little more at retail.

Just Us Girls

While this chapter is aimed at the estrogen-dominant among us, don't feel like you need to skip ahead if you're a guy, or a gal who's not particularly keen on painting her toenails. The fact is, I'm a lady myself, so I can speak only to what women do when there aren't any boys around—I can't really do the reverse. If nothing else, turn the page for a recipe for white sangria that really shouldn't be relegated to girls' nights on the couch only. It's perfect for cookouts and summer parties, when the weather is warm, and fresh herbs and juicy fruit are in season. Read on for some ideas for your next girls' night, or for a peek into what the women in your life might like to drink when they're left on their own.

'A Trashy Girls' Night,

Sometimes, you just need to let loose with your lady friends, whether you're on the couch or attempting to mimic normal social skills out on the town. Sometimes it's fun to just be unapologetically girly. Here's to white sangria and bitches who brunch.

"Clubbing." If you're going to wedge yourself into something more revealing and stylish than usual and actually go to a "club" because there's that one woman in your friend group who still does that kind of thing and you want to prove you're not a fossil yet, you'll need something for the long metro/cab/waiting-in-line journey before you get there. It's up to you to find out if this is illegal where you live, but paper coffee cups work, as do empty iced latte–type drink containers. If it's summer, no one will suspect a Nalgene bottle. Fill your vessel with something crisp and neutral that won't make your breath smell too weird, like an inexpensive **Verdicchio** from Italian producer **Santa Barbara**. It's tart and has faint hints of pineapple and fennel, and it'll quite possibly give you the courage to hang with the young whippersnappers for at least an hour or two. Hey, it's wine, not magic.

Vegging out to bad reality TV. What is so addictive about reality TV? Why are we all so transfixed by the Kardashians eating mediocre-looking takeout salads in Kabuki makeup? For staying in and watching bad reality shows in worn-out yoga pants with your friends, you need something that goes well with snacks and that you can sip over a long period of time

Here's to white sangria and bitches who brunch.

without getting too drunk or bored with what you're drinking. Satisfy everyone with a batch of **white sangria**. Unfortunately, sangria, especially the white variety, is a little . . . looked down upon. No need to look down on this version, which is refreshing and not too boozy, so everyone can slurp away with abandon, and you won't end up with your entire group of friends passed out and drooling on the decorative pillows on your couch.

WHITE SANGRIA

Serves 7–8

Can easily be scaled up.

1 bottle crisp, citrusy white. (Look for a Sauvignon Blanc or a Picpoul de Pinet, but an inexpensive Pinot Grigio will do in a pinch.)

¼ cup orange liqueur, like Cointreau

½ cup fruit juice in the citrus or tropical family, like orange or pineapple

1½ cups cut-up fruit (I like peaches, mangoes, and sliced citrus fruits like oranges or lemons)

1 cup whole-leaf fresh herbs, like basil, mint, or tarragon

Club soda or seltzer

Macerate all the ingredients but the club soda for a few hours or overnight, if you can. Pour over ice, top with club soda or seltzer, and enjoy with a colorful straw! This is not a serious beverage—you may as well go for broke with the girliness.

For a long (hopefully boozy) catch-up session over dinner, you'll need a red, so that drinkers who think only red is acceptable to have with a main course will be satisfied, but one that isn't too heavy for that person who always orders a grilled chicken breast with no oil or butter. The 1990s are over, Karen—fat is in! Try one of Italy's most underappreciated reds, **Grignolino**. Many producers who make (much more expensive) Barolo or Barbaresco from Nebbiolo also make the light, perfumy Grignolino. It has the elegance and aromatic qualities of Pinot Noir, but has a little bit more tannin

KNOW YOUR GRAPES

Grignolino (gree-nyoh-LEE-noh)

REGION: Northern Italy's Piedmont region—the specific DOCs are Asti and Casale Monferrato.

DEFINING FLAVORS/AROMAS: Smells like ripe cherries warmed in the sunshine, roses, fresh strawberries, and there's often a hint of clove or some other type of warm spice in the mix. It's got mouthwatering acidity in spades, and nicely grippy tannins that are a bit surprising given its lighter color, and tastes like just-ripe strawberries, tart cherries, and cranberries.

PERFECT FOR: Pasta with a bit of meat and cheese going on in the sauce, roast chicken, pork chops, charcuterie

WHAT TO TRY: **Crivelli** makes a wonderfully fruity Grignolino that smells almost exotic, like an expensive room candle that's fig-scented, and is $15–$20. **Rovero**'s (about $17) has a bit more tannin and a little more of a smoky, savory bent to its aromas and flavors.

and is a lighter color. But don't let that light color fool you into thinking it's light on flavor! Most Grignolinos are $18–$25, and go with almost everything but the very heaviest dishes. **Crivelli**'s feels a bit lusher and fuller-bodied on the palate than some other producers, and its aromas are really flamboyant—think rose petals and Rainier cherries. It's the kind of wine you just want to keep sniffing. **Enrico Rovero**'s Grignolino is a little less about ripe Rainier cherries, and a little more about sour cherries and sandalwood.

House parties. Sure, sophisticated dinner parties make you feel like a real grown-up, but a down-and-dirty house party can be just as great, no matter when you finished college. The faint sweat that collects on your forehead from being smashed against a bunch of people, the feeling that you could make out with anyone at any time. It's exhilarating . . . for about two hours, and then you'll probably want to be at home in your pajamas. For this kind of mash and mingle deal, you need something you can absentmindedly sip and not get too hammered, because God knows you probably won't be sensibly drinking a glass of water for every drink. Take a cue from the Spanish and try a **Tinto de Verano**—literally "red wine of summer." It's equal parts inexpensive red wine and lemon-lime soda drunk over ice with a lemon wedge, so it's easy to put together in a Solo cup with people knocking into you every 30 seconds. If adulterating wine sounds blasphemous, remember that people have been doctoring their wine with various herbs and flavorings for centuries. So relax!

The morning after an epic night. So your dinner out turned into a slumber party, and now everyone's in their pj's at your place and needs a little something to eat while they regroup and, most importantly, rehash what happened the night before. This calls for brunch! It's a little classier than showing up bleary-eyed at a diner (although you will miss out on the people-watching), and brunch is a great way to entertain. It's usually cheaper than throwing a dinner party, but the food is just different and festive enough that people are still impressed.

Brunch obviously calls for bubbles, but Champagne is a little on the nose—not to mention expensive. For something a bit different, try a **lambic**. These Belgian beers are known for their tarty, fruity flavors and dry, Champagne-like finish. If your girlfriends have a sweet tooth, the super-fruity and sweet lambics from **Lindemans** (Pêche and Framboise are especially delicious)

will go over well, but for something a little more interesting that will pair better with food, more traditional styles will be less sweet and more quaffable. **Brouwerij Boon Geuze Mariage Parfait** is a more complex take on raspberry lambic and perfect for brunch. It tastes like the love child of Champagne and a lighter Belgian beer. **Lindemans Gueuze**, a blended lambic style, is refreshing, drier than the fruit lambics they make, and has a gorgeous amber color that looks great in a flute.

All of these beers are tart and fruity, rather than bitter like an American pale ale or an IPA, and all that acidity will make your mouth water and hanker for another bite of egg strata or fried chicken and waffles.

Secret Single Behavior

O ne of the few things that *Sex and the City* really got right was that episode about "secret single behavior." The descriptions of all of the women's private rituals were so wonderfully specific, especially that image of Carrie standing at her kitchen counter, eating saltines with grape jelly on them and reading fashion magazines. After some rigorous, rosé-fueled polling of friends, the results are in and have been matched with their ideal beverages. Whether you're single or coupled, here are some ideas for beverages to pair with your inner weirdo.

Calgon, take me away. Is there anything better than a long bath, a glass of wine, and a juicy novel? Unless you add the real-life version of the Brawny man feeding you snacks and telling you how beautiful you are, probably not. You'll want to drink something aromatic, so that you can still smell it over the lavender bath bomb you've used, and something that will become a bit more complex as it gets warmer. Try a **dry,**

electrifying Riesling from Austria. If a Riesling is from Austria, you can be 99.99 percent sure it's dry—this is the dominant style for Riesling in that country. Other places, like New York's Finger Lakes region or Germany, make Rieslings in a range of styles, from bone dry to syrupy sweet, but with many landing in the murky zone we call "off-dry." Off-dry means a little sweet, but not dessert-wine sweet. But if you're looking for Austrian Riesling, you don't really have to worry about all these distinctions.

The dry Riesling from **Huber** retails for around $15, and is so tart and zippy it will keep you from dozing off in the bathtub. **Schloss Gobelsburg** is an iconic Austrian producer, and their single-vineyard Rieslings are bananas delicious—especially **Gaisberg**. Their texture is reminiscent of a great white Burgundy, in that yes, they are white wines, but they have the richness, depth, and power—that ability to make you sit back and say, *damn*—that reds do, but the aromas are textbook Riesling: white peaches, subtly floral, fabulous. One of the things about this style that's so compelling is that the aromas will make you think you're going to get something sweet, and then once you put it in your mouth you get this whiplash effect of something dry, tart, and very serious.

Master of your domain. You know how you get into those moods where you think if you could just get this ONE THING squared away, everything else in your life will just fall into place? *Tonight, I will organize all of my nail polish,* you think. You might get really obsessive and wash your walls, or fold every. single. piece. of laundry in your apartment, down to thongs that can't really be folded, but you put them into a more orderly shape, because you're getting your life together, goddammit. Something bracing, like the piney blast of an **American IPA**, will keep you from abandoning this project halfway through, annoying anyone else who lives with you when they enter the kitchen the next morning and wonder why the spices are spread out all over the floor, or, more importantly, why you've fallen asleep on the couch with a label maker by your head.

And if you're prone to snacking while engaging in compulsive behavior (because of course you are), an IPA will provide the perfect counterpoint to

KNOW YOUR STYLES
India Pale Ale (IPA)

REGION: As the name suggests, these originated as the beer of choice for British expats in India. Legend has it that the hops, which are an antibacterial agent, kept their brew from spoiling on the long, hot journey. But this high-gravity (read: boozy!) beer really came into its own in the United States, where craft brewers have used this hop-centric style to highlight the much more assertive flavors and aromas of American hop varieties.

DEFINING FLAVORS/AROMAS: These beers are all about showcasing hop aromas and flavors, which can range from citrusy (think juicy grapefruits and lemon zest) to piney, to floral, to almost soapy, kind of like cilantro.

PERFECT FOR: Foods with assertive flavors work best with the boldness of hop-heavy beers, so Indian and Mexican dishes are great. Fried foods are also wonderful with IPAs—the bubbles and bitterness are a nice counterpoint to rich, fatty, and crunchy foods. Anything from snack mix to fried chicken wings are great.

WHAT TO TRY: **Deschutes Fresh Squeezed IPA** is brewed with Citra and Mosaic hops, varieties known for their refreshing, citrusy qualities, and they really come shining through here with aromas of zesty lemons and flavors of white grapefruit juice. If you've had IPAs in the past and found them overwhelmingly bitter, this is a great one to try. **Stone IPA** is an American classic, with aromas and flavors that lean more toward the piney, resiny side of hops (think camping in the woods and maybe a little rosemary).

your super-salty blend of Chex Mix and Marcona almonds—plus these beers pack a pretty hefty alcoholic wallop, so snacks are a good idea, anyway. You might actually make it to bed and remember to put the label maker away.

Your favorite sandwich everyone else hates. Riesling is one of the most food-friendly wines on the planet. Though we associate it mostly with sweet wines, it has very high natural acidity, a quality that makes your mouth water and plays a big role in what makes wine great with food. So it almost doesn't matter what's in your crazy sandwich, as long as you're pairing it with something that will make you hanker for the next bite. Whether you love cream cheese and pickles, a grilled cheese with four different kinds of cheese, peanut butter and jelly with bread that's buttered, or a Monte Cristo, something with lots of mouthwatering acidity will be just what you need to cleanse your palate for the next bite of decadent trashiness. For a change of pace, try one of off-dry Riesling's many cousins like **Müller-Thurgau** ("MULE-er TUR-gow"). A cross between Riesling and another white variety, this unusual grape is aromatic like Sauvignon Blanc, but with less of a citrus edge—think papayas, underripe peaches, and orange blossoms. On the palate, it tends to be more tart than it smells.

Müller-Thurgau shines in northern Italy's Alto Adige region. Many producers in this area make one, but the version from **Kellerei Kaltern** (about $16) really shows the floral characteristics of the grape—the aromas remind me of lime skin and orange blossom. And **Muri-Gries** makes one with some of those trademark floral Riesling aromas, but with the volume turned down just a little.

Buy now with one click! Any site that requires you to pull out a credit card should have a Breathalyzer somehow involved. But for now, you'll need something to sip while you peruse discount beauty products, weird used books, and all of the new perfumes that have been released in a roller ball on the Sephora website. **Muscat** isn't just for Moscato d'Asti anymore (that's right, Drake). As one of the most ancient grape varieties, it's made into a wide range of styles, many of them dry. I like the sweet styles, too, but the dry ones are cool because they have the same heady, floral aromas, but are crisp and tart once you actually taste them. The aromas pull you in, all sweet and appealing, like really well-styled photos online. Then you're hit with this whiplash of acidity—sort of like that feeling you'll get a few days later when all the weird crap you ordered actually comes to your door, and all you're left with is a credit card bill and some glittery nail polish you'll never wear.

Italy's **Manincor** makes a dry Muscat that has all the floral craziness of the sweet, fizzy Moscato d'Asti, but is dry and tart. For $25–$30, you can drink something that is basically the equivalent of expensive perfume.

KNOW YOUR GRAPES

Muscat (muss-CAT)

REGION: In northern Italy, it's made into Moscato d'Asti (see page 35), and in the south of France, it's made into sweet dessert wines that are sometimes fortified. In other parts of southern France and in Greece, it's made into a fascinating dry white.

DEFINING FLAVORS/AROMAS: The whole perfume store, baby! Muscat is known for its flamboyant aromas—from exotic flowers like jasmine and orange blossom to juicy peaches and apricots.

PERFECT FOR: Sweet Muscats are great with lighter, non-chocolate desserts, like fruit tarts, or just by themselves. Dry Muscats, with their combination of heady, flamboyant fruit and floral aromas and dry, tart flavor, are wonderful with similarly aromatic cuisines, like Vietnamese, Laotian, or Thai.

WHAT TO TRY: **Arnaud de Villeneuve** is a producer based in southern France who makes a very dry, but floral-scented Muscat that manages to be refreshing despite all that perfume (about $12). **Domaine Weinbach** makes a fuller-bodied **Muscat Reserve** whose fruit flavors tend more toward golden raisins than tropical perfume, which retails for about $20 and is fantastic with Indian food.

Time-Consuming Beauty Rituals,

Why does all the pruning and landscaping required of modern womanhood take so damn long?! At least a nice beverage will pass the time—here's what to drink while primping. You can put on Jay Z's "Big Pimpin'" and sing along, substituting "primping," but that's a personal choice.

Pre-date landscaping. Getting ready for a date, especially one where you might actually get naked, can feel like being confronted with a garden that's gone fallow for several seasons. So much hair to remove, so many scaly spots to moisturize, so much concealer, so little time. Why not make all this scaling and trimming an event in and of itself? Am I recommending turning on music and taking a cocktail into the bathroom with you?

Why, yes, yes, I am. A great **vermouth**, like **Perucchi** or **Dolin**, is a perfect choice—it isn't just for martinis anymore! Vermouth is a fortified wine that includes the bonus of not just extra alcohol, but also botanicals and spices, which give it an herbaceous and sometimes astringent bite. Try a good-quality white vermouth over ice with a splash of soda and a grapefruit or lemon twist—it'll put a spring in your step and make you feel sexy and interesting.

If you're an adult, then you know all those at-home avocado masks are useless, but they are so fun! Is it the kid in us that just likes an excuse to smoosh mayonnaise through our hair? **At-home facials and beauty treatments** require something cooling and vaguely tropical to go with the scents of all the various goos and potions you're using. Try Argentina's **Torrontés**, a white grape that's the result of a cross between the Mission grape and the aromatic Muscat of Alexandria variety—but make sure to serve it really cold or it can taste too heavy and boozy. **Recuerdo** makes a wonderful one that is floral and exotic, but unlike some Torrontés wines, doesn't end up tasting like those little decorative guest soaps no one actually uses. Ask your local wine store for something that's not too fruity, and that should steer the sales assistant away from anything that smells like the latest Herbal Essences scent.

At least when you do your **manicure and pedicure** at home, you can wear sweatpants and watch old episodes of *Twin Peaks*. A nice fleshy **Pinot Gris from Oregon** is great to sip alone, and won't combine in an unpleasant way with the fumes of varnish and nail polish remover. **Ponzi** makes one that is fruity and fun to drink, but not *too* fruity, and **Elk Cove** is ubiquitous on restaurant lists and retail shelves for a reason—it's one of those wines that almost everyone likes. It's not oaky like some California Chardonnays, it's not pungent like a lot of Sauvignon Blancs, it just tastes like ripe, juicy pears and apples, and that's hard to object to! Both retail for around $20, and taste of ripe fall stone fruits, with a slight hint of sweetness reminiscent of rock candy.

Dye job. Having your hair dyed by competent professionals will make you look like a shampoo commercial, at least for a couple of weeks, but while you're sitting in that chair breathing in the toxic fumes, you'll feel like your life is just sliding through your fingers. It takes so long! Why?! Christ, it's like they mix and paint on a specific shade for every single separate hair on your head. Sip something slowly that feels rich and expensive, like a really good **Zinfandel**.

Poor Zin has gotten a bad rap, but the good ones, like those from classic producer **Ridge**, are blended with other grapes like Carignan (a grape grown in northern Spain and the south of France that's known for its tannic grip and dark blueberry flavors) and Petite Sirah to keep things from going too over-the-top jammy. A BYOB approach probably works only at a really nice salon, where they are used to crazy rich people who carry their dogs around in their purses and make all kinds of strange requests, so you arriving with your own wine will barely register as eccentric.

KNOW YOUR GRAPES

Zinfandel (ZIN-fan-del)

REGION: Brought to the United States in the 19th century, Zinfandel evolved from Italy's Primitivo grape. It's found a new home and a unique expression in California. The Napa Valley, Sonoma's Dry Creek, and Lodi are all regions known for this grape.

In the late 20th century, White Zinfandel, a semisweet rosé made from Zinfandel, became hugely popular, and while wine nerds turn up their noses at it, 85 percent of Zinfandel is made into White Zin. While not the most complex beverage in the world, White Zin is a "gateway wine" for many people, and its popularity has kept many older Zinfandel vines in the ground producing grapes that date from the late 19th century—had it not been so popular, they would have been ripped up and replaced by a more popular grape for red wine like Cabernet Sauvignon or Merlot.

DEFINING FLAVORS/AROMAS: When made into red wine, Zinfandel is big on alcohol and ripe, brambly, jammy fruit flavors, but lower in tannin and lighter in color than other popular red grapes grown in California like Merlot or Cabernet. It'll smell like super-ripe strawberries, raspberries, and sometimes kind of, well, leafy. Have you ever smelled an actual berry bush, or the top of a fresh tomato when it's pulled off the vine? Kinda like that. Zinfandel is also often aged in American oak barrels, so you'll get notes of vanilla, coconut, cedar, and dill, too.

PERFECT FOR: Foods with that savory/sweet combination like barbecue and gently spiced curries

WHAT TO TRY: **Ridge Three Valleys** ($21–$25) is a little darker-colored and fuller-bodied than some of the jammier, fruitier Zins you might see at the local grocery store. **Dashe Cellars** makes a line of really interesting Zinfandels made from single vineyards called **Les Enfants Terribles**. These are lower in alcohol, subtler, and more perfumy and elegant, kind of like a weird combination of Pinot Noir and Zinfandel. At about $75, they're not cheap, but for a special occasion are worth seeking out. For a modern take on White Zin, **Storybook Mountain** makes a **Zin Gris** ($15–$17) that's made in a dry style, so you get some of those sweet, strawberry jam flavors, but with a dry, refreshing finish.

Growing Up and Getting Older

Marking life's occasions and milestones is one of the oldest and most important uses of beer and wine. Unfortunately, most of us won't be inheriting a manor stocked with Claret that's ready to be opened at the peak of maturity, so we've just got to muddle through on our own.

What to drink with those intimidating, round-number birthdays, and other big-deal events like graduation, will be addressed here. But perhaps more importantly, we'll look at how to toast those moments that aren't covered in the greeting card section of the drugstore. Being ma'amed for the first time, or the affront to dignity that is discovering varicose veins, definitely merits an adult beverage. And if you're graduating but don't quite know what to do next, or wallowing in that wistful feeling that arises when you realize there's absolutely no way you'll accomplish most of your childhood dreams because you're too old to become an astronaut and were terrible at science anyway, we've got you covered for that, too.

Your "Big" Birthday

Although no one likes getting older, it is an excuse to celebrate, and usually someone else is buying what you're celebrating with. Whether you're drowning your sorrows at being one year closer to death, or toasting a momentous birthday, now is the time to splurge on an iconic bottle, or just treat yourself to something you love, even if everyone else thinks it's weird. Here are some special wines and beers to put on your wish list—or to file away for the next time your dad or best friend has a big-deal birthday to celebrate.

Turning 21. If you happen to be this young, or have friends or family members celebrating this milestone birthday, do everyone a favor: no car bombs and none of those weird "shots" where they take everything in the rail and mix it together and try to make you throw up. No, your 21st should, ideally, be a time to be ushered into the world of legal-drinking adulthood with something delicious and momentous like a great bottle of **Champagne** (see pages 80–81). Save your pennies, or convince your friends to go in on a bottle or two. You won't regret it.

27: You're almost there (wherever *there* is). Age 27 is sort of a way station on the road to true adulthood. Some people really have their shit figured out by then, and some are still living like 19-year-olds. Both are perfectly acceptable these days—not sure what that says about our generation, but there's a limit to how much we can tackle in just one book, so let's move on.

Even if you haven't started stocking away cases of first-growth Bordeaux, you can at least graduate to decent beer. Try a couple of **classic American craft brews** and see which one should be your new go-to beer to keep on hand. You may just have a mini-fridge in your parents' basement, but you can start to accumulate some of your own stuff that will make you

Even if you haven't started stocking away cases of first-growth Bordeaux, you can at least graduate to decent beer.

feel like an independent person, and not an overgrown child. **Dogfish Head 60 Minute IPA** is a pungent, hoppy, yet balanced take on an American IPA. It's a good option when nothing else on the draft list looks appealing, both because it tastes great and because it's popular, so it's probably fresher than most of the other options. And while we don't really think of **Samuel Adams Boston Lager** as being craft beer anymore, we wouldn't have all the nut-bar chipotle and peanut butter ales we do today without this American classic. Sometimes, clichés exist for a reason, and this is one of them!

One of the best things about the American craft beer movement is how thoroughly it has proliferated into almost every part of the country, so consider this encouragement to find some breweries near you. Their flagship brew might just become your house beer.

The Big 3-0. When you turn 30 you are, even in our society that tends to extend adolescence indefinitely, unequivocally an adult. Your teens and 20s are often about trying on a series of personas and habits to find what really fits, but once you're 30, you usually know what kind of life you want, even if you're not quite there. One of the things you may not have figured out yet is how mature you like your wine. So for your 30th birthday, buy yourself (or ask someone to gift you) a **case of wine in a style you like that's known for aging well, and pop open a bottle every year thereafter**. Each year,

Champagne (sham-PAYNE)

REGION: Champagne is in northern France, about an hour away from Paris. The climate is so cold that growers often have to bury their vines during the winter to protect them from the snow. It's not an easy place to grow grapes, which is one of the many reasons why Champagne is so pricey!

GRAPE: Chardonnay, Pinot Noir, or Pinot Meunier—most are a mix of these three grapes. Pinot Noir and its cousin Pinot Meunier (also red) are usually made into white sparklers by pressing the juice out of the skins right away so as not to impart any color.

HOW IT'S MADE: To be called Champagne, it has to be made in a specific way and meet certain quality standards. The French are serious about their wine bureaucracy! Here's a quick summary of the *méthode champenoise*:

1. Start with still wine. Most still wines made in the Champagne region are so tart they'd take the enamel off your teeth.

2. Bottle said still wine with a little bit of sugar and additional yeast (this mixture is called *liqueur de tirage*) and close the bottle with a crown cap.

3. A second fermentation will begin in the bottle now, creating those famous bubbles. They'll stay in the bottle because of that crown cap.

4. Special racks called gyropalettes, or riddling racks (if the producer is really old school), help move all the dead yeast cells that accumulate during this second fermentation down to the neck of the bottle. The bottles are tilted and turned slowly during this process so that all of that sludge moves toward the neck. If riddling racks are being used, someone comes and turns the bottle a little bit each day. These dead yeast cells are called lees, and Champagne must age for at least 12 months on said lees before the next step. This process is called *sur lie* and it's a bit like bottle-conditioning beer. Other types of sparkling wine that are made in the same basic method as Champagne don't spend nearly as much time *sur lie*. As you can imagine, it's expensive

to have so much inventory just sitting there, aging, so while this step adds to the complexity of Champagne, it's one of the things that makes it so pricey.

5. Dry ice is used to freeze the neck of the bottle so that the dead yeast cells form a plug, and when the crown cap is popped off, the yeast plug shoots out. A mixture of sugar and a little base wine, known as the *dosage* (also called *liqueur d'expédition*), is added before a specially shaped Champagne cork is shoved into the bottle.

6. You now have Champagne!

DEFINING FLAVORS/AROMAS: Many of the aromas that make Champagne famous are the result of that long aging *sur lie* process. This extended contact with dead yeast cells (kinda gross if you think about it, right?) gives Champagne a—you guessed it—*yeasty* aroma. These aromas remind critics who make their money writing fanciful wine reviews of more exciting things than "yeast" or "bread." Often it's referred to as "brioche." Hookay, Marie Antoinette. Once you actually get the fizz into your mouth, it's usually pretty tart and sassy. That tartness, in addition to the bubbles, is what makes Champagne such a great predinner drink, because when your mouth waters, it signals your stomach that it's food time and gets your gastric juices flowing. *Bon appétit!*

PERFECT FOR: What ISN'T Champagne perfect with? Seriously, Champagne isn't just for toasting at weddings and New Year's Eve. It's great with anything fried, crispy, or crunchy and with creamy, unctuous foods like smoked salmon. Try it with fried chicken. Or just those delicious crispy chicken strips from Popeyes with plenty of that sweet, gloopy mustard stuff and biscuits. It's the perfect high/low food-and-wine pairing, and totally decadent and delicious.

WHAT TO TRY: Champagne is home to a growing number of independent producers who are giving big houses like Veuve Clicquot a run for their money.

Guy Larmandier Blanc de Blancs is made from all Chardonnay grapes (hence the name, "white from whites") and is light and crisp without being wussy. This handmade Champagne from Cramant, one of the villages in Champagne with the highest quality ranking, just makes you feel fancy. At about $60, it's pretty reasonable for great quality Champagne.

Pierre Péters Cuvée Spéciale Les Chétillons will knock your socks off. It's got that bracing, effervescent quality that all good Champagne has, but with an extra note of depth. This all-Chardonnay cuvée may be a beautiful blonde, but she's got a doctorate in theoretical physics, too. It usually retails for around $100, but for a special occasion, it's worth it.

make a note of what it tastes and smells like, and whether you like it more or less than the previous year. This will help you figure out whether you like your wines young and fresh, or you're more into the distinguished, silver foxes of the wine world. This is a good opportunity to enlist help from your local wine-shop. Once you give them the details of your little project, they'll probably be super excited to help you.

Bordeaux and wines based on Nebbiolo are especially known for their ability to age. However, stay away from the following styles of wine/grapes, because they are likely to taste like poo after a few years no matter what: Viognier, Sauvignon Blanc, Pinot Grigio, Prosecco, Beaujolais Nouveau or

What's the Deal with Aging Wine?

It would be great to be able to give some magic formula for how long to hold every type of wine for maximum pleasure, but the truth is, there is no such thing. The best way to figure out how long to hold your wines is to taste as many as possible.

Whenever you get an opportunity to taste older wines (keep an eye out for older wines being poured at local wineshops during their free tastings—it doesn't happen super often), jump on it, and really think about whether or not you like the aromas and flavors. Whether it's just a few years past the normal release cycle for that style of wine (say, five years for a California Cabernet instead of two or three), or a true library release that's 10 or 20 years old or more, it's always a great opportunity.

It's absolutely OK to not enjoy older wine, or to enjoy most styles younger.

Wine critics are notorious for putting these incredibly specific "drink windows" at the end of their reviews, and while they are sometimes helpful, usually they end up sounding ridiculous: *OK, sure, just because this old white dude says so, I'm going to wait to open this bottle until the second Tuesday of 2073 when there's a full moon.*

The only reason to age a wine is if you think it'll get better than it is right now. So, for example, if you enjoy the flavors, but the tannins are a bit too strong, aging it for a few years will soften those tannins, and you might like it better (tannins and pigment from grape skins are mostly what form that sludge at the bottom of older bottles). But if what you love about a wine are its fresh, fruity aromas, well, those will be the first to go as it ages, so drink it up ASAP!

Villages, and Dolcetto (usually). And while you don't have to go nuts and spend $100 a bottle, you should probably spend at least $20.

Ready to retire: 65. As you're nearing retirement age, go for something classic, like a rich, fleshy **Pinot Noir from northern California**. The Pinot from **Robert Stemmler** is delicious—deep, full-bodied, and tasting of cherries so ripe and dark red they're ready to burst, as opposed to sour cherries you'd normally use for pie, but still balanced. It'll run you about $50. If that's a little too pricey, **Siduri** in Russian River makes a fantastic Pinot Noir at around $30 with the signature spicy aromas, reminiscent of those fancy "artisanal" colas. Yum!

Wine nerds like to hate on this style of Pinot Noir, but even though it can veer a little too far into cherry lollipop territory, it's very easy to like (and drink!). So enjoy indulging in a Pinot that tastes a little like cherry pie while planning all of the exotic vacations you're going to take now that you have the time.

A grande dame of 70. At 70, you can officially stop giving a shit what anyone thinks, can't you? You can also start wearing capes unironically, and just say fuck it and eat chocolate cake and whiskey for breakfast. But most people who reach age 70 probably are more sensible than that, so hopefully, you will be, too. Try a stately, expensive **Sauternes**, a famous style of dessert wine that manages to taste delicious and indulgent while still being sophisticated and fancy. Made from tart white grapes that have been intentionally left to rot, which only happens in exactly the right way in the best years, Sauternes tastes like candied apricots and dried pineapple, but usually lacks that sticky, cloying feeling. Sauternes is from Bordeaux, and it carries with it

all the weight of that famous region. And like Bordeaux, these wines range from the stupid expensive, like **Château d'Yquem**, to the very reasonable. So break out the fancy cheese and pour yourself a glass. You've earned it, and you've probably earned the right not to share, either.

KNOW YOUR STYLES

Sauternes (saw-TERN)

REGION: Bordeaux, France

GRAPE: Sémillon, Sauvignon Blanc, or Muscadelle. These wines are generally blends of these three grapes. Each producer has their own style—some use almost all Sémillon, some use more Sauvignon Blanc, and many use no Muscadelle at all.

DEFINING FLAVORS/AROMAS: The aromas in Sauternes are often reminiscent of those sticky candied apricots you get around the holidays. It will feel luxuriously thick in your mouth, but there should be a little "pop" of bright, fruity flavor toward the end that keeps it from feeling annoying and sticky after you've swallowed.

PERFECT FOR: Foie gras, runny cheeses, strong blue cheese, or just by itself! At this point in your life, you've probably had enough birthday cake, but who among us has really eaten her fair share of super-fatty goose liver?

WHAT TO TRY: **Château d'Yquem** is the undisputed best producer in the region of Sauternes (French winemakers can be fiercely proud when it comes to what they produce, but even other winemakers in Sauternes are like, "Yeah, Yquem is the best, no one else even comes close," probably followed by one of those typical French-dude shrugs). Depending on the vintage and where you buy it, it can range from really expensive to stupid, astronomically expensive. Happily, there are lots of more sensibly priced producers out there.

Château Doisy Daëne is around $45 per bottle—a reasonable price for a delicious, balanced Sauternes from a classic producer.

Château Guiraud is unctuous and sweet, but with a bright note of pineapple that helps keep it all in balance. You can find half bottles pretty easily for around $25, sometimes less.

'Discovering Signs, of Aging

I f ever there was a situation that merits a drink, it's discovering disturbing evidence of your slow decline and eventual death. Found a new wrinkle or gray hair? Slap on some hair dye, and drink to forget—and to mask the suffocating dye fumes.

Gray hair where?! Gray hair on your head is one thing. You can dye it, or you can let the streaks grow in and enjoy looking like an eccentric middle-school art teacher who has the class make dream catchers every semester. But a weird, wiry gray eyebrow hair that won't lie flat and play nicely with the rest of your brows (why?!), or, worse, one in the, er, bathing suit area? That calls for a drink, or possibly something even stronger! Attempt to embrace being older with a distinguished **off-dry German Riesling**. The Kabinett (the least sweet of the sweet Riesling styles—think lemonade sweet, not cough syrup sticky sweet) from **Joh. Jos. Prüm** is especially known for its ability to age, but many wines in this off-dry category (a little sweetness balanced by bright, tart acidity) age well also. Acidity and sugar both contribute to a wine's ability to age. These Rieslings wear their grays with élan and are excellent with pork sausages. So open up a bottle, pluck that weird eyebrow hair, and revel in your mature sophistication.

You can't be old enough to drink!! Realizing just how recently some 21-year-olds have been born is terrifying. In the presence of younger people, it's easy to forget everything that's great about being older, and one of the best things about getting older is appreciating the subtler things in life, like an **under-the-radar classic Chardonnay**. Grown on a historic vineyard on Spring Mountain in the Napa Valley, **Stony Hill Chardonnay** was one of the first wines to gain a cult following here in the United States. Basically it was hipster wine before skinny jeans existed.

Stony Hill Chardonnays (around $40 retail) are a world away from the richer, more "buttery" style of producers like Rombauer. It's a subtle style of Chardonnay that is easy to overlook, especially in an area like the Napa Valley, where flashy reds and heavily oaked whites are often what get all the attention. It's lemony and fresh, but with more depth and weight than Chardonnays made in stainless steel tanks. The folks at Stony Hill have been doing things their way for a long time, and they have earned the respect of wine geeks all over the world. Their oak barrels are old and crusty looking, but the wines are clear and pure as a church bell. Let the young whipper-snappers have their short shorts—pour yourself a glass of old-school Chard and go to bed at 10:30 p.m. You've earned it.

That first time someone calls you ma'am, in that, ugh, overly respectful tone is just the worst. You start feverishly thinking back to your younger days, remembering all those concerts you crowd surfed at, all the clubs you snuck into underage. *I had a great fake ID once!* you want to shout to the kid who just rung you up for almond milk and the "supergrains" mix you use to make a healthier version of tabbouleh you pack for work almost every . . . oh, fuck. You are totally, totally old. Remember those frosty, comfortingly bland cans of anonymous, fizzy water that approximated beer that you drank at all those crazy, loud punk shows you used to go to? Well, American craft brewers have reclaimed this style, and have reimagined the PBR of your youth as something light and drinkable, but flavorful enough that you still know you're drinking beer. Now that you're officially old, try one of these **lagers for grown-ups**:

- **Victory Helles Lager** is an homage to the German-inflected beer styles that have always been popular in its home state of Pennsylvania, and if you could bottle the taste of a sunny, open field, this would be the way. The barest hint of hop bitterness and a pleasing fizz make this a high-quality lager that will make you regret all those watery beers of your youth.

What's the Deal with Buttery Chardonnay?

Buttery is a term that's often used to describe Chardonnay, especially Chardonnay from California, but what does that actually mean? Is there butter in the wine?

Not quite, but close! Most red wines and some whites like Chardonnay actually go through two fermentations. The first is the traditional fermentation we think of, which turns sugar into alcohol. The second is what's called malolactic fermentation. This turns malic acid into lactic acid. You know how when you bite into a super-tart Granny Smith apple, it's so sour that it almost sends a little shiver down your spine? That's malic acid at work. Lactic acid is softer—it's what gives yogurt its tang. In red wine and in white wine styles like fuller-bodied Chardonnay, lactic acid is more pleasant and jibes better with the over-all profile of the wine. Winemakers can play with the fermentation

temperatures and types of yeast they use to induce these secondary fermentations and create the effect they're after—butter bomb, or a softer hit of creaminess. Each style has its fans!

A by-product of this process is a compound called diacetyl. It's what makes cultured dairy products like European butter taste, well, buttery. The scary yellow stuff you put on movie theater popcorn also contains lots of diacetyl, created in a more . . . industrial way. The presence of diacetyl also creates a rounder, fuller mouthfeel, which in Chardonnay like you find in California, is desirable. I find that my customers who like to drink Chardonnay on its own prefer a style that has a more amped-up diacetyl/buttery factor, and folks who drink their Chardonnay before or during a meal prefer less of this influence.

So, all those "buttery" California Chardonnays really are! The more you know...

- **Brooklyn Brewery** was one of the first craft breweries to bring back this style, and their **Brooklyn Lager** is still their flagship beer. Lightly bitter from dry hopping and smooth and easy going down, it's a session beer that's way too easy to drink.

- **Stillwater Classique** proves that you can make a flavorful beer using ingredients usually eschewed by quality-focused craft brewers, like corn and rice. Also brewed with a yeast strain used for farmhouse ales (known for their sour tang) and Cascade hops, this modern spin on your grandpa's lager is refreshing and lemony, kind of like a beer version of those preserved lemons you see in Moroccan cuisine, or the olive bar at Whole Foods. It'll make you feel hip and nostalgic all at the same time.

Varicose veins. You work out regularly, moisturize obsessively, occasionally go outdoors and get some sun. You thought your legs looked fine. Then you decided to get a little wild and try on a short skirt, and getting a good look at them in that unforgiving fluorescent light was a rude awakening, like staring at a terrifying road map to your own sexual irrelevance. So, what to sip while you're perusing expensive vein treatment therapies on the Internet?

> *It's like staring at a terrifying road map to your own sexual irrelevance.*

Try a **traditional English ale**—something from a country where TV stars have wrinkles and slightly crooked teeth seems appropriate. It will never taste quite as good as it does fresh from a real English pub, but if you're not taking a flight to London anytime soon, try **Samuel Smith Nut Brown Ale** or **Yorkshire Stingo**. These beers are rich and malty—with flavors of hazelnuts, brown sugar, and raisins—but they finish clean, with no lingering stickiness on your tongue. And maybe order some of those compression socks. It can't hurt.

°Class Reunions,

How did anyone even plan or attend their high school reunions before Facebook, let alone do the extremely important ground-work of stalking former classmates to see how you measure up? Whether you're gloating about your success or hoping no one notices that you haven't done anything with your life except allow your ass to get a little bigger, you'll definitely need a drink.

Five-year reunion. The concept of a five-year reunion is just cruel and unusual. No one has their shit together by 22 or 23. The people who do will gloat about their Peace Corps assignments, or how they won a grant to study something in an exotic location, or how they have a real, grown-up job with an office already, and the fact that you were rejected by Starbucks will come into awful, painful relief. Whether you've got it together or not, just skip the whole thing. It'll just be attended by obnoxious show-offs and organized by the hyper weirdos who ran the yearbook.

Instead, surround yourself with your real friends from your youth, the ones you actually talk to and don't just stalk on Facebook. Gather in someone's basement to eat terrible junk food like you did in high school, and instead of pairing it with wine coolers or pilfered gin from your friend with the lax parents' liquor cabinet, have some fun, fizzy red from Italy, like **Lambrusco**. Perfect for a night of indulging, Lambrusco runs the gamut from fairly sweet and tasting of ripe cherries and plums, to dry and tart, almost reminiscent of cranberries and rhubarb. (Some will say on the label whether they're dry or sweet, but in my experience the labeling isn't consistent, so if you're not familiar with the wine, it's best to ask.) Traditionally this style is drunk with cheese and char-

Whether you've got it together or not, just skip the whole thing.

cuterie, so it's a natural match for pizza. If you and your friends really want to treat yourselves, order one draped in salty prosciutto and maybe with some arugula thrown on top for

a nice bitter contrast to all that meat and cheese. A little nostalgic music like you used to listen to when you had more time to obsess over the relative cool factor of bands wouldn't hurt, either. So what if your net worth consists of a huge pile of job applications and a half-broken sofa bed from IKEA?

Cleto Chiarli e Figli Lambrusco di Sorbara Vecchia Modena Premium is a very dry, tart version of this style. It's almost like fizzy Pinot Noir, with its super-bright sour cherry and cranberry flavors. Delicious, but best with food. **Vigneto Saetti Lambrusco Salamino di Santa Croce** is made in the method used in traditional Champagne (most Lambrusco is made in a more industrial method), and the handwork shows, because in addition to its darker color, it smells and tastes earthier, like mushrooms and grilled meat—sort of like someone threw cherry sauce over your grilled boar sausage. Yum!

Ten-year reunion. Your best friend's dad was this gruff Italian guy who had a great record collection, and always had a six-pack of **Peroni** in the refrigerator. You may have grown apart from your friend—but as soon as you see her across the auditorium all those great memories come rushing back. Sneak out back to the bleachers where you used to sit and gossip about your teachers, read, and eat too many of those terrible for you Otis Spunkmeyer cookies that were three for a dollar. She'd smoke, you'd lecture her about the dangers of smoking. Good times. Sneak a six-pack of Peroni out and let the memories flow. This pale, anonymous lager always smells a little funky and almost skunked, even when it's not. Feel free to substitute your favorite beverage that, while it doesn't taste great, brings back great memories.

At your **20-year reunion**, everyone has gotten boring. Deep into childrearing, caring for aging parents, or both, your late 30s are a time where the shit kind of hits the fan and you can't even pretend to be young anymore. To really catch up with all your old friends, make a quick and dirty **shandy** with whatever lager is on offer at the bar, and lemonade. You'll be able to drink these all night, and not get that "I'm too old for this" feeling in the morning.

40-year reunion. You may have been captain of the debate team and alone on prom night during high school, but a few decades out, you've already retired. All those football players are a little worse for wear, while just last year you learned how to paddleboard while vacationing at your apartment in Puerto Rico. You may have been an afterthought in high school, but now all those long nights you spent studying have paid off. Let's face it, the selection at these things leaves something to be desired and you don't have your wine cellar or humidor at your disposal. Just remember that the safest bets at events like these where the wine selection is dubious at best are crisp whites that traditionally don't see any oak. So, **Pinot Grigio** or **Sauvignon Blanc** is usually your best bet. Crummy Pinot Grigio may not blow you away with complexity, but it's rarely actively bad. And if you're in a crowded, stuffy banquet room, go ahead and drop an ice cube in it. Hey, if you're CEO of a successful company or created a TV show or something, you don't need to show off. Hold your head high and don't pay attention to the former cheerleaders sniggering at you. Go find the kids from the French Club and have some real fun.

A Shandy by Another Name

Shandies and their assorted variations have become very popular in the last few years—and it's about time! Quite a few breweries are making bottled versions, but I still think this is a drink best made on your own. Here's a rundown of some terms you might see and how to mix one yourself:

- **Shandy** = beer + lemonade. For a super-easy shandy, I like **Long Trail Summer Ale** and Newman's Own lemonade, in a proportion of about one-third lemonade to two-thirds beer. Cheers to a long, sunny summer!

- **Radler** = beer + citrusy soda. Austrian beer giant **Steigl** makes a prepackaged **Radler** with their light pilsner mixed with grapefruit soda. It's not the most complex beverage on the planet, but for a picnic on a hot summer day, that slightly bitter hint of grapefruit zest is super refreshing. I like to put an amped-up, American-style spin on this classic with a half-and-half mix of San Pellegrino orange soda and **Deschutes Brewery Fresh Squeezed IPA.** You get the sweet, tangy orange flavors of the soda up front, and the bitterness comes rushing in on the finish. Super refreshing and fun to drink. Where's my hammock?!

- **Diesel** = beer + cola. There are a few different drink recipes that go by the name Diesel floating around, but I like the German version, which is half lager and half cola. I like a mixture of a mild but not too watery lager, like **Blue Mountain,** and a slightly spicy artisanal cola, like Boylan. Fevertree is another delicious change of pace from the usual Coke or Pepsi, but its assertive, almost peppery flavors tend to take over in mixed drinks.

These are all drinks that are meant to be fun and not taken too seriously, so feel free to experiment! Some people like to stick with a traditional half-and-half ratio, and some people like a little more beer and a little less soda/lemonade.

˙Graduation˳

Graduations are one of those milestones that are often kind of a letdown. You know how sometimes you feel like you're going to sneeze for what seems like forever, and instead of getting that satisfying sneeze out of your system, it just . . . never comes? It's kind of like that. There's all this buildup, and the frantic writing of papers, and then, what was supposed to be a leap into the great, wild, wonderful unknown is more like stepping into an empty, airless waiting room in a metaphorical beige dentist's office, and it all leaves you wondering, what next? If you can't find a sexy older woman to have an affair with, you can at least drink something decent.

Your law degree. Although a law degree isn't exactly the ticket to the good life that it once was, still . . . you're a lawyer! So pony up and spring for a bottle of expense-account wine—something bold, so dark you can't see your fingers through it, and that comes in a bottle so heavy it seems criminal to use the fuel to ship it. Big, rich Napa Valley Cabernet is a good choice for this, but if you want some bang for your buck (say, you haven't landed that sweet gig yet), try a **Cabernet blend from Washington State**. You'll get a lot of the oak spice and richness that you do from Napa Cabernets, but for a fraction of the cost.

Efestē Final Final is blended with a bit of Syrah, like many Washington State Cabernets, giving it a hint of smokiness. It's a wonderful combination of ripe, dark fruits like plums and blackberries, with those spice box aromas from oak (hints of sandalwood, cinnamon, chocolate, and even cola). It's great with steak crusted with peppercorns, and usually around $30.

Basel Cellars Estate Claret is a fantastic value for a Cabernet-based blend. As much as I bitch and moan about overuse of oak in wine, this is one place where lavish oak treatment really works, and those vanilla and cedar aromas meld perfectly with ripe blackberry flavors. There's a nice little pop of mouthwatering acidity here, too, that is often lacking in wines made in this style. Customers of mine routinely guess that it is way more expensive than it really is! (It usually retails for around $23.)

Your Ph.D. If ever there was a project that requires dogged determination against all odds, it's finishing a Ph.D. Most people who have completed one will tell you it's just something you have to chip away at, a little each day, and even when you're finally done, you rarely get the accolades or attention you deserve. The wines of **Beaujolais** are the same way. They may have earned a bad reputation based on the gallons of crappy Beaujolais Nouveau churned out every November, and there may be only a handful of people who recognize the better producers, but hardy French farmers have been working that land for centuries, harvesting by hand every year (harvesting by machine is illegal there) and turning out honest, food-friendly wine that rarely gets big scores or splashy wine magazine covers, but is an excellent dinner companion. **Jean-Paul Brun**'s earthy Beaujolais are worth checking out, as is the gutsy, yet still fruity and fun to drink **Brouilly** from **Château Thivin**.

> *When you're finally done, you rarely get the accolades or attention you deserve. The wines of Beaujolais are the same way.*

Your useless liberal arts degree. At 17 or 18, you wanted to choose something that really inspired you. You figured that four years is a long time—you'd have it all figured out by the end. Maybe you majored in conceptual art, or philosophy, or early 20th-century theater, or poetry. Whatever it is, it's great knowledge to have, but now you can't, well, get a job. You'll need something comforting and hopeful, and there is no more comforting and hopeful color

KNOW YOUR STYLES

Beaujolais (bo-jo-LAY)

REGION: Just north of Lyon in France

GRAPE: Gamay or Chardonnay

DEFINING FLAVORS/AROMAS: When it's young, red wine made in Beaujolais has what I think of as "fresh" fruit aromas. Think raspberries and cherries that are just barely ripe enough to eat, as opposed to super-ripe fruit that's been sitting in a fruit salad bowl for a few hours. As reds based on Gamay age, they tend to get more mellow and earthy, as most red wines do, but they do so in a way that reminds many people of their neighbor to the north, Burgundy, and they take on some of the same qualities Pinot Noir does as it ages—aromas of mushroom and forest floor, and an affinity for duck.

PERFECT FOR: Charcuterie, roast chicken, and—this is my guilty pleasure—hot dogs. Just think of them as American charcuterie.

WHAT TO TRY: **Jean-Marc Lafont Domaine de Bel Air Brouilly** (about $15) is the perfect summertime red. Its aromas remind me of raspberries and fancy violet soap, and it tastes even better after it's been in the refrigerator for a few minutes. I also love the wines from **Domaine de la Chapelle des Bois**, especially their **Fleurie "Grand Pré"** (usually in the low $20s). It's a great example of Beaujolais that is a little less light and fruity, and takes on more of those earthy characteristics. It's the absolute perfect style of wine to take to a dinner party, because it's dark enough and has enough tannin and "oomph" to seem like "real red wine," but it won't overwhelm roast chicken.

than pink. Try a delicious **off-dry rosé from France's Loire Valley**, specifically from a little subregion called Anjou. **Champteloup** makes a delicious, inexpensive (usually around $10) off-dry rosé. You may be feeling bitter and dejected, but you can still drink something sweet, and you'll always be the smartest person at any dinner party, so at least you have that?

Your sensible major. So you were smart and practical, and majored in something that isn't stupid—like computer engineering or nursing. You may seem boring on the surface, but everyone is really just jealous of how much you have your shit together. You may as well just keep going with this, and

Pinot Gris vs. Pinot Grigio: What's in a Name?

One of the more confusing aspects of the wine world is that sometimes the same grape is grown in different countries and so, logically, you end up with that grape having different names. The name for the pinky-gray clone of Pinot Noir is Pinot Gris in French, and Pinot Grigio in Italian—*gris* and *grigio* both mean "gray." What makes things even more confusing is the fact that the style in which this grape is made into wine has evolved differently in France and Italy. This means that when winemakers in other parts of the world use this grape, which name they choose often tells you which style they're going for. This isn't true 100 percent of the time, but it's usually true.

When you see **Pinot Gris** on the label, it means the producer is going for a somewhat fuller-bodied, riper style popular in Alsace, the region in France where you most often see Pinot Gris. The flavors here are more golden apples, pears, and other fruit flavors I put in the "fall fruit" category. Wines in this style sometimes have a teeny bit of sweetness to them, too. Don't freak out, they don't taste like dessert wines—it's just a touch, and it makes this style great with roasted fall and winter vegetables.

When you see **Pinot Grigio** on the label, it means that the producer is going for the Italian style. Alto Adige is the most famous region in Italy for Pinot Grigio, and white wines there are made in a crisper, fresh style. The fruit flavors will usually remind you more of Meyer lemons and crisp, tart apples. Some producers in Alto Adige have been ramping up the ripeness and richness of their wines, and have been letting the juice sit with those pinkish skins a little longer to give the wine more color and flavor, but most Italian Pinot Grigio falls into the more "dry, citrusy, quaffable" category.

choose a new go-to wine that mirrors your personality. **Pinot Grigio** is one of those wines that people dismiss as boring, overly reliable, watery, and bland. But they don't have to be! A well-made Pinot Grigio is like the perfect dinner party guest—subtle enough to not dominate the conversation, but always with something interesting to say if you ask. Pinot Grigio has a pretty wide range of flavors—from ripe golden apples and juicy pears to crisp lemons—that present in different ways depending on where it's grown and how it's made. It will please almost anyone who likes white wine, so it's perfect to keep on hand for unexpected guests, like that friend who always shows up at your door with an intense life crisis. Maybe this time she'll actually take your advice.

Nals Margreid Punggl has that perfect combination of richness and depth of flavor that people who claim to not like whites look for, but with mouthwatering acidity that really revs up your appetite. It's around $16, but feels much more sophisticated. **Di Lenardo Pinot Grigio** shows off the more citrusy, refreshing side of the grape, with flavors of Honeycrisp apples and Meyer lemon. It's right around $12 and even sports a convenient screwcap. (How practical are you?) It's great with sautéed chicken thighs with a bit of sauce, or any number of simple weeknight meals. And don't forget the Pinot Grigio from **Kellerei Kaltern**. This producer's wines are such great values for the money. For $11–$12, you have something that is easy and refreshing, but also has some interesting pear and kind of candy apple flavors if you pay a little more attention to it.

Thwarted Childhood Fantasies,

Sure, you love your career in library science or real estate, but every once in a while it's fun to fantasize about the amazing things you thought you'd do with your life when you were a kid. Sometimes reverting to all of those daydreams can be a good thing. What you dreamed about doing as a kid can tell you a lot about who you are now and what you should be doing. Besides, listening to music is so much better when you're fantasizing about being the really sexy lead singer. Plus, what goes better with daydreaming than a nice drink?

Fancy businesswoman. You remember that scene in *Kill Bill* when Lucy Liu's character has that meeting in that fancy boardroom/criminal lair, and cuts off that guy's head? Or all the killer suits and shoes Bette wore in Season 1 of *The L Word*? Being that kind of fancy businesswoman is the ultimate fantasy—no one's life is like that all the time, but it's so fun to dream about being the kind of person who gets luxurious pedicures while yelling self-importantly on an expensive cell phone, or strides confidently into boardrooms. Something so deep and dark it's almost intimidating is what you need. Try a full-bodied style of Italian red called **Amarone**, or, for a lighter, less expensive version, its younger cousin, **Valpolicella Ripasso**.

Amarone ("am-ah-RO-nee") is made from grapes that have been dried out on purpose, so it tastes like dried strawberries and cherries. Traditionally that "big gun" wine you bring out at the end of the evening, it's not a dessert wine; it's more of a "dessert alternative" wine that you have with cheese, dried fruits, and nuts after dinner when you're sitting around talking and don't want the night to end. They can go above 16 percent ABV, so sip slowly! **Prà Amarone della Valpolicella** is made in a very classic style: inky dark in the glass, with aromas of dried cherries and plums, with some floral notes as well. At around $60, it's a splurge, but well worth it. **Musella Amarone della Valpolicella** will be a little lighter on your palate and your wallet—it hovers around $40.

Ripasso has some of the same dried-fruit flavors, but in a lighter package. **Allegrini Ripasso Valpolicella** (around $20) has some of that raisiny, dried-cherry flavor that Amarone has, but not as much of the tarry, smoky bass notes. It's perfect by itself when you want a glass of something warming and sexy to curl up with on the couch.

These are what old Italian men with big watches, possible Mob connections, and visible chest hair drink after dinner.

These are what old Italian men with big watches, possible Mob connections, and visible chest hair drink after dinner. Drink yours while looking at sky-high heels and suits you can't afford on the Internet.

If you're the kind of adventurous person who day-dreamed about being **an astronaut** as a kid and now get your science on with a trip to a museum or by watching *Cosmos* or *Through the Wormhole*, try a **crazy, adventurous beer** from one of America's creative craft breweries. Go arty with something from **Stillwater Artisanal**; their **Vacuum Readymade** (the label is a little nod to Marcel Duchamp) is a double whammy of dark roasted malts and hoppy bitterness. And **Rogue** has made crazy-sounding beer mainstream by throwing everything from doughnuts to peppers into their brews, but their Farm series, that highlights single ingredients from, you guessed it, their farms, is a nice marriage of experimentation and drinkability. The **Chipotle Ale** has a nice, subtle, smoky heat that doesn't really kick in until a second or two after you've swallowed. When it comes to craft beer in the United States, creative brews you can still sip with dinner seem to be the final frontier.

Famous novelist. Fantasizing about being a famous writer usually involves great clothes and some kind of modernist cabin in the country somewhere, or writing while traveling to exotic locales. You're wearing linen pants in Greece, with the breeze blowing in through the half-open windows. Unfortunately, the reality of writing is more like an overcaffeinated, unwashed siege that takes place in coffee shops while eating things you shouldn't, or at home, on your unmade bed, the only light from the laptop, in your stained yoga pants—also usually involving eating things you shouldn't. Whether you're meeting a deadline or just daydreaming about it, a **Gewürztraminer** from Alsace will make you feel more creative just saying the name of the grape ("geh-VERZ-trah-MEEN-er"). **Zind-Humbrecht** is a producer known for its pioneering approach to farming and winemaking, and their Gewürztraminer has plenty of exotic spice aroma and full-bodied flavors of pears and lychee. **Domaine Weinbach Cuvée Theo** is a truly special Gewürz—just barely sweet, flamboyant, and perfumed. It's a wine to drink all by itself while you think philosophical thoughts.

You may never be **a rock star**, but you can at least drink like one. So put on something loud and obnoxious, like Grinderman, or an early White Stripes album, and sip a little **Tannat**. **Bodegas Carrau** makes a great example of the earthy, tannic Tannat that comes out of Uruguay, which has become this big, bold red grape's new home. Tannat's flavors remind me of tart blackberries and damp, dark brown soil, plus a little bit of smoke. The bass notes of the flavor world, if you will. Belt out your favorite songs at the top of your lungs, never mind your stained teeth. Or your love handles.

So you think you can dance? Even if you haven't stuffed your feet into pointe shoes in years, just seeing Misty Copeland interviewed somewhere brings all those memories flooding back. Watch videos of Russian dance students on YouTube while drinking a lithe, sophisticated **Pinot Noir from Sancerre**. Everyone associates Sauvignon Blanc with this little region in France's Loire Valley, but red is made there as well, and if you've mostly had California Pinot Noir thus far, this version's light body and aromas of just-barely-ripe red fruit and tart flavors of cranberry and sour cherries may be a bit of a shock, but soon you'll be drawn in by its elegance and poise. It packs so much flavor into a light-bodied package, just like those slim dancers. How do they manage to have super-human strength? **Domaine Vacheron Rouge** is one of the best versions of this style available, and is usually a little over $25.

Pinot Noir (pee-no NWAR)

REGION: Burgundy, France; Oregon's Willamette Valley; Chile; and New Zealand—just to name a few

DEFINING FLAVORS/AROMAS: Of the mainstream red grapes (Cabernet Sauvignon, Merlot, etc.), Pinot Noir is the lightest in color, and the most aromatic. What makes it such a popular grape, and so fascinating to wine drinkers, is how it marries these seductive, pretty aromas of cherries, ripe raspberries, and cranberries, with more earthy, funky aromas like mushrooms and damp fall leaves. A great Pinot Noir often smells so incredible that you almost don't want to drink it.

PERFECT FOR: Pinot Noir's lighter color translates to lighter body and fewer grippy tannins, so it can play with a lot of different dishes at the table, making it the perfect go-to red wine for restaurant situations where everyone is ordering something different. I know I'm supposed to do this wine thing for a living and all, but being handed the list at a nice restaurant while all my friends wait expectantly still gives me major anxiety. Pinot is a great cure for that! European, less fruity versions are great with duck and anything involving mushrooms. Fruitier versions from warmer climates are great with salmon and pork.

WHAT TO TRY: **Evesham Wood** makes a range of gorgeous, classic Oregon Pinot Noir, but their **La Grive Bleue** ($25–$30) is what Pinot Noir is all about for me: light, elegant texture, but packed with flavors of ripe cherries, raspberries, and a whiff of forest floor. Pinot Noir from France is almost always lighter in body and has tangier fruit flavors. **Domaine Jean-Michel et Laurent Pillot Mercurey** (around $30) is a perfect example of this style. Light on color, but not on flavor, it reminds me of underripe strawberries and cranberries, and is delicious with cured meats.

The Holidays

Awkward family gatherings. Last-minute shopping. Telling yourself that you can pull off an elaborate menu from the issue of *Bon Appétit* full of "updated" holiday classics, only to end up in a crumpled heap on your kitchen floor in a stained sports bra and yoga pants covered in cat hair minutes before guests arrive. The holidays are rife with reasons to drink.

Here we'll be discussing wines and beers that work well for gifts and celebrations for a variety of budgets. If you want recommendations for the best full-bodied Napa Cabernets that retail for $30–$75, go get a copy of *Wine Spectator*! If you want to give gifts your friends and family will actually enjoy, conquer your holiday-hosting fear, or curl up with something delicious while you're handing out candy to trick-or-treaters on Halloween, read on.

Avoiding Mall Vertigo: Choosing Wine and Beer as Gifts

What's Mall Vertigo, you ask? You've never had that woozy, headachy feeling after spending hours in the mall trying to hack through your holiday gift list, overwhelmed by the too-bright lights, crowds, and nauseating perfume sprayed in your face at department stores, subsisting on nothing but a Starbucks Peppermint Mocha because you're shopping in this hellhole instead of having a nice dinner at home? If you haven't, you're lucky. If you have, you probably want to avoid it. Your local purveyor of fine adult beverages is guaranteed to be a little saner than the mall.

Too often gift-giving becomes more about status, or fulfilling an obligation, than it does about finding something that the recipient will actually, you know, enjoy drinking. While it's nice to knock someone's socks off when they open the box (or if you're lazy like me, pull it out of the gift bag), what you really want is for them to have their socks knocked off when they actually *drink* the stuff, so here are some suggestions for wines and beers for the important people in your life—no vertigo required.

The parental units. No matter your age, your parents usually want to spend more time with you. So, why not get a great bottle of wine that will go well with a meal your mom or dad likes? Enclose a note with a promise to come over and cook. Or, if you're not into cooking (seriously, though, you should at least learn how to roast a chicken! Come on!), you'll bring over takeout. Sangiovese is a famously food-friendly red grape, and **Brunello di Montalcino**, with its naturally high acidity and beautiful ripe cherry flavors, is considered to be its most noble expression. So splurge on an expensive hunk of grass-fed meat at that fancy butcher you always say you'll shop at more often, and cook for Mom and Dad for a change. And don't forget to clean up!

KNOW YOUR STYLES

Brunello di Montalcino (broo-NELL-o dee mont-al-CHEE-no)

REGION: Tuscany, Italy

GRAPE: Sangiovese—however, since it's a grape that tends to mutate under different conditions, the subvariety (what wine geeks call a "clone") in Montalcino is called Sangiovese Grosso.

DEFINING FLAVORS/AROMAS: Sangiovese smells like tart red fruits (think slightly underripe cherries), and there is often something a little herbaceous, and sometimes dusty, in there as well. On the palate, you'll taste those same cherries, in addition to feeling some pretty strong tannins.

PERFECT FOR: Grass-fed beef, especially rubbed with a little rosemary. You can get away with red-sauce Italian food or pizza, but make sure there is some serious hard cheese or meat in the dish, otherwise all the acidity from the tomatoes might make your delicious Brunello taste a little tinny and flat.

WHAT TO TRY: If you really want to go for broke, the Brunello from **Valdicava** is around $110, but well worth it. This is a big, full-bodied Brunello with plenty of tannin, so do not try to sip this without food. **Ciacci** is another classic producer. Their style is a little less tannic and more lush and elegant. The aromas and flavors tend to be fruitier and less herby/savory. Ciacci makes really high-quality wines at various prices, so for a less expensive introduction to their style, try the **Rosso di Montalcino**. It's delicious, very consistent from year to year, and retails for $20–$25.

That couple who has everything. Forget trying to find someone's birth year, unless that person is a toddler. The urge, when buying gifts, is to be very "on the nose," especially if you don't feel like you know a lot about wine. Like, your friend loves cats so you get her a wine with a cat on the bottle, or you try to find the *exact wine* she had on her honeymoon in Greece. Trying to find a specific birth year, or an obscure wine that someone had at their wedding 20 years ago, is often more trouble than it's worth. So don't even try to play that game. Instead, **enlist the help of your local wineshop or beer store and ask them what would bring back memories of a given vacation or milestone**. We love open-ended questions like "What would remind someone of their Greek honeymoon?"

Let's say your friend did go on that Greek trip. Find a great Greek wine, even if they probably never had it on their trip, and enclose a heartfelt note, telling them that you hope this bottle brings back memories of Santorini. Then move on, and have a much happier holiday season. Should you choose this route, **Domaine Sigalas** makes a fabulous Assyrtiko-Athiri from Santorini that would please anyone who loves Sauvignon Blanc or Albariño and will transport them to vacations past. Just don't try to hunt down the traditional pine-flavored Retsina wines you can still find in Greece. They're an . . . acquired taste, and definitely something that would only taste OK with sand in your flip-flops.

So get creative! Your local wineshop and beer store can help you find a gift to tie into almost any locale, except maybe space. Are astronauts even allowed to drink in space?

Significant other. Nothing turns a humdrum Tuesday into a great night (with probably some great nookie afterward) like an excellent bottle of **Champagne** and some popcorn or potato chips (trust me on this). Another great accompaniment for your future date night is fried chicken (but not too much—remember, nookie). Bonus points for truffle salt on the popcorn— consider it an investment in your relationship. A couple of special bottles to consider: **Pierre Gimonnet "Special Club de Collection" Brut** (this will have a vintage date on the bottle as well, but don't worry about the specific vintage too much because vintage Champagne is released only in really good years) is made from all Chardonnay, and has a savory, almost briny quality that makes it great with food. **Krug Grande Cuvée** is a powerhouse Champagne. Its barrel aging makes the wine bold and rich, perfect for guys who think sparkling wine is for girls!

MVPs. If you live in the First World and make enough money to have some of it to spend on wine, then you've got a team, whether you realize it or not. You may not have an assistant, butler, or personal yoga instructor, but there are people who frequently perform services for you whose absence you would definitely miss. Is there a sandwich shop you love where they always get your pain-in-the-ass modifications on the menu exactly right? Do you visit a hairdresser who strikes the perfect balance between creepy silence and too much chatter? Has your therapist saved you from trashing your relationship and moving to another state just because you're feeling a little anxious more times than you can count? These people deserve a little something, and they would probably appreciate a bottle of wine a lot more than oatmeal cookies from your grandma's secret recipe. By the first week in December, everyone's usually had enough sugar to put them in a diabetic coma anyway.

Bordeaux has a bad reputation for being expensive, but the truth is, it's a big region that pumps out tons of quaffable red that can be a fantastic value. Another bonus is that the wines are medium-to-full-bodied reds that are pretty widely appealing, and the labels on even inexpensive producers' wines tend to look stately. In other words, you can bring them to dinner parties and people will think you spent a lot more than you did. If you paid less than $25 for a bottle of Bordeaux, there's a good chance that the stately château on the label is fictitious and the wine is really made in giant stainless steel tanks in a huge, anonymous facility somewhere in southwestern France, but no one has to know that.

If you're buying high-end Bordeaux, sure, you'll want to look for specific, iconic producers. But under $20, you'll want to ask your local wineshop or an

What the Heck Is a Bordeaux?

Bordeaux is a big, diverse region in Southwestern France, and unfortunately, because of famous, super-expensive producers like Pétrus, etc., it's gotten the reputation among American consumers as being "fancy" and out of reach, but this is not true! Lots of affordable wine is made there.

Red Bordeaux is the most famous type of wine made in this region, so we'll stick with that here. (For information on the renowned sweet wines made in this area, see the Sauternes section on page 84.) Bordeaux can be made from five different grapes: Cabernet Sauvignon, Cabernet Franc, Merlot, Petit Verdot, and Malbec.

LEFT BANK VS. RIGHT BANK

Every producer has their own take, but in general Bordeaux can be broken into two camps: the style employed by producers on the left side of the Gironde River and the style used by those on the right side. Those on the left side of the Gironde make wines with a larger proportion of Cabernet Sauvignon. These **Left Bank Bordeaux** tend to have more tannin, more aging potential, and more aromas of tobacco, cedar, and that slightly musty (in a good way!) antique-bookstore smell.

Wines made from areas on the right bank of the Gironde tend to be made from a higher proportion of Cabernet Franc and/or Merlot. These **Right Bank Bordeaux** tend to have softer tannins and are more immediately drinkable. Wines with more Cabernet Franc especially have aromas that are often described as "leafy"—think leaves in a blackberry bush or that wonderful green smell you get when you pick a fresh tomato off the vine.

DEFINING FLAVORS/AROMAS

In general, Bordeaux can have some of the same flavors that we associate with Cabernet Sauvignon or Merlot from other parts of the world, but usually the volume is turned down on the fruit, and turned up on the non-fruit aromas and flavors like green, woody, smoky, and tobacco-like. If a Merlot or Cabernet-based wine from the New

World is a voluptuous, Jessica Rabbit kind of gal in a pushup bra, a wine made from those same grapes from Bordeaux might still be wearing trashy lingerie, but she's got it hidden under a Miss Moneypenny tweed suit with her hair in a bun.

If a Merlot or Cabernet-based wine from the New World is a voluptuous, Jessica Rabbit kind of gal in a pushup bra, a wine made from those same grapes from Bordeaux might still be wearing trashy lingerie, but she's got it hidden under a Miss Moneypenny tweed suit with her hair in a bun.

FINDING THE RIGHT BORDEAUX FOR YOU

When it comes to inexpensive Bordeaux, what's available from these big-volume producers will change year to year, so if you're shopping in the $10–$20 range, it's best to ask your friends at your local wineshop. But just for reference, here are a few producers that I particularly love:

Château Recougne Bordeaux Supérieur is about $15 and made from Merlot and Cabernet Franc. With aromas of plum and cedar, but in a lighter-bodied package than you might expect from Bordeaux, you could even have this with roast chicken and the wine wouldn't overwhelm it.

Château Larose-Trintaudon Haut-Médoc Cru Bourgeois ($25) is made from about 60/40 Cabernet Sauvignon and Merlot, and is fuller-bodied and has more of those "Grandpa's study" aromas—pipe tobacco and old books—along with blackberry and plum flavors.

Château Fonbadet is a small producer in Pauillac (a town on the left bank of the Gironde River), whose vineyards neighbor those of prestigious producers like Château Lafite Rothschild. Their traditional blend of mostly Cabernet, with Merlot and Cabernet Franc as supporting players and a dash of Petit Verdot and Malbec, is full-bodied and often has a hint of minty herbaceousness that really gives it character. It's a steal at around $40.

online retailer you trust what's good. Buy a case, tie a bow around each bottle, and spend December showing the people who help your life run a little more smoothly just how much you appreciate them.

Neighbor. In addition to being great for date night, sparkling wine is one of those festive things that people always enjoy when it's handed to them, but they rarely buy for themselves. It's also a good thing to buy for someone whose taste you don't know well, because even if you totally got it wrong and your neighbors don't even like wine that much (Who are these monsters?! Move immediately!), they'll still probably have a celebratory moment down the road where they'll want something bubbly to pour. Champagne is expensive, but as you've probably learned if you've made it this far, there are lots of other styles of sparkling wine that are delicious and affordable. You can still send that festive signal to the recipients even though you haven't spent $50+ dollars, which, for your new neighbors whom you don't know very well, you're probably not ready to shell out—unless your sex noises, food smells, or animal noises/excrement have been particularly egregious. You people know who you are. Anyway, **Cava**—like Prosecco and all the other wonderful sparklers in the world that go for less than $30—is great because it says "party!" but in a less pressured way than Champagne.

Let's say you've just started dating someone and you don't want to give them the false impression that being with you is going to be all puppies and rainbows. Sometimes you'll have horrible PMS. Sometimes you'll be a backseat driver. Maybe you'll yell at the TV screen when you watch golf, or refuse to blow your nose when you have a cold as some kind of bizarre moral stand. Give a gift that says, "I'm thoughtful, but I'm no milquetoast pushover" with a six-pack of an interesting **rye-based beer**. These beers have a significant amount of malted rye added to the grains, creating a sour, spicy character. **Southern Tier 2xRye** is an IPA/rye hybrid, but the spicy rye flavor really pops out on the finish, despite all the piney flavors and heft that you'd expect in an IPA. **Atlas Brew Works Rowdy Rye** has lots of peppery rye flavor,

KNOW YOUR STYLES

Cava (CA-va)

REGION: Penedès, Spain

GRAPE: Usually one or more of the following Spanish white grapes: Macabeo, Xarel-lo, and Parellada

DEFINING FLAVORS/AROMAS: Cava is made in the "traditional method" (i.e., the same way Champagne is made), so it often has some of those same toasty aromas. Light, tart, crisp, and zippy, with notes of light citrus and yeast, it is great for those of us with Champagne tastes on a beer budget!

PERFECT FOR: Cava is the ultimate party wine, the perfect fizzy backdrop for crispy, crunchy snacks and appetizers. It's also great with one of those decadent sushi rolls with crispy panko crumbs and spicy mayonnaise that would make a real sushi chef faint in horror.

WHAT TO TRY: **Finca Valldosera** is a fantastic small producer, whose entry-level Brut Nature will run you about $15, and is a great option for a big New Year's Eve party where you don't want to shell out for Champagne for a big crowd! It's got a hint of that yeasty goodness that Champagne has, and a citrusy brightness reminiscent of fresh lemon peel. And you know what? **Freixenet** ($10–$12), despite those cheesy commercials and even cheesier black bottle, is not bad in a pinch!

but a crisp finish—the bitterness doesn't linger, and hopefully, neither will your fights.

Hosting Thanksgiving

Hosting is, shall we say, fraught, at the best of times, but for this quintessential American holiday, the stakes are especially high. People act like their whole day/year/life will be ruined if they don't get their cranberry sauce exactly the way their grandma made it, or if there aren't biscuits, or mashed potatoes, or whatever. If you're not cooking, you should eat what you're served and like it—not just because that's the polite thing to do, but because it's not about the freaking biscuits, dipshit. It's about people and companionship and making memories.

Menu planning. What's more fun than paging through recipes and creating ambitious plans in which everything comes together perfectly instead of ending with you sweating and crazed, while everyone waits expectantly in the living room wondering what the fuck they've gotten themselves into? Nothing, that's what.

Since everyone is in that sweaters-and-pumpkin-spice-everything frame of mind, this is a great time to explore **seasonal beers** that don't taste like someone melted a Yankee Candle into your glass. **Uinta Punk'n Harvest Pumpkin Ale** has enough roasted malt and hop flavor to balance out the pumpkin pie spices and hints of vanilla. It's delicious with pork chops, and even pumpkin pie! **Bell's Winter White Ale** is sort of the anti-seasonal beer, brewed without spices so that the naturally occurring fennel and clove flavors of the traditional Belgian yeast they use can shine through. If you're suffering from spice and clove overload but still want something that pairs with hearty food (or just thinking about it!), this is one you'll want to hoard so you can enjoy it all year long.

So kick back, and enjoy the shit out of planning your fantasy menu while you sip your seasonal ale. It all might be a disaster, but for now while it's just in your mind, it's perfect.

For a traditional meal with the family, do yourself a favor, and don't serve anything too crazy or unusual. When the whole fam is there, drama is bound to erupt, whether it's because someone is trying to micromanage the green bean casserole, or your grandmother won't stop bugging you about when you're going to settle down, because you're not getting any younger! So, yeah, you'll need a lot of wine. For your aunt Tracy who loves White Zinfandel, try an **off-dry Riesling from Germany**. Off-dry just means semisweet, and wines like these will have that same sweet-tart balance that lemonade has. They are very refreshing in between bites of stuffing with sausage and rich sweet potato casserole, so buy a few bottles! Many producers, like the Pfalz region's **Klemens Weber**, make liter-size bottles of this off-dry quaffer for around $15.

For those who need a red with their main course, **Zinfandel** is full of soft, ripe fruit flavors that will marry well with all the sweet spices at the table. California producer **Dashe Cellars** makes a range of Zinfandels that are lighter and more food-friendly than most traditional American Zinfandels, so they won't overwhelm the (let's face it: usually kind of dry and bland) turkey.

A quirky, gourmet Thanksgiving. Want some wine street cred? Got some discerning gourmets coming to dinner, and want to impress them with your reimagined Thanksgiving classics and impeccable taste? **Grignolino** is where it's at. Though Italy's Piedmont region is known mostly for Barolo and Barbaresco, it is also home to a host of other interesting grapes. Grignolino is kind of like what would happen if Sangiovese and Pinot Noir had a baby. It's got the tart acidity and slightly grippy tannins that make Sangiovese so great with food, but the body is a bit lighter, and the aromas are more exotic—think rose petals and fall leaves to go with those tart little cherries— and while it won't dominate the turkey or the conversation, every time you

stop to contemplate a sip, it has something interesting to say. **La Mondianese** makes a fantastic Grignolino that has a bit of tart cranberry flavor to it—perfect for Thanksgiving, no matter what kind of crazy gourmet brine you used on your heritage turkey.

Friendsgiving. When you're having all your degenerate friends over, you want to strike a balance between quality and, you know, not bankrupting yourself. A soft, easy-drinking red pleases almost everyone, even vegans with gluten allergies who brought some scary casserole that everyone just sort of gingerly takes an inch-square piece of to be polite. For something a little different, try a **red from Portugal's Alentejo region**. Although the country's known for Port, many winemakers there are experimenting with using the same full-bodied red grapes they use to make their famous dessert wine (Touriga Nacional, Tinta Roriz, and Touriga Franca to name a few) to make regular table wine. The fun, fruity results go down easy, but still look dark enough to please people who think it's not real wine if they can see their fingers through it. It's sort of like a Côtes du Rhône, but with the fruit factor turned up just a little bit. Look for something from Alentejo (Vinho Regional Alentejo is the general designation you'll see on labels) that is less than $12—you will be pleasantly surprised!

Cleanup. The end of the night, when everyone has gone home or to bed, is the perfect time to treat yourself to a little something special. And if you've still got a few bites of pumpkin or pecan pie, so much the better. While you're puttering around picking up napkins, sip a delicious **Madeira**, an obscure style of fortified wine that sommeliers keep convincing themselves is going to have its moment in the sun. This will probably never happen, but it's kept

KNOW YOUR STYLES

Madeira (ma-DEER-uh)

REGION: Madeira, an island off the coast of Portugal

GRAPE: The most famous grapes are the white Malvasia, Verdelho, Malmsey, Bual, Sercial, and Terrantez, but Madeira's workhorse grape is the red Tinta Negra.

DEFINING FLAVORS/AROMAS: Madeira's origins are one of those great stories like the invention of chocolate chip cookies—created by accident, but now we can't imagine life without it. Fortified wine from the Madeira Islands was sent on long sea voyages, where it was heated in the hold of the ship. The unique characteristics the wine took on became a feature rather than a bug, and for a long time folks thought that there was something magical about the distance the wine traveled. Eventually, we figured out that those signature aromas of stewed, jammy fruit and caramel come from heat, not distance, and now Madeira is heated in a controlled way in special facilities. There are many, many different styles, but they all share the signature aromas of wine that is heated like this.

PERFECT FOR: Older, sweeter Madeiras (usually with the words "Boal," "Malmsey," or "Colheita" on the label) are great as an after-dinner drink. Younger Madeiras (look for "Verdelho," "Sercial," or "Rainwater" on the label) are less sweet and more on the tart, dry side. The younger ones will remind you of a really intense version of a regular dry white wine and are great chilled with cheeses and nuts.

WHAT TO TRY: **Bartholomew Broadbent** is an importer of Madeira who has done the work of sorting through all the dozens of styles and grades to bring in the best stuff. His **1996 Colheita** is fabulous for a sweeter, after-dinner sipper that's not too cloying.

The Rare Wine Company makes a historical line of Madeiras that are based on the style that was popular in port cities in the United States in the 18th and 19th centuries. Their **Charleston Sercial** (about $50) is a great example of a lighter, more tart style of Madeira. You can imagine that you're being transported back to the colonial era, except without all the slavery and lack of sanitation. Because Madeira has already been aged and heated, you really can't ruin it. So go ahead and splurge on that $50 bottle, because you could leave it on your kitchen counter for a month, and it would taste just like it did when you bought it.

prices from becoming totally astronomical, so that's not a horrible thing.

There are a few different styles of Madeira that range from fairly dry and light bodied with super-high acidity (these are usually labeled **Verdelho** or **Sercial**) to very sweet, unctuous, and nutty. For after-Thanksgiving sipping, look for a sweeter, richer style like **Boal** or **Malmsey**. It's like dessert in a glass, but interesting and less cloying than pecan pie.

Leftovers. For a hodgepodge meal with bits of everything, or, better yet, a sandwich with a bit of everything on it, you want the little black dress of wine: **unoaked Chardonnay**. Often Chardonnay is associated with the buxom, buttery versions popular in California, but in many other parts of the world, it's made in a more crisp, refreshing style. In the Loire Valley, the region in France where Muscadet (a tart, crisp wine perfect for seafood) is made, some producers are experimenting with Chardonnay to produce wines that have a great combination of the light body and crisp character that area of the Loire is known for, along with the riper, apple-y fruit you'd expect from Chardonnay. **Domaine de la Fruitière** and **Les Frères Couillaud Le Souchais** are both crisp and refreshing enough to wash down that sandwich you went ahead and put stuffing on, and usually go for less than $15.

Halloween.

Who says Halloween is just for kids? Whether you're putting together a cheesy costume, handing out candy for your neighborhood rugrats, or going to a party where you know you'll cringe at the photos the next day, something to wash down all the candy you tell yourself you won't eat is essential.

If your costume is based on **a literary reference no one understands**, the wine you drink before hitting the town should be similarly misunderstood. Most people roll their eyes when they hear the word "**Beaujolais**" because they think all Beaujolais is like the fruit cocktail–esque abomination Beaujolais Nouveau, but they don't understand, man, that Beaujolais from one of the special, higher-quality villages in the region (Moulin-à-Vent, Fleurie, Chiroubles, and Brouilly are ones you see imported into the United States fairly often) is a cut above the rest. Sorry, no one gets your Humbert Humbert costume and the darkly ironic statement you're trying to make. Sip on a **Fleurie** from **Domaine de la Chapelle des Bois**—it tastes like tangy, almost-underripe blackberries with maybe a hint of pink peppercorns. Or try **Jean-Marc Lafont Domaine de Bel Air Chiroubles**—sexy and fruity, but not too heavy. Next year, maybe don't try to combine a pun *and* a reference to a novel whose protagonist was a skeevy pedophile, especially if you're a woman. It's just confusing. Keep drinking Beaujolais, though, because it's fucking delicious, and people are starting to catch on and the prices are creeping up and I won't know what to do with myself if it gets as expensive as Burgundy and life is so *hard*.

Hey, I'm not judging—if you're going to **slut it up**, Halloween is the time! But if you're going to be wearing something tight and revealing, you certainly don't want to down beer before you go out, or you'll feel like you're carrying a carb baby all night. The solution? A quick and dirty **white wine spritzer**. Try inexpensive Sauvignon Blanc, a splash of grapefruit juice (most citrus has mild diuretic properties, which help flush out any water weight you might not want showing in your slutty mermaid costume—pineapples are great for this, too, plus, you know, delicious!), and soda water. It'll be kind of like Fresca, but with a little kick.

If you're at home handing out candy, coziness is a priority. Try a **tawny Port**—its flavors of caramel, baking spices, and vanilla will go perfectly with all that candy that's "for the kids." And even if you're not a fun-size addict (how did you develop such self-control?), a nutty, warming tawny Port will keep you feeling snug even if there's a fall-ish nip in the air that rushes in every time you open the door. **Fonseca 20 Year Old Tawny** is like the wine equivalent of a big, warm cardigan sweater the color of oatmeal. **Graham's 10 Year Old Tawny** (about $30) is a little less sweet than some tawny Ports, and is great for sipping alongside a bowl of roasted or spiced nuts.

A nutty, warming tawny Port will keep you feeling snug even if there's a fall-ish nip in the air.

Couple costume. First of all, if you're the kind of couple that does a costume together, you guys are gross—stop it. But since you're into sharing everything, try sharing a rich, full-bodied brew in a large-format bottle that'll be enough for both of you. **Belgian-style strong pale or blonde ales** often come in bottles sized for sharing. They've got the alcoholic heft of a tripel (see page 177), but with a drier finish and a bit more hop character—after all, you two are sweet enough, your beer doesn't need to be! **Allagash Confluence**, brewed with both a Belgian yeast strain and brettanomyces, has some richness up front, but is dry-hopped for a crisp finish. **3 Sheeps Brewing Roll Out the Barrel** is aged in oak barrels that previously housed Chardonnay, giving the beer some of the apple and vanilla flavors from the wine. Both of these come in big bottles perfect for sharing and are combinations of two great things—just like you two. *Aww!*

For a witty, pun-based costume, try a pungent, herbaceous **wet-hopped ale**. Most of the time, the hop flavor in beer comes from hops that are dried so that they are shelf stable and can be shipped to any brewery in the country. But in the fall, some brewers use the just-harvested hops (the hops often go

KNOW YOUR STYLES

Wet–Hopped Ale

REGION: Any hop-growing region, namely the Pacific Northwest

DEFINING FLAVORS/AROMAS: Most beer is treated with hops that have been dried, but in the fall, when hops are harvested, brewers scramble to make beer with hops that have just been picked. This has to be done within about a day of harvest, or the fresh, delicate little hop blossoms lose their freshness and start to break down. You can think of the difference between dried hops and wet hops as the difference between dried herbs and fresh herbs—cooking with fresh herbs will give you a more delicate, grassy "green" flavor and less of the harsher base notes that come out when herbs are dried. Fresh hops are also a little less potent than dried, so the resulting beers are a little more delicate in flavor. Sometimes the aromas of wet-hopped beers almost remind me of fresh-cut grass. If you're not always a fan of some of the aggressively hopped beers coming from American craft breweries, wet-hopped beers are worth a try!

PERFECT FOR: Seafood, and hot and spicy foods like curry because the hop character is a little softer and it won't amplify spices in quite the same way a traditional IPA might.

WHAT TO TRY: **Deschutes Brewery Hop Trip** shows off grapefruity citrus and gingery spice, while **Sierra Nevada Northern Hemisphere Harvest Wet Hop** showcases the lemony citrus and floral aspects of Centennial hops.

from field to kettle in less than 24 hours) for an earthier, grassy flavor profile. The ideal way to taste these is on draft at the brewery, just after they're made, and there are festivals celebrating these delicious brews all over the Pacific Northwest. But if you can't make it to Washington State in the fall, give a bottled or canned version a try—just check the date and make sure it's not from last year! If you're the kind of nerd who brings a cringe-worthy pun to life in a homemade costume, you can handle a little research, and you'll appreciate the unique flavor of these beers. **Great Divide Fresh Hop** is a great example of this style and brings out more of the floral and tropical-fruity characteristics. It's the perfect thing to sip while you slip into your Cereal Killer costume.

What's the Deal with Fortified Wine?

Fortified wine is a big umbrella of a wine category. Basically, it goes down like this: Fortified wine is doused with some kind of spirit, usually brandy, during or after the fermentation process. This does a few things. First, it stops the fermentation. This means that whatever sugar the yeast hasn't consumed will stay in the wine. This can be done at almost any time during the process, so how much sweetness gets left in depends on the style of the wine and the vision of the winemaker. The second thing fortification does is increase the ABV of the wine. Most fortified wines are in the 20 percent range, rather than regular table wine, which usually falls between 11 and 15 percent. Thirdly, the addition of spirits and the remaining sugar ups the aging potential.

There are many styles of fortified wine, but here are a few of the major ones:

- **Port** is made in Portugal's Duoro Valley and is usually made with red grapes (there is a little bit of white Port, but not a ton). It ranges in color from dark red to nutty brown depending on how long it's aged.

- **Sherry**, from Andalusia, Spain, is made from white grapes. Made in a range of styles from dry and light to sweet and heavy, Sherry has been exposed to air or—believe it or not—yeast on purpose, which gives the wines a unique range of flavors. Salty, nutty, and cider-like, Sherry's singular aroma and flavor profile is kind of like stinky French cheese: At first, it tastes wrong, but it quickly has you coming back for more!

- **Madeira** is made from red and white grapes, in a range of styles from dry to sweet, on islands off the coast of Portugal. What makes Madeira different than, say, Sherry, is that it's heated on purpose. Controlled exposure to heat, long aging, and the natural acidity of the grapes used to make Madeira add up to a really exciting drink—you'll smell and taste everything from roasted walnuts, to stewed fruit, to caramel.

- **Vin Doux Naturel**, from France, is made in basically the same way as Port and can be made with red or white grapes. The styles you'll see most often are Muscat de Beaumes-de-Venise, made from the white Muscat grape, and Banyuls (see pages 225–227), made from mostly the red Grenache.

- **Vermouth** can be made with red or white grapes and doesn't have to be made in a specific country. In addition to being fortified, botanicals and spices are added, giving the wines an herbaceous and sometimes astringent edge.

Because both sugar and alcohol are preservatives, fortified wines can really go the distance when it comes to aging, so they're great candidates for something to give when your best friend has a baby—a nice bottle of Port has a much better chance of being good on the kid's 21st birthday than some random $30 Cabernet you picked up on a trip to Napa, trust me.

Fortified wines are also, of course, great for after-dinner sipping and for cold, blustery nights. Who needs a Slanket when you've got a glass of Sherry?

'Your New Year's, 'Resolution Diet,

New Year, new you, blah blah blah. No matter how much you scoff at silly concepts like New Year's resolutions during the holiday crush of cookies and Champagne, once that New Year's Day hangover hits, it's easy to let the guilt over the previous night's or week's debauchery make you feel like you need a fresh start, and what better way to maintain the illusion that you have control over your life for a few weeks than a shiny new diet?

Most diets will admonish you not to drink, but then if you look at the fine print, it'll say something like, *Well, a thimbleful of Merlot once a week probably won't kill you, you big lush—now drop and give me 20!* Exploit this loophole by finding something to wash down your weird diet food. Just don't go too crazy, because that's how you end up face-planting into a box of Cheez-Its.

Dr. Weil, with his Santa Claus–esque beard, is all about an anti-inflammatory diet. His recommendations are pretty measured and sensible, if a bit austere, and pretty similar to food guru Michael Pollan's: Eat your veggies, and try not to overdo it on the dense, calorie-rich stuff. So balanced! So boring! Well, if you're going to be eating a lot of fish full of healthy oils, vegetables, and grain salads, a **tart Sauvignon Blanc** is just the thing. New Zealand Sauvignon Blanc is going to be too overwhelmingly pungent—you need bolder food for that stuff.

Something from the Loire Valley, with just the right touch of grassiness and refreshing citrus, is what you want. Look for lesser-known appellations like Touraine and Menetou-Salon on the label for a good value below $20.

But is it Paleo? As obnoxious as the whole Paleo/Crossfit subculture has become, the general idea of eating mostly whole foods and avoiding processed ones is pretty sane. Some of those strange, date-based "blondies" look

Drinking and Dieting

As delicious as wine and beer are, they do not metabolize in a way that is optimal for dieting. Alcohol isn't *exactly* a sugar, but when it comes to the way your body processes it, it might as well be. Not only is too much bad for your health, but it can lead to the same kind of belly bloat that too many carbs can.

For both your overall health and your waistline, here are some tips for moderating your consumption so you can have a long life of adult beverage enjoyment.

Slow it down. Often we overdrink, especially in warm weather or at the end of a long day, because of thirst. So if you've just had a hellish, nonstop day, have a tall glass of water before diving headfirst into wine or beer. And once you pour your beverage of choice, sip slowly and savor it. Notice how it looks and smells, in addition to how it tastes. It sounds hokey, but practicing a little mindful drinking will help you get more enjoyment out of less booze.

Dilute it. If you're drinking inexpensive white wine or rosé and it's hot as Hades out, dilute your wine with ice cubes or sparkling water. It'll keep colder longer, and you'll drink less and stay hydrated.

Make it count. Though this book does include advice on how to choose the best wine or beer when presented with limited options, if you're watching your weight, just say no if what you really love isn't available. If you're a full-bodied-reds girl, and you're at a party that offers only cheap sparkling wine, skip the extra calories and wait until another day when you can get your hands on a bold Châteauneuf-du-Pape and really enjoy it.

Watch the sugar. Beverages with extra sugar will add calories, and can also make you hungrier later in the evening, leading to the drive-through or drunken grilled cheese sandwich experiments. So if you're watching your weight, say no to punches, sugary cocktails, dessert wines, and wines labeled demi-sec or off-dry.

disgusting, and some schools of Paleo thought eschew drinking altogether, but those people are crazy and we're not concerned with them here, obviously. What we are concerned about is this: What are you going to drink with all that bacon?

Choosing a big-gun red for steak is easy, but for bacon and other delicious, fatty pork products, you'll want something that cuts through all that richness. A **dry Gewürztraminer** will pick up any spice notes in the bacon or sausage you're noshing on, and will do such a great job of cutting through all that fat and smoke that you won't even miss that din-

ner roll. OK, you'll probably still miss the dinner roll, but Oregon's **Brandborg** makes a fantastic Gewürztraminer that feels light and refreshing on your palate, and is filled with classic Gewürz flavors of lychees, rose petals, and a hint of clove.

The best thing about the *4-Hour Body* diet is the fact that you get to have a cheat day. It makes having beans as your only source of carbohydrates a little more doable. So, what to pair with all the delicious pastries and sweets you'll shove into your pie hole? A **rich stout** is perfect with dessert—its roasted, coffee-like flavors complement that second slice of cheesecake you'll have before going back on the straight and narrow tomorrow. **Samuel Smith Oatmeal Stout** is delicious and great with desserts with baking spices in them, like carrot cake. For chocolate desserts, it's gotta be **Bell's Special Double Cream Stout**. Who needs whipped cream when you can just have a lick of that rich, delicious foam?

Raw food. For all those salads and legumes, you'll need something that can stand up to crisp vegetables, tart dressings, and vibrant flavors. And let's face it, a lot of "health" food tends to be kind of bland and underseasoned. To perk things up, choose a quirky **Chenin Blanc from France's Loire Valley**.

Chenin is very high in acidity, so it won't end up tasting weird and bitter against all that fresh, zingy food. Additionally, wines from this part of France are more likely to be made from organic or biodynamically grown (kind of like organics on steroids) grapes, which, if you're on a raw food diet, may be important to you. Look for **J. Mourat**, a great Loire producer, whose bottles are delightfully weird looking as well, the design based on antique bottles found in their dusty cellar. Their Chenin Blanc/Chardonnay blend is racy, refreshing, full of personality, and usually less than $15.

Minor Holidays

W hy should Christmas and New Year's get all the love? Less "big deal" holidays deserve some hoopla as well. Whether you're trying to survive the emotional minefield that is Valentine's Day or find a saner way to party on Cinco de Mayo, what better way to celebrate than with something delicious in your glass? Here's how to toast smaller occasions.

For the vernal equinox, in late March, depending on where you are, things are juuuust starting to thaw. You might actually be thinking about boning someone and peeling off a layer or two. People are starting to wear light enough clothing that you can actually check them out, and maybe even develop a spring crush—after all, that's tough to do when we're all reduced to walking L.L.Bean overcoats and scarves on the subway. But the best part about the vernal equinox is that it means the days are definitely getting longer, and we can all start shaking ourselves out of the season-long funk we've been in.

To celebrate, try a fresh, spritzy **gose** ("GO-suh"), an obscure style of German beer that's sour, salty, and spiced with coriander. That sounds totally weird, I know, but gose has the same addictive quality as salt-and-vinegar chips. The first bite is like, what?! And then all of a sudden the bag is empty and you kind of hate yourself. Anyway . . . **Anderson Valley Blood Orange Gose** is a refreshing take on this style, with tangy, juicy blood oranges added during the brewing process to add a little citrusy acidity to balance that potentially off-putting saltiness. **Victory Kirsch Gose** tastes kind of like cherry pie without the crust, or like a really fancy artisanal cherry soda. It's a good way to ease into this style and it's almost a little too drinkable. And if you can find it, a more traditional take like the **Leipziger Gose** from **Gasthaus & Gosebrauerei Bayerischer Bahnhof** will taste a bit more mellow, and doesn't have the fruit and aggressive herb additions that many of the American versions do.

Whatever you choose, the refreshing tartness of gose will wake you right up out of those winter doldrums!

On **Presidents Day**, honor our Founding Fathers by trying a **native North American grape variety**. Though most wine snobs will tell you that only *Vitis vinifera* grape varieties (basically all the "normal" ones you know, like Cabernet Sauvignon and Chardonnay) are capable of making good wine, our great nation is home to many interesting, flavorful grapes. Sure, their aromas and flavors might be different from what you're used to, but that doesn't make them bad. Norton, a full-bodied, dark red grape first cultivated in Richmond, Virginia, is *Vitis aestivalis*, a wild native North American grape species. It's now grown in several states, and is the official state grape of Missouri. Norton doesn't have the "foxy" (read: musky and kinda skanky) aromas that so many find objectionable in North American grapes. Virginia's **Chrysalis Vineyards** makes a series of wines from this grape, ranging from soft and fruity to serious and suitable for steak night, and from $15 to $35. These can be a little tricky to track down, so ask the nerds at your favorite store for suggestions for native or locally made wines if you can't find them near you.

For **Cinco de Mayo**, skip the tequila and try something lower-octane that you can sip all day without ending up wearing nothing but a sombrero. Thankfully, a country with its fair share of warm weather has come up with plenty of

beer-based drinks to keep you refreshed for your next round of gua-
camole. Try a spicy **Michelada**, which is sort of like a beer-based
Bloody Mary. It starts with a one-to-one ratio of a mild
Mexican lager like Corona and tomato or Clamato juice,
and is finished with a healthy squeeze of lime and a few
dashes of Worcestershire and hot sauces. Rimming
the glass with a mixture of chili powder and salt is also
traditional, and some bartenders even add bouillon powder. Sounds disgusting, but on a hot day, all that salt and
tomato juice will keep you hydrated if you're sweating on
someone's deck or a restaurant's sunny patio.

Celebrate **Valentine's Day** with your favorite girlfriends,
and open something as dark and mysterious as your hearts: a **dark, smoky
porter**. This dark beer doesn't have as creamy a mouthfeel as a stout, but it's
got many of the same rich, roasted flavors. Try one with some bloody steaks
while you watch *Fried Green Tomatoes* and complain about the opposite (or
the same—we all kind of suck sometimes, really) sex. **Anchor Porter** has a
thick, creamy texture, sweet maltiness, and roasted coffee flavors. Don't forget the chocolate for dessert.

KNOW YOUR STYLES

Stout and Porter

REGION: Both originated in London in the late 17th and early 18th centuries. The styles have since spread, with stout becoming a popular product in Ireland, the United States, the Caribbean, and Africa. American craft brewers have really embraced both styles, and there are so many variations that the lines between porters, stouts, and Black IPAs are kind of blurry.

DEFINING FLAVORS/AROMAS: One of the things that makes a stout so delicious on tap is that it's poured from a nitrogen keg, giving it its ultradense, creamy head and luxurious mouthfeel. Stouts smell and taste kind of like they look—like coffee, dark chocolate, and sometimes a little smoky. Porters usually have a finish that comes across as more dry and crisp, while still having those roasted caramel flavors that stouts do. What makes a stout and a porter different is the subject of some debate, and the most prevalent theory is that they are variations of the same basic style. However, the main difference is that stouts are a little bit lower in alcohol, and there are "sweeter" variations—milk, cream, chocolate, and so on.

PERFECT FOR: Both are great with chocolate desserts, ice cream, and oysters. Porters pair especially well with blue cheeses and smoky, grilled meats.

WHAT TO TRY: **Murphy's Irish Stout** is one of the "other" Irish stouts besides Guinness, and has a much sweeter profile. Forget dessert—this milk-chocolaty number IS dessert. With more roasted coffee flavors and a hint of vanilla, **Maine Beer Company Mean Old Tom** tastes much, well, nicer than the name implies. **Fuller's English Porter** has a note of something fruity, almost like raisins, or brandy, to go along with all those dark-chocolaty flavors, while **Great Lakes Brewing Company**'s award-winning **Edmund Fitzgerald Porter** has a bit of smoky pipe tobacco thrown in with all that dark chocolate.

come over for DRINKS

DATE _____
TIME _____
PLACE _____

Home and Hosting

"You'll drink what I serve and like it" is a highly useful entertaining/life philosophy to adopt. It sounds harsh, but your guests will be happier, more beverages will be drunk, and a merrier time will be had by all if people are given fewer choices.

This doesn't mean that when you have people over, you should throw a six-pack of Bud on the table and be done with it, though. It means that like most things in life, a little confidence goes a long way. If you're secure in what you like, other people will be as well, and will thus enjoy themselves more.

Whether you're feathering your nest, soothing cranky roommates, hosting a dinner party, or hunkering down for a scary storm, your home is where you (and your friends!) will do a lot of drinking. Here's what to stock up on after you've got the basics like toilet paper and a bed covered.

Roommates

A h, roommates. Love them or hate them, they're often a fact of life. And what better way to induce bonding with people you're hopefully not sleeping with (if you are, well, that's a whole other chapter), but have to share a bathroom with, than alcohol?

Estrogen overload. Here's some advice: If you're a girl, don't move in with all girls! Like workplaces, group houses and shared apartments are better when there's a little, shall we say, hormone balance. Too much estrogen is just bad juju. One of the things that tends to happen with too many girls is competitive nesting. Rolling towels, hotel-style, in the bathroom, leaving passive-aggressive Post-it notes about not putting their shitty knives back in their proper cardboard sleeves, and other overly fussy, borderline psychotic behavior starts to crop up. But ply these bitches with enough **Lagrein** and you'll all be back to watching reruns of *30 Rock* in your pj pants in no time. No one will even notice that your one towel is covered in hair dye stains and doesn't match *anything*.

Ply these bitches with enough Lagrein and you'll all be back to watching reruns of 30 Rock in your pj pants in no time.

Alto Adige is the place to look for this delicious red, which is like a cross between Beaujolais' soft, fruity Gamay and the smokier, meaty Syrah.

Kellerei Kaltern makes a great one that tastes of super-ripe blackberries that's about $14. The Lagrein from **Muri-Gries** is more expensive at around $20, but is a bit more sophisticated—it's fuller-bodied and has more of those peppery aromas and less simply fruity ones. You know, if the pizza you ordered is from a slightly nicer place and there are some fancy mushrooms on it.

Snow day. There's no better way to weather a winter storm, or just a cold, blustery day when no one wants to go outside, than to lounge around in your pajamas with your roommates, chewing through some weird old TV shows like *Twin Peaks*, or the early seasons of *The X-Files*. These shows are so hilarious to go back to—the cell phones were almost as big as Scully's shoulder pads! Throw together some **mulled wine** before the power goes out to keep warm. Here's a basic recipe.

COZY MULLED WINE

Serves 6 or so depending on the size of your mugs and just how cozy you want to feel.

1 bottle (750 ml) of red wine (suggestions: Grenache or Tempranillo)

1 peeled and sliced orange

Zest from said orange (it's easier to zest it with a sharp knife or vegetable peeler before peeling)

¼ cup brandy (Laird's Apple Brandy, which is American and much less expensive than its French counterparts, is quite tasty)

8–10 cloves

⅓ cup sugar, honey, or maple syrup

4 cinnamon sticks

1 teaspoon fresh ginger (use a microplane to grate this)

1½ cups apple cider or pear juice

Bring all ingredients to a boil and simmer for 10–20 minutes. Your house will smell so good you'll no longer notice the funk of the last fish dish you attempted or the litter box that needs to be cleaned.

Sunday dinner. A weekly dinner with your roomies is a great tradition to start, and pizza and pasta are kind of go-to group foods. Carbs are cheap, they're customizable to accommodate vegetarians and even vegans (here's hoping he or she doesn't leave "helpful" pamphlets around or give you the stink eye for putting honey in your tea), and they're easy to share. Similarly, inexpensive **Sangiovese** is chuggable, cheap, and cheerful. Sangiovese is all about sour cherries—some styles emphasize that sourness more than others, but that's the thread that runs through almost all wines made with this grape. It also has fairly high acidity for a red, making it a natural wine to pair with food, because higher acidity will make your mouth water and you want to reach for another bite! Plus, it has enough tart zing to stand up to tomato sauce.

Sangiovese is the main grape in Chianti, but for school-night glugging, try fresher-tasting, less heavy (and cheaper!) versions usually labeled Toscana Rosso. One of my favorites is from **Giuggiolo**. Their Toscana Rosso is 100 percent Sangiovese grapes and fermented in squeaky clean stainless steel tanks to preserve all those bright cherry flavors. The vintage should be recent, and the flavors like almost-underripe, sour cherries. Throw it in the refrigerator for 20 or so minutes before drinking—when they're too warm, high-acid wines like Sangiovese can cross over into unpleasantly sour territory.

KNOW YOUR GRAPES

Albariño (al-bah-REE-nyo)

REGION: Rías Baixas in northern Spain, and northwest Portugal, where it's called Alvarinho

DEFINING FLAVORS/AROMAS: Peaches that are still a little crunchy and tangy, Meyer lemon, pineapple, and that kind of briny "beach" smell

PERFECT FOR: Seafood, especially garlicky shrimp, mussels, and salads

WHAT TO TRY: **Albariño de Fefiñanes** is around $20 and is worth every penny. It comes in that long, skinny type of bottle we normally associate with Riesling, but don't be scared, it'll still taste like citrusy, refreshing Albariño. **Veiga Serantes** is a little spendier at about $30, but it's richer, and has a hint of fresh almond to go along with all those tangy peach and lemon flavors.

Accidental nudity. You forgot to bring a towel into the bathroom, and no one was home when you got in. So, you think you'll get away with a mad dash to your room, damp and naked, with wet hair and mascara still streaming, Iggy Pop style, down your cheeks. Wrong! One of your roommates is coming up the stairs the moment your bare ass is in the middle of the hallway. Busted! A white wine like **Albariño** is cooling and a little lemony, which will help put out the fire in your cheeks. **Viña Taboexa** makes an Albariño that has aromas of ripe citrus and even a little bit of that sandy, salty aroma reminiscent of the shore. Which is probably where you'd rather be, so . . .

Moving out (and on). Whether it's because you and your significant other broke up, or because your roommate has decided to get serious with her girlfriend and she's shoving you out of the nest, it sucks to have to move when it's not your idea. In awkward situations like this, it's important to keep up a sense of optimism and forward motion. As you figure out your next move, something bracing as well as bitter will fuel you. A **Black IPA**, also sometimes called **Cascadian Dark Ale**, is the perfect combination of chocolaty flavors, for comfort, and bitterness, to jolt you out of any wallowing. **21st Amendment Brewery Back in Black** combines espresso flavors with refreshing grapefruit for something truly unique, that's also great with steak tacos. **Southern Tier Iniquity** is reminiscent of baking chocolate, pine, and ginger. Things may be dark now, but like that burst of hop brightness, your perfect new apartment and/or soul mate could be right around the corner!

'Stuck Inside: 'Hurricanes,'Tornadoes, and Other Climate Change– 'Induced Severe Weather

Whether it's a snowstorm, hurricane, or an earthquake, there's always an impulse to stock up on food and toilet paper before or during a disaster. And what people tend to buy is delicious, empty-carb-laden junk food. The end is nigh, might as well eat up! Plus, you're being sensible, because it's nonperishable! Right, that's the reason . . .

Why not pair your favorite guilty pleasure junk foods with great wine and beer? If this is really the end, you may as well go out with a bang.

Cheddar & Sour Cream Flavored Ruffles. Are these laced with crack in addition to dehydrated cheese powder? Because they are really, really hard to stop eating before you're practically ill. Diabolical Ruffles call for something crisp and refreshing, yet assertively flavored, to stand up to that artificial cheese powder. This calls for sparkling wine, obviously. **Cava** is great, but pop some **Champagne** if you've got it. Remember, this might be the end!

Don't save that bottle for a special occasion. Because all we've got is THIS MOMENT, and EACH OTHER (you'll drunkenly say to your roommate, hugging her and making her feel awkward while she reassures you that this is just a power outage during a not-even-very-big summer rainstorm).

For **Brown Sugar Cinnamon Pop-Tarts** (no frosting, for the love of Christ!), try a **white Port**. Tawny or ruby Port can be a little heavy or overwhelming. After all, you wouldn't want to drown out the subtle wheat notes of the Pop-Tart pastry. White Port is a fortified dessert wine just like regular Port, but it's made with white grapes, so it's lighter in body and color, and doesn't share the red versions' drying, tannic grip. The result is a wine that tastes sort of like marmalade and toasted hazelnuts. **Rozès** makes a delicious white Port that's great chilled if your toaster works and you've heated up your Pop-Tart, but you can drink it room temperature as well.

For **Pizzeria Pretzel Combos**, you'll want something that marries with the powdered oregano and rich, delicious cheese product. Try a classic **Chianti**! If it's good enough for takeout pizza, it's good enough for its flavor-crystal equivalent. **Fiore** makes an affordable Chianti Classico, but if you want something that's really structured, dark-fruited, and serious, try the Chianti Classico from **Castello dei Rampolla**.

Honey Mustard & Onion Pretzel Pieces call for a light, yet assertive red that won't get lost when up against mustard's punchy, vinegary flavor. A wine heavy on **Mourvèdre**, a grape from the south of France known for aromas like leather, barnyard, and smoke, would be the perfect thing to wash these down, in addition to lots of water, because they are incredibly salty (not that that is usually a deterrent). **Mas d'Alezon** is a unique small estate in France's Languedoc region, and their **Faugères Montfalette** is earthy and full of ripe, brambly, wild berry flavor, yet doesn't feel heavy or cloying. If only you could say the same thing for that sticky honey mustard coating...

For the sweet, smoky, salty wallop that **Barbecue Fritos** pack, a smoked beer will amplify those flavors. The newfangled Honey BBQ Flavor Twists are also great for their more substantial texture, but the old-school regular barbecue flavor is damned delicious, too. **Rauchbier** is a German style of beer that harkens back to the good old days when all malt was dried over an open flame, giving the resulting beer a smoky flavor. Go classic with the **Aecht Schlenkerla Rauchbier Märzen** from **Brauerei Heller-Trum**. They make beers brewed from smoke-kilned malt in a couple of different styles, but they'll all have that distinctive charred flavor, which really brings out the sweetness of the Fritos. If it's too difficult to track down an authentic Rauchbier, **Stone Smoked Porter** is one of the first smoked beers made by an American brewery. A darker take on this style, it gets its flavor from peat-smoked malt, so it has a bit of that salty funk that peat has—a perfect complement to salty corn chips.

Your New Home

Whether you've bought a real grown-up house (go you!) or you're renting your first crummy apartment in a dubious neighborhood, a new place to live is cause for celebration. Unfortunately, it can also be rife with unexpected disasters, like pipes bursting, crazy neighbors, or getting sucked down the expensive rabbit hole that is home decor and organization!

Braving IKEA. Stores like IKEA don't really sell affordable couches and stackable storage bins. They are selling the fantasy that you might become the kind of person who would effectively use color-coordinated magazine holders. Or decorative mini trash can liners for the bathroom trash can. But what IKEA really does, better than selling storage bins or meatballs, is test your relationship. Think you and your boyfriend get along great because you never argue about directions and share the same political views? Try finding the dresser you picked out in the display area once you get to the scary warehouse section, and then wrestling all of those weird cardboard boxes into your car. How much do you like him now?

Once you get home, a serious white wine like **white Grenache from Spain** (**Xavier Clua** makes a wonderful one for about $30) will help you unwind. It has that nice full-bodied feeling that oaked Chardonnay does, but it's crisper and doesn't have that buttery character. It might even inspire you to organize all of your DVDs using the "Glak" storage system you bought, if you haven't used it to impale your significant other.

Remodeling. You'll need something both soothing and cheap to get you through the weeks (months? years?) of banging and clanging and being over budget—you'll get to the point where you dread phone calls and emails from any of the contractors. **Dry Sherry**, like the bracing **Puerto Fino** from **Lustau**, lasts much longer than regular table wine if you keep it in the refrigerator (about two weeks), so you'll never feel like you're pouring money down the drain when you don't finish a bottle. It's got the dry, crisp character that white wine does, but with a salty, nutty note on

Sherry's perfect with nuts, crackers, and other nibbles that are appealing when you can't cook an actual meal, either because your kitchen is torn apart, or because you just can't deal anymore.

the finish, and it's a bit higher in alcohol, which you'll probably appreciate at this point in your life. Next time you feel like you're just hemorrhaging money, pull the bottle out of the refrigerator for a bracing, refreshing little nip. Sherry's perfect with nuts, crackers, and other nibbles that are appealing when you can't cook an actual meal, either because your kitchen is torn apart, or because you just can't deal anymore.

Big girl (or boy) furniture. It's hard to believe that this day has come. You're buying a big, solid piece of furniture, one that doesn't have to be assembled and contains no particleboard. You're even paying people to deliver it. You have arrived! And while all this furniture buying is great, you big grown-up, you, let's not forget your booze collection. Because now you've got a real couch that's not from IKEA, or a four-poster bed that you can actually have sex on comfortably without always worrying in the back of your mind that if you get too into it something will snap and then you'll have to throw yourself out the window in shame.

That's all great. So why are you keeping your wine and beer in a collection of moldering cardboard boxes you pilfered from the shop where you bought them? If you have more than 25 or so bottles of wine or large-format

What's the Deal with Sherry?

Sherry is a fortified wine (see page 120) from Spain that comes in enough styles to give a wine nerd with all of her flashcards a little shiver of pleasure. A lot of its character hinges on the way it's aged, whether it's under a protective layer of yeast called *flor* or from slow air exposure in large casks. Here's a rundown of the main styles:

- **Fino** is super light, but still has a slight twang of nutty, aged flavor on the finish. It's great chilled with little appetizers at the beginning of the night. **Tio Pepe** is about $20 and has a salty, almond character to it that makes it perfect for nuts.

- **Manzanilla** is very similar to Fino, but made specifically in the coastal town of Sanlúcar de Barrameda. **Hidalgo La Gitana** is an affordable classic ($15–$17), and has this briny, salty flavor—it tastes like being at the beach.

- **Amontillado** is made from Sherry where the *flor* has broken up, so it's been exposed to more oxygen. It's dry and heavy on umami flavors that will remind you of toasted nuts and sautéed mushrooms. **Valdespino Amontillado Tio Diego** is about $30, and has some interesting orange peel notes along with all the savory action.

- When the Sherry cellar master doesn't allow the *flor* to form, **Oloroso** Sherry results. Usually a bit darker and higher in alcohol (around 19 percent) than Amontillado, Oloroso Sherries are almost always dry, but their aromas may remind you of roasted, caramelized nuts. **Lustau Don Nuño Oloroso** is dry, about $24, and has really interesting flavors of toasted walnuts and nutty, nubbly grains like buckwheat.

- **Cream** and **PX Sherry** are both sweet styles, closer to the sweet, syrupy style that many of us think of when we think of Sherry. (The PX stands for the Pedro Ximénez grape.) Less expensive Cream Sherry is often just Oloroso with sweet grape juice added, while higher-quality ones sometimes start with dried grapes to make a really thick, unctuous wine. **Alvear Pedro Ximénez Solera 1927** is about $40 for a 500 ml bottle and is super complex, with flavors of praline, maple syrup, and ginger. Delicious and indulgent.

KNOW YOUR STYLES

Pilsner

REGION: Originated in Plzeň, Czech Republic

DEFINING FLAVORS/AROMAS: Pilsner is just the embodiment of the word "refreshment." With a faint biscuity aroma and a little grassy hop flavor, pilsner is all about those lively, scrubbing bubbles and a clean, dry finish.

PERFECT FOR: By itself—it's the ideal afternoon or pre-dinner quaffer. It's also great with light food like salads or a turkey club.

WHAT TO TRY: **Würzburger Hofbräu's** pilsner has a super-dry finish and subtle, earthy hop flavors. **Firestone Walker Pivo Hoppy Pils** uses a combination of West Coast and German hops for a spicier earthy character, with some citrus and pine from the American hops. It's a pilsner with the volume turned up just a bit. **Mama's Little Yella Pils** from **Oskar Blues** is a little richer, with a slightly darker yellow color and more hop character; it's a pilsner for folks who want crisp flavors, but a bit more body.

beer and your house or apartment gets warm in the summertime, it's time to upgrade and invest in a **wine fridge** to protect your delicious beverages! **Sub-Zero's** fancy dual-zone wine refrigerators with wooden shelves are really nice, I'm not going to lie, but they are also usually built-in units that run in the thousands of dollars. I've also had good results with no-name wine fridges that are considerably smaller that I bought from, like, staples. com or something for $175–$250.

In my experience, the ones that have two temperature zones, one for white, and one for red, tend to break a little more often, and you'll also want to read through online reviews and watch for models that are said to be noisy. It's one of those things that you might not think of initially, but will start to drive you bananas. Whichever route you choose, you'll feel like such a solid, prepared grown-up the first time someone comes over and you pull out a bottle of wine that's been stored at the perfect temperature in your little fridge.

Moving day. Moving is one of those tasks that seems to magically expand the longer you're at it. I swear, every time I move, my stuff breeds more stuff, and every time I think I have it all packed there's another closet that still has a bunch of old winter coats in it I didn't even know I had! Once everything is finally ready, it's time to have your friends over and ply them with beer so they'll help you load the truck and get all your crap into your new place. Now is not the time to introduce your friends to the unique oxidative wines of France's Jura region. Now is the time for cheesy pizza Margherita and a light, crisp **pilsner**.

Theme Parties.

As much as people groan and roll their eyes, when you're trying to introduce friends from disparate social groups, a wacky theme that requires dressing up and/or participating in games or trivia is a great way to break the ice. You know how people bond when faced with a common enemy? In this situation, you, the host, are the common enemy, and your friends will all bond over thinking you're lame. Is this why no one's been texting me lately?! Anyway, here are some fun/silly party themes and what to drink with them.

For **a brunch party** where you force everyone to wear their pajamas, make a fun DIY fizz bar. Make sure said fizz bar and all the delicious food you've made (or bought—store-bought bagels and cream cheese never hurt anyone!) is within very easy reach, otherwise you'll end up with too much leftover sparkling wine, which can get one into trouble on a humdrum weeknight. Buy a case of a fun, fruity **Prosecco** like **Villa Jolanda** (retails for $12–$13) or **Casabianca** (around $10) and set out an array of juices and cocktail ingredients. Mango, peach, and pear juice are great, and you can also put out sugar cubes, bitters, and brandy so people can make their own sparkling cocktails.

How Bubbly Is That Bubbly?

There are a few shades of gray—er, bubbles—between still wine and fully sparkling wine. You may see words on bottles or menus that describe how fizzy a wine is, so here's a little primer on the most common ones:

Fully Sparkling: *Spumante* is the Italian term for fully sparkling wine. Champagne, Cava, and Prosecco all fall into this fully sparkling category. In French, fully sparkling wine is referred to as *crémant* or *mousseux*. The German term for fully sparkling wines is *sekt*.

Somewhat Sparkling: A wine like Moscato d'Asti, that has a slightly lower level of fizz, is called *frizzante*. In French this is referred to as *pétillant*.

Lightly Sparkling: Something with a very light, just barely tongue-prickling level of fizz, like the Portuguese Vinho Verde, would be called *aguja* in Spanish, *vivace* in Italian, *perlante* in French, and *perlwein* in German.

Back-to-school–themed party. There's something about that fall, back-to-school season that makes you feel like you're getting a fresh start, even if you haven't been in school for years. Celebrate with mini pizza bagels and peanut butter and jelly sandwiches. Since it's your party, you don't have to worry about anyone's peanut allergy. If you think people wouldn't be interested in such pedestrian snacks, you would be wrong. Also shockingly popular: Popeyes chicken tenders. Disgusting, but they disappear every time. Make sure to pick up an array of dipping sauces. For a grown-up version of apple juice, try some fun **dry and off-dry hard ciders. Crispin** is widely available and is—you guessed it—crisp and refreshing, but has a pleasing hint of sweetness. It won't knock your socks off with complexity, and it is better undiluted rather than over ice as the makers recommend, but it does taste nicely of crisp, juicy apples! If you really want to walk on the wild side, styles from France will taste like the weird love child of Champagne and apple cider—like biting into a Honeycrisp when you first take a sip, but they finish dry, and a little yeasty. **Eric Bordelet** makes wonderful ones that even come in fancy-looking Champagne bottles. Not the apple juice from snack times of yore, that's for sure!

A wedding-themed party is one of those themes that definitely forces people to wear their tackiest. Tell your guests they have to wear either a thrifted tux or the worst bridesmaid dress they can find at the Goodwill. The photos alone are worth it. For something festive and a little bit retro, make **Kir Royales**. A blend of sparkling wine and the blackcurrant liqueur crème de cassis, this bubbly, purply-pink cocktail is perfect for cheesy wedding attire. **Langlois Père et Fils** is a great brand of crème de cassis—it's so concentrated and bright magenta, that you need only a few drops. After that, just add the sparkling wine of your choice. Try one from Burgundy, the Kir cocktail's place of origin: Look for Crémant de Bourgogne on the label for something that will taste a lot like Champagne, but will be much less expensive—usually in the $20–$25 range.

A holiday-card party, where everyone makes handmade holiday cards, is a great theme that seems horrible and dorky and like no one will participate, but trust me—get people liquored up enough, and even folks you would never guess have a crafty streak get INTO it. Set up a few clotheslines or corkboards so you can display everyone's cards and vote on the best ones. The winner should of course get a six-pack of beer or a bottle of wine to take home! This is a great excuse to put out an array of fun **Christmas- and holiday-themed beers**. While you're getting crazy with the glitter glue, you can discuss which holiday beers were the most successful that year. One of my favorites is **Anchor Brewing Christmas Ale**, which is sort of like pale ale with sweet baking spices added. The label is classy and not cartoonish, and it's not cloyingly overspiced like some holiday special-edition beers, so you can drink it through making cards for your whole list of friends and family. **Brouwerij Huyghe Delirium Noël** is a Belgian strong ale that tastes like super-boozy fruitcake—toffee and dried fruit are the main flavors here. At 10 percent ABV, sip slowly or your aunt Suzy might end up getting a Christmas card with some off-color language and un-invite you to the family reunion!

How Much Should I Buy?

Figuring out how much wine, beer, and other beverages to purchase is a daunting task. It seems so mysterious and murky and so much harder than just doubling that lasagna recipe to feed 12 instead of six. Here are some things to keep in mind when you're shopping for your next shindig.

Consider context. How much alcohol people drink has a lot more to do with the general atmosphere of the party and the mood people are in than anything else. So if it's a Saturday night with all your closest friends, you might want to buy a little extra. If it's a Sunday afternoon and you've invited over all the parents from your kids' school, things will probably be much tamer and you won't need to buy as much.

Break it down. Beer is easy because one bottle or can equals a serving, more or less. Each bottle of wine contains about five glasses/servings. When I'm trying to get a ballpark idea of how much to buy, I calculate based on 1.5 servings per person per hour. So if you're having 20 people over and you think they'll be there about three hours, you'll want 90 servings available. You likely won't use that much, but this is a conservative way to estimate that will give you hosting peace of mind. You can divvy that up among wine, beer, and other beverages depending on the theme of the party and your guests' preferences.

Overbuy with confidence. Many stores will let you return bottles of wine you don't use for an event as long as the labels aren't damaged. So if you're buying for a really big event, ask about this policy so you can stock up and not worry about it!

Weather matters. People tend to drink more white wine and beer in the warmer months, and more red wine and spirits in the cooler months. At an outdoor event, you would be shocked at how much white wine your friends will go through!

Pretending to Be a Grown-Up (Dinner Parties)

T he thing to remember with dinner parties is that no one cares as much about how everything turns out as you do. No one's analyzing the texture of your sauce, or secretly thinking critical thoughts about the wine you paired with the main course. But the social component of dinner parties is a much grayer area, since our rules of etiquette aren't as rigid as they used to be. In our modern world of eating takeout while bingeing on Netflix, sitting down at a deliberately set table can feel awkward and overly formal. Suddenly, you don't know what to say to friends you've known for years, because it seems inappropriate to launch into a story about the woman next to you on the elliptical at the gym who wouldn't stop audibly farting, while you're sipping wine out of nice stemware. And if coworkers are involved, it can be even worse—definitely NOT the time to bring out Cards Against Humanity! Here's what to serve as you navigate this modern social minefield.

Your coworkers/boss. Your boss has had you over already, so you feel like you need to return the favor. Or you're close with your coworkers and invited everyone over, and now you're panicking. What if someone sees embarrassing pills or cream in your medicine cabinet that you forgot to remove? What if your dog fishes your period-stained underwear out of the hamper and drags it all over the house and then you have to throw yourself off a bridge?

While you can't control who snoops in your bathroom or what your pets do, you can make sure your wine game's on point. You want to show that you're interesting, but still a team player, so serve a full-bodied red that's made in a style people generally like (dark fruit flavors, rich mouthfeel, lots of spice notes from oak aging), but from a place they wouldn't expect: **Priorat**. Wines in this Spanish region are grown in slate soils called *licorella*. Imagine a field of dark gray shards of rock, not much rain, and the hot sun beating down on you, and that's the life of a grapevine in this area. As you can imagine, the vines have to work very hard to survive, let alone produce grapes, so the few grapes they do produce tend to be deep in color and possess a distinctive, spicy, white-pepper character. If these vines can produce something this delicious in such a harsh climate, you can certainly still make some small talk even after someone sees the huge collection of self-help books you forgot to hide.

Game day. Even if you couldn't possibly care less about sports, the food associated with sporting events is generally fattening and delicious, so have everyone over to "watch the game" anyway. Hopefully someone else will know what channel it's on. Do your part by making chili with all sorts of fun toppings—people love being able to customize their meal before ambling back to the couch. Sure, everyone's probably expecting beer, but the people who really care if there's beer available will probably bring it themselves! Instead, why not offer something unexpected that's great with chili and spicy wings: a rosé that's fuller-bodied than the pale salmon-colored ones you usually see all over restaurant menus in the summer. **Tavel**, a region in the south of France known for its rosé, makes a style that's a little fuller-bodied and darker, so its raspberry and blackberry fruit flavors won't get lost when it's drunk with spicy food. It's also perfect for sweeter barbecue sauces and Chinese food that have a bit of that darker, sweet/spicy balance going on, like Chinese-style ribs or moo shu pork.

Château de Ségriès makes a Tavel ("tah-VEL") that's about $12, is a little lighter in color, and has a more tart, mouthwatering character. It has a bit

KNOW YOUR STYLES

Priorat (PREE-o-raht)

REGION: Priorat, a zone in northeastern Spain (Catalonia)

GRAPE: These wines are almost always blends. Garnacha and Cariñena are the most widely grown grapes and usually make up the biggest percentage of the blend, with Syrah, Merlot, and/or Cabernet Sauvignon generally playing supporting roles.

DEFINING FLAVORS/AROMAS: In addition to the aromas and flavors of ripe blackberries, blueberries, and dark cherries that you would expect from these grapes, there is a peppery aroma and quite a bit of tannin in these wines, which result from their unique growing conditions.

PERFECT FOR: Big food with lots of flavor—think braised short ribs, pepper-crusted steak, or braised pork shoulder. Anything with a charred character would be great, too, like grilled mushrooms or octopus.

WHAT TO TRY: **Viñedos de Ithaca Akyles Black** is about $30, but tastes much more expensive—its name is inspired by Greek mythology, even though it's Spanish. With its sophisticated nutmeg and vanilla notes and dark plum flavors, it will please any Napa Cabernet lover. The Priorat from the iconic **Clos Mogador**, the most famous estate in the region, will cost $75—$85, but if you really want to impress, this is a great wine to serve because its full body, deep color, and famous label all scream "fancy."

---

of that musky aroma that a nice, ripe melon does, but tastes more like sour cherries. **Sol'Acantalys** makes a great one that's about $13 and tastes like ripe, sweet strawberries and juicy watermelon when you first take a sip, but finishes refreshingly dry.

An ambitious menu. You know how magazines always tell you, when giving makeup advice, to emphasize either your lips or your eyes, but not both? That applies here, too. Try to go balls-out with a crazy ambitious menu AND a big-deal wine, and you'll end up with the dinner party equivalent of Kardashian-style makeup. Just too much. So when you've got a big menu planned, go with an understated wine, and try a food-friendly, lighter-style red like **Schiava** from Italy's Alto Adige region. It's a light-bodied red like Pinot Noir, but even more delicate and fresher. It's the wine equivalent of that great party guest who's easygoing and gets along with everyone. In warmer weather, stick it in the fridge for 20 minutes before serving. **Manincor Kalteresee Keil Schiava** tastes just like biting into one of those farmers' market strawberries when it's just barely ripe: fresh, fragrant, and mouthwatering.

Date disaster. So, what to do when you were invited to a dinner party with your significant other, but you break up in a flood of fighting and tears three days before . . . and you're not quite comfortable enough with your coworker hosts to tell them what happened, so you just have to lie and say your boyfriend is sick and not that you want him to die in a fire, and you have to slap some concealer over your puffy eyes, throw on a dress, and make the best of it?

Bring beer. Lots of beer. Maybe have one before you go and take a cab there? Obviously, this applies to other awkward dinner situations—like maybe you're the coupled one, and one of your friends is newly divorced, and it's the first time he's coming to a social gathering solo in a long, long time. A mellow, food-friendly beer that's not too bitter and has a bit of a pleasant tang, will get everyone's mouths watering and make those cheese straws you put out taste even better. Try a variation on the saison called a **grisette**, named for the drab gray uniforms of the Belgian factory workers who used to hand the beer out to miners to enjoy back in the day. **Smuttynose Hayseed** is very light, with a less pronounced tang than most saisons, and has a smooth, almost velvety mouthfeel that makes it go down real easy. There's a lovely note of fennel in there as well that would make this great with food or on its own. **Sly Fox Grisette** is a bit higher in alcohol (5.6 percent to Smuttynose's 3.8 percent) and has more fruit flavor, like citrus and banana, but is still a great easy-drinking pre-dinner sipper. Doesn't just reading about these make you feel more relaxed?

How to Open Sparkling Wine

So your dinner party guests were kind enough to bring you a bottle of something sparkling. Here are a few tips for opening it like a pro:

1. First, loosen the cage. Technically, you're supposed to keep it on tight, but no one's grading you on your performance. (Remember that *Seinfeld* episode where Elaine keeps asking, "What are you writing?" while the doctor scribbles away on her chart? That's sort of what taking a service exam for your sommelier certification feels like.) And if you have to open several bottles, the metal from the cage will start to hurt your hand.

2. Point the bottle away from you and anyone else you wouldn't want to pelt with a cork flying out of the bottle. It's unlikely, but it does happen.

3. Grip the base of the bottle (that indent at the bottom is called the punt—sounds kind of dirty, I know) with your nondominant hand, and with your dominant hand, make sort of a fist over the neck of the bottle and the cork, so that you'll be able to feel the cork coming out and control its exit.

4. Start twisting the base and the cork until you can feel the cork start to loosen a bit, and gently twist it out. You want a gentle hiss, not a big pop. Those bubbles should be in your glass, not all over the floor!

Movies and Television

Sure, in Europe they are all thin and sophisticated and wear black turtlenecks and don't eat while walking or while watching their arthouse movies, but here in the trashy US of A, we like something to sip and/or eat while we watch TV or movies. And since we're already in our sweatpants on the couch, why even maintain the pretense of being classy? Here's your chance to trash it up. All those snotty Euros might look better in designer jeans, but are they having as much fun?

Classic-Movie Night

S nacks seem almost required for watching movies, but what you'll wash them down with is just as important. And since most of these classics aren't available in theaters anymore, you can feel free to imbibe to your heart's content, without fear of being scolded by ushers.

Classic sci-fi. The original *Star Wars* trilogy really stands the test of time. Some things are popular for a reason! Others, like *Duck Dynasty* or stirrup pants, are more of a mystery. Back in the 1990s, **Shiraz** was what the

---

KNOW YOUR GRAPES

Shiraz/Syrah (shi-RAHZ and sih-RAH)

REGION: Rhône Valley, France (Syrah); Australia and South Africa (Shiraz). One of the maddening aspects of the world of wine is that many grapes have different names depending on location. It's like people speak different languages or something! So frustratingly inconsistent!

DEFINING FLAVORS/AROMAS: Ripe blackberries, plums, licorice. The Rhône Valley's cooler climate tends to bring out the smokier, bacon-esque side of Syrah, while that same grape grown in Australia tends to express itself with more of that licorice element.

PERFECT FOR: Barbecue, steaks, burgers, and other bold, red meat–based food

WHAT TO TRY: **Fox Creek Short Row McLaren Vale Shiraz** (about $23) is like one of those really dark, matte MAC lipstick colors: a little over the top, but pretty sexy. Like blackberries rolled in vanilla sugar and crushed velvet. For something 180 degrees from Fox Creek, try **Vincent Paris** and his super-elegant Syrahs from the northern Rhône Valley. His **Côte-Rôtie** (about $30) has all the classic Syrah flavors—blackberries, black raspberries, and smoky bacon—but the texture and mouthfeel are more like a wine made from a much lighter grape like Pinot Noir. Try both of these to get a feel for just how different the same grape can taste!

future was supposed to look like: Australia's wine bubble would never pop, and we'd spend the rest of our days drinking dark purple wine out of bottles adorned with cute animals, grinning our ghoulish stained teeth at one another. Thankfully for good taste and wine variety, this didn't turn out to be true, but Shiraz is still good for another spin around the block, just as it's fun to watch hokey sci-fi movies from the past and laugh at what we thought the 2000s would look like in the 1950s, 1960s, and 1970s. **The Boxer** from **Mollydooker** is the quintessential Aussie Shiraz—bold, rich, over-the-top, and great with a burger with blue cheese. For something a little more restrained, **Fowles** makes an earthier, lighter-bodied Shiraz in the cooler Victoria region called **Ladies Who Shoot Their Lunch**.

You know, when you look back on **classic chick flicks** like *Clueless* and *Dirty Dancing*, they're surprisingly progressive, beneath the frothy dance routines and too-teased hair. Cher becomes an activist, and Baby's dad helps a total stranger who's had an abortion! To channel your inner girly teen queen, try something that's light and sweet, but also has a bit of substance. Instead of drinking wine coolers like you might have as a teenager, here's a recipe for a drink that tastes suspiciously similar to a **wine cooler**, but—unlike the scary bottled ones—you can rest assured it contains actual wine.

WINE COOLER FOR GROWN-UPS

Serves 1

Ice

4 ounces Sauvignon Blanc

1 ounce blood orange liqueur

Juice of 1 lime (or another citrus fruit)

3 ounces tangerine soda (like the Switch)

Combine all ingredients besides soda in a cocktail shaker. Pour into a tall glass filled with ice, and top up with soda.

What would Audrey Hepburn do? There was just something about Audrey, wasn't there? An Audrey movie deserves a wine that's poised and elegant, but doesn't take itself too seriously—just like her. As much as Beaujolais in general gets a bad rap, **white Beaujolais**, made from Chardonnay, almost has it worse, because no one's even heard of it! That's a shame, because Beaujolais is basically just a less-famous, slightly warmer part of Burgundy, and the wines reflect that. So if you like your whites with a bit of weight and texture, but find full-throttle Cali Chards a little too much, white Beaujolais is perfect. **Jean-Paul Brun**, from quirky import company **Louis/Dressner Selections** (If you're looking for some cray-cray Italian red that's still stomped by sweaty guys in their underwear, that's where to look.), is elegant and subtle, and tastes like a fresh golden apple. Poised and pretty, but in an understated way.

For **classic camp** like the *The Birdcage* and *Hedwig and the Angry Inch*, try something frothy and playful, but with a real message at its core. **Sparkling Riesling**, usually labeled "sekt" (which is just the German term for sparkling wine), is the way to go. When you put your nose in the glass you'll get all those typical flamboyant (ha), floral Riesling aromas, but most sparkling Rieslings are fermented quite dry, so they won't finish sticky and cloying. **Klemens Weber** makes one that is a perfect example of how delicious this style can be. Its flavors are pure Riesling: peaches, pears, and fragrant flowers. It's a party in a bottle, but the kind that doesn't leave too much of a mess to clean up in the morning. **Knauss Wurttemberg Riesling Sekt Zero** (about $30) is very citrusy and dry, and has a little bit of Champagne-like yeastiness.

OK, if you've made your boyfriend watch *Clueless* 87 times with you, it's time to throw him a bone and watch a **classic action movie** with a nice cold beer. How about a flick with a kick-ass heroine? *Mad Max: Fury Road* features the

KNOW YOUR GRAPES

Riesling (REES-ling)

REGION: Germany; Austria; Alsace, France; Washington State; and Australia

DEFINING FLAVORS/AROMAS: Riesling is high in natural acidity and very aromatic, throwing off showy aromas of peaches, lime skin, white flowers, and even funky stuff like asphalt or rubber. The types of aromas and flavors will vary depending on where it's grown and how it's made, but like other aromatic varieties like Sauvignon Blanc (page 195) and Gewürztraminer, Riesling has a signature fruity/floral aroma that once you get to know it, you almost always can identify.

PERFECT FOR: God, what ISN'T Riesling perfect for? Its high acidity makes it a great match for much richer food than you'd normally pair with a white wine—think fatty pork, like the kind you get in delicious, soft steamed buns at Asian restaurants, or a big, juicy pork chop with mustard sauce. But its delicacy and light body also make it great with Vietnamese and Thai food and sushi. Seriously, if you're stumped for what to drink, unless you're having a porterhouse, you can probably have Riesling with it.

WHAT TO TRY: Pewsey Vale Eden Valley Riesling (about $18) will turn everything you thought you knew about Australian wine on its head. It's lean, crisp, taut, and tart, and tastes like lime zest dropped into icy cold seltzer. **Domaine Weinbach Riesling Reserve Personnelle** (about $25) is super elegant, and the aromas, like fresh peaches and gardenias, are so lovely you could just smell the stuff all night. For a taste of a semisweet German Riesling (for a rundown of German sweetness levels, see page 18), try **Mönchhof Mosel Slate**, a Spätlese that's about $25. You know those super-sticky candied apricots that you see in gourmet stores around the holidays? It's like drinking one of those. All those snobs who say they don't like anything sweet are seriously missing out, because this stuff is delicious.

fierce Imperator Furiosa and a crew of awesome old-lady bikers. Or kick it a little more old school with the original *Alien*—you would not want to mess with Sigourney Weaver's Ellen Ripley. Go for a similar mix of traditionally masculine and feminine in your drink with a **Black Velvet**. A simple half-and-half mix of a dark, roasty stout, like Guinness, and Champagne, it looks great in a tall, narrow glass like a Collins glass. Start by filling the glass halfway with your stout, and then top up (slowly, this can create a lot of foam!) with Champagne. The addition of lighter sparkling wine actually highlights the flavors of the stout, and the whole thing ends up reminding me of really good iced coffee. There's a great balance of dark, roasted flavors, and a bright, clean, tart finish. My go-to for less fruity cocktails that call for Champagne like this one is Cava; for fruit-based sparkling cocktails like mimosas, Prosecco tends to work better. Even the most stereotypically macho and kick-ass things, like super-dark beer and explosive action movies, are better with a touch of something lighter.

Dress Snarking: Sparkling Cocktails for Awards-Show Season

I n a perfect world, you'd be able to serve top-quality Champagne to all your friends, with lobster or fancy sushi, and you'd all nosh like kings while you judged celebrities on the red carpet while wearing your finest stretchy pants.

But let's get real here. You want to serve something festive and a little bit glamorous, but you don't have as much money as all those people invited to after-parties at awards shows. A sparkling cocktail is a great way to stretch your bubbly budget while still getting into the spirit of things.

The Oscars, aka the Academy Awards, are the Mac Daddy of awards shows. Celebrities pull out all the stops when it comes to their gowns and suits, someone always goes way too long with their acceptance speech and gets shooed off the stage by music, and there's always some kind of crazy Björk-like situation

THE FRENCH 75

Serves 1

½ ounce simple syrup

½ ounce lemon juice

1 ounce gin

3–4 ounces sparkling white wine
(Older recipes will call for
Champagne, but let's be realistic
here: Cava will do just fine.)

Lemon twist, for garnish

Combine simple syrup, lemon juice, and gin in the bottom of a Champagne flute. Top up with sparkling wine and garnish with lemon twist.

where someone wears something nuts that commentators on E! can obsess about for hours. For the Academy Awards, you want something timeless, classic, and glamorous, like the **French 75**. If you can't afford bonkers expensive Champagne, you can at least get schnockered on this stiff sparkling cocktail.

Eurovision might be in first place when it comes to costumes, but the **Country Music Awards** have the market cornered on hair. There are all the ladies with big blonde 'dos, but it's really the men who just have a ton going on in the head area. Nouveau mullets, big beards, cowboy hats with suits. For a refreshing nod to the South, try a fun, fruity, wine-based beverage that isn't quite a sparkling cocktail, but it's still delicious. To make a **Boozy Peach**, combine a cup of a crisp, citrusy white wine like Sauvignon Blanc with a handful of frozen peaches and whizz it up in the blender. If you really want to get crazy, you can float a little crème de cassis on top. Drink with a straw so as not to smudge your inch-thick makeup. Enjoy, y'all!

The Grammys are always just a little more wild than the Oscars, and slightly less formal. Plus the musical performances usually include at least one medley that's so bad you can't help but laugh. Really, you

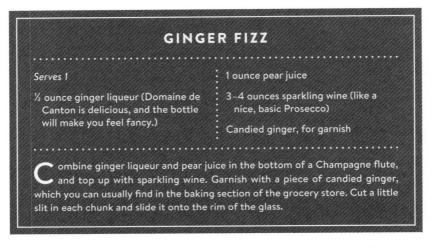

GINGER FIZZ

Serves 1

½ ounce ginger liqueur (Domaine de Canton is delicious, and the bottle will make you feel fancy.)

1 ounce pear juice

3–4 ounces sparkling wine (like a nice, basic Prosecco)

Candied ginger, for garnish

Combine ginger liqueur and pear juice in the bottom of a Champagne flute, and top up with sparkling wine. Garnish with a piece of candied ginger, which you can usually find in the baking section of the grocery store. Cut a little slit in each chunk and slide it onto the rim of the glass.

don't have to slam every one of the singles from an artist's latest hit album into one performance. While you take bets on when and how Kanye will let loose on someone, you'll want a drink with a little more pizzazz, and since the show airs in the winter, something with warming, spiced flavors will keep that festive mood going even though the holidays are over. This calls for a **Ginger Fizz**.

The Eurovision Awards call for something fun and a little bit trashy. The outfits at this awards show are so insane, you almost can't snark. You have to respect the commitment to tacky craziness. Since Eurovision performers are competing against each other and have a time limit, their outfits have become almost as important as their performances, if not more so. Just like silver pleather pants, mango-flavored drinks are a little dated, but admit it—they're fun. The **Mango Madness** is a sparkling, spicy take on all those drinks using Absolut Mango that were flooding bars there for a minute in the early aughts, except without the Absolut, because let's face it, that stuff kind of tasted the way air freshener smells. Thank God those days are over. This sweet and spicy little number will make you want to run off to a resort in the Côte d'Azur and strut around in a Pucci bikini and giant sunglasses. With a kick of cayenne pepper, it should also keep you awake through all those speeches.

MANGO MADNESS

· ·

Serves 1

Orange or lemon juice

Sugar

Cayenne pepper

1 ounce amber rum

1 ounce mango juice

Sparkling wine

· ·

First, rim yo' glass: Dip your flute in a small bowl full of orange or lemon juice, then dip it in a mixture of sugar and cayenne pepper. Add rum and mango juice (if you're feeling really fancy, use one of those expensive juices like Suja, which has a little pepper and sea salt in it as well as a bunch of good-for-you shit, so you'll feel better about drinking on the couch all night . . .), then carefully top up with sparkling wine. The little hit of spice on the rim keeps things exciting with every sip!

ʼYour Next Netflix Binge,

Sometimes it's impossible to deal with going on a real date, attending a cultural event where you might actually have to think, or doing whatever else you're supposed to be doing with your leisure time to be a well-rounded human being. Sometimes you need to binge-watch your favorite television shows in slipper socks and mismatched pajamas. Here's what to drink with what you're watching. (Note: Streaming services do change their offerings periodically, so if Netflix, Hulu, Amazon, or your service of choice doesn't have these shows, I've included some alternate suggestions.)

If you're in the mood for a brainy sci-fi series like ***Battlestar Galactica***, you'll need something as tense and nervy as the show, especially for nail biters like the early episode "33." **New Zealand Sauvignon Blanc** is appropriately tart, taut, and citrusy, and it's generally made in the most modern and squeaky clean of methods. It's fermented in stainless steel tanks and bottled under screwcap almost 100 percent of the time. Most wineries even use

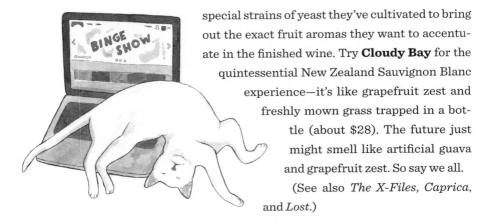

special strains of yeast they've cultivated to bring out the exact fruit aromas they want to accentuate in the finished wine. Try **Cloudy Bay** for the quintessential New Zealand Sauvignon Blanc experience—it's like grapefruit zest and freshly mown grass trapped in a bottle (about $28). The future just might smell like artificial guava and grapefruit zest. So say we all.

(See also *The X-Files*, *Caprica*, and *Lost*.)

The late-1990s USA series ***La Femme Nikita*** is awesome for so many reasons, from Roy Dupuis' smolder to the delightfully insane outfits they put on Peta Wilson. But the best thing about this show was Alberta Watson's portrayal of Madeline. Do not even talk to me about the CW's version of this show. It is a monstrosity, and their Madeline 2.0 is all hauteur and pencil skirts and no substance. Madeline was ladylike, and at times kind, but had a badass core so ruthless it sometimes made you gasp. I mean, she shot her husband! Traditional **Rioja**, with its aromas of tobacco and fine leather and ability to age almost indefinitely, perfectly captures her stateliness. No one does old-school Rioja better than **R. López de Heredia**, but there are other good producers who capture this style a little less expensively, like **Hacienda López de Haro** (the Reserva is well under $20). Drinking one of these and watching Madeline strut across that scary white interrogation room will have you wondering if you can pull off shoulder pads. You can't, but enjoy the fantasy.

(See also *Alias*, *Damages*, and *House of Cards*.)

An iconic girl-power series like ***Buffy the Vampire Slayer*** cries out for **semisweet Riesling**. Look for feinherb, Kabinett, or halbtrocken on the label, and don't be afraid of inexpensive liter bottles. Like *Buffy*, on the surface, off-dry Riesling is all fun and lightness and floral aromas. I mean,

KNOW YOUR STYLES

Rioja (ree-OH-ha)

REGION: Named for the Rioja region of northern Spain

GRAPE: Tempranillo is the main grape here, but it's usually blended with Garnacha, Mazuelo, and/or Graciano.

DEFINING FLAVORS/AROMAS: Most traditional Rioja is aged in American oak barrels, which lend the wines a distinct profile. The dusty cherry and cedar aromas of the Tempranillo grape have become intertwined with the flavors of vanilla and coconut from American oak so much that it's kind of hard to imagine them separately.

PERFECT FOR: Spain is definitely a country that loves its pork products, so everything from fatty pork belly to salty, chewy *jamón ibérico* are great matches with Rioja.

WHAT TO TRY: **La Rioja Alta Gran Reserva 904** is super complex and elegant, with aromas of fancy balsamic vinegar and coconut. Sounds weird, but it's good, trust me. It's usually aged for quite a while at the winery, which is typical for this style, so expect the current release to be around ten years old and about $50. For something a little more affordable and with more fresh fruit (i.e., that you could conceivably sip without food at a party), try **Bodegas Luis Cañas Crianza**. It's usually less than $15 and is a great example of the oak influence Rioja is known for in a bit more modern package—think ripe, juicy cherries with a faint whiff of coconut oil and sandalwood.

you know homegirl wore body spray from Bath & Body Works or The Body Shop White Musk, right? Not to mention those nail polish colors that just had to be Revlon Street Wear (RIP). A good *Buffy* episode has a lot to say, while keeping you distracted with fun and monsters and breaking the fourth wall in a completely endearing way. Good Riesling's the same way—well, with flavors and aromas instead of demons. It's a good beginner wine, but unlike Franzia Chillable Red, it's one you'll likely never outgrow.

(See also: Just about anything in the Joss Whedon canon.)

An intense documentary series like **Locked Up Abroad** is horrifying, but you just can't look away. You need something similarly absorbing, but a little scary. This might be the time to try a **dry Sherry**. Try Fino for something light to have with snacks or Amontillado for something with a bit more body and heft. (For a full rundown on Sherry styles, see page 139.) It will taste weird and wrong at first, like slightly old apple cider and toasted nuts, but you'll find yourself returning to the glass again and again. Sherry can get up toward 20 percent ABV, so don't forget to pour a little lighter (a 3-ounce pour is standard if you order a glass of Sherry in a bar in Spain). Plus, if you become a Sherry lover, there are—comparatively speaking—some good deals to be had, because no matter how hard sommeliers and boutique retailers try, it will probably never be a very popular category.

(See also *I Shouldn't Be Alive* and *I Survived*.)

For the BBC's cop drama **Luther**, it's got to be something brooding and intense, like a big, chewy **Syrah**. Some wine grapes are prone to oxidation during winemaking, and some are prone to reduction. Oxidative grapes are sensitive little guys that start to smell stale and flabby if they are exposed to too much air while they're being made into wine. Reductive grapes, like Syrah, are burly and need lots of air and exercise, and tend to have these savory, sometimes downright dirty aromas that some people learn to love, but can be overpowering.

Basically we're describing Idris Elba's role as police detective John Luther here. Could he be any foxier? Good God. There is just something about that roiling tension all bundled under tweed jackets.

Feral, dark, and meaty, Syrah has the body of other "big" grapes like Malbec or Grenache, but not as much friendly fruit, especially when it's grown in France's Rhône Valley and not in Australia. Basically we're describing Idris Elba's role as police detective John Luther here. Could he be any foxier? Good God. There is just something about that roiling tension all bundled under tweed jackets. You might need a cold shower after a couple of hours with a Côte-Rôtie and all that desk pounding. Try **E. Guigal Côte-Rôtie "Brune et Blonde de Guigal"** ($75) for a traditional take on Syrah (one sniff will help explain why people always say Syrah smells like bacon!), and for something a tad less intense, **Arnot-Roberts North Coast Syrah** ($40-ish) has a bit less smoke, and riper blueberry and blackberry fruit flavors.

(See also *Breaking Bad*, *Mad Men*, *The Sopranos*, and *The Shield*.)

Every once in a while it's fun to scroll through the myriad offerings on Netflix, Hulu, or Amazon, and discover a quirky foreign sitcom like Denmark's *Rita*. It's like *Nurse Jackie*, but with a sassy schoolteacher instead of a nurse, and less, like, actual scary crime and more cigarette smoking in the bathroom. For an obscure comedy like this, try something with a similar sweet/sour balance, like **Berliner Weisse**, a tart, low-alcohol (so you can sip while bingeing through a whole season) German style of beer. With fresh, lemony citrus flavors and very little hop bitterness, it's often doctored with raspberry or green woodruff syrup to balance out its tartness. Woodruff syrup has that kind of sweet, yet herbaceous flavor that's a bit reminiscent of Ricola cough drops. But it can be a little tough to find in the United States, so raspberry syrup from a company like Monin will work just as well.

For the true classic, try **Berliner Kindl Weisse**—it's light, with a sour-citrusy tang, and at 3 percent ABV, you could have one at lunch and not fall asleep under your desk. **Bell's Oarsman Ale** is an American take on this style, and its combination of light, citrus-inflected hop character and tangy finish makes it really refreshing.

(See also the spinoff *Hjørdis*, *Coupling*, *Peep Show*, and the short-lived show *Spaced*.)

Music

Of all the subjects and hobbies people tend to geek out about, nothing inspires passionate infighting and emotional attachment like music, wine, and beer. People who love wine, beer, and/or music love to sit around and argue about their top ten albums of the 1990s, or their desert island wines, in a way that people who are into, say, cross-stitch, don't.

Both beverages and music tap into that very powerful sense, memory. Often when we remember wonderful or horrible or embarrassing times in our lives, we remember songs, or we remember smells, and most of what defines a wine or beer experience is smell. So whether you're at a concert, a music festival, or just listening to weird shit no one else likes at home by yourself, drinking something while humming along seems natural!

Your Favorite Music

If you spent your high school years trolling used-record stores for Smiths albums and worked for your college radio station, you're probably used to people calling you pretentious. Why not go all the way, and find the perfect beverage to pair with your favorite music?

Indie rock. Going through your old Pavement albums or collection of Sonic Youth side projects? Something similarly offbeat, yet refreshing, is the perfect accompaniment to all those fuzzed-out guitars and impenetrable lyrics. This calls for an **Austrian rosé**. Though France is known for its classic rosés, Austria is turning out some interesting pink quaffers that provide a fun change of pace from the usual Grenache, Syrah, and Mourvèdre drill. Look for rosés made from the quirky red grape Zweigelt ("SCHVAI-gelt") for something with sweet red fruit flavors and an intriguing whiff of herbs.

Austrian producer **Tegernseerhof** makes a tart, refreshing rosé from Zweigelt that is sort of like alcoholic cranberry soda. It's great for summer! **Anton Bauer** makes a very light, tart rosé that tastes like grapefruit and blood orange. It's the perfect rosé for a Sauvignon Blanc lover. Sure, Austrian rosé might seem a little obscure, but the difference between oddball and underrated classic is just a few years—no matter what the guy at the music store says when you try to sell your massive, maybe slightly scratched, collection.

Loud, thrashy punk to annoy your neighbors. If you spent many nights in tiny clubs damaging your hearing and listening to bands like the Yeah Yeah Yeahs (before Karen O came out with a line of overpriced nail polish and performed at the Oscars), the Coachwhips, and Fugazi, you probably drank watered-down, anonymous beer like Pabst Blue Ribbon. It has this sort of weird, hipster, so-bad-it's-good appeal, but come on, people! Trust yourselves! We all know this stuff tastes like crap. For something clean and refreshing that you can drink all night, a true **pilsner** is what you want. If you're lucky enough to live on the West Coast, **Trumer Pils** is the best, so fresh and clean it'll make you forget about who you're rubbing up against at that grimy club. On the East Coast, **Victory Prima Pils** is a little heavier and hoppier, so it feels a bit more satisfying, which will help you suspend disbelief if you're just in your basement, rocking out while you fold laundry.

The sweetest taboo. Classy lady crooners like Jane Monheit, Jessie Ware, Adele, and even Sade (what?!) cry out for something fizzy, pink, and a little sweet. Anytime I recommend a sweet wine to someone, I get a similar expression, that of a disdainful, slightly nervous badger. "Oh, I don't like anything sweet," they say. OK, sure, you are the only mammal in the history of everything who isn't hardwired to love sweets. Something like **Jean Vesselle Cuvée Friandise**, an off-dry (usually labeled "demi-sec"—see page 169 for a rundown of sweetness designations for sparkling wine) **all-Pinot Noir rosé Champagne**, is complex, interesting, a gorgeous raspberry color, and will blow apart everything you thought you knew about sweet wine. Not to mention it goes down way, way too easy for a bottle that's definitely a splurge (about $50). Split it with someone you really like. For an all-Pinot sparkler that's a little more affordable, the **Secco** from Austrian winery **Leo Hillinger** is about $15, and the perfect "girls' night" wine. What better to drink while you're listening to Adele's new album and experimenting with outlandish eye makeup you'd never wear outside the house? Both are proof that something pretty polished can also be interesting.

Classic folk like Bob Dylan, Joan Baez, or Woody Guthrie deserves the kind of wine that can fade into the background if it needs to, but always has something interesting to say if you listen closely. A **Garnacha** from Spain that's as simple and stripped-down as a great folk song goes with a surprisingly

KNOW YOUR GRAPES

Garnacha (gar-NA-cha)

REGION: Spain; southern France (where it's called Grenache)

DEFINING FLAVORS/AROMAS: Red fruit like raspberry, strawberry, or cherry, with spice aromas and flavors

PERFECT FOR: Barbecue, not-too-spicy Asian food (like Indian), or a juicy burger from the grill, especially with a few crumbles of blue cheese

WHAT TO TRY: When you need to grab something to bring to a party and you know there's a good chance red Solo cups will be involved, this is the style to go for. This is one category of wine where you should just ask your local wineshop what inexpensive Spanish Garnacha they're liking, because what's available and the best value in your area will change from year to year. They do the work of sifting through dozens of wines that are released in a given category every year to find the best ones. In the same way that famous chefs always say that they judge a fellow cook's skills based on simple dishes like roast chicken, the best test of a wineshop is its inexpensive wines. They're the hardest to get right, and show that the buyers are doing their jobs.

DON'T FORGET THOSE BOXES!
Some producers are also making boxed versions of their cheapie Garnacha, and most of them are pretty good! Stay away from anything less than $20 for three liters, and anything that mentions oak aging or "spicy aromas of oak." There's no way most of these producers can afford real oak barrels for these inexpensive wines, so instead they use oak chips, and those taste terrible. Better to go for the wines that just ferment in stainless steel tanks and let those nice fresh, fruity aromas and flavors shine!

wide range of foods and, more importantly, can be drunk out of juice glasses. Garnacha's a fun, fruity grape that grows well in Spain's warm climate. As a result, the country pumps out an incredible amount of the stuff, and I've tried dozens of delicious, sub-$10 bottles. Savor or gulp, it's up to you. Open up a bottle and see if it doesn't go perfectly with Bob Dylan's *Desire*. It's moving and often sad, but still somehow fun to listen to.

A sound track to brooding. There are lots of musical artists who seem to permanently exist under a dark gray cloud. Thom Yorke always sounds like a sad, funereal dove is about to burst out of his chest, and Kate Bush is a lady brooder if there ever was one, but if you really want to contemplate the void, the worst parts of humanity, and the dark night of your soul, it's got to be Nick Cave. Whether you're going for the dirty-old-man grunge of Grinderman or more classic Bad Seeds material, it's got to be a wine from Malbec's ancestral home, the Black Wine of Lot, **Cahors**. Brooding, dark, and tannic, Cahors is a style of wine that's very different from the Malbecs we've come to expect from Argentina. Most people like the Argentinian style of Malbec because they like ripe, jammy fruit, as well as the vanilla and spice aromas and flavors in boxed versions that come from lots of oak aging. There's nothing wrong with this, but these qualities have much more to do with winemaking than the grape itself. When made in a more traditional style, Malbec is deep, dark, inky, and

How Sweet Is Your Fizz?

The sweetness designations you see on bottles of sparkling wine date from a time when it was made much, much sweeter than it is today. Since then, much drier styles have come into fashion, rendering designations like "demi-sec" kind of confusing. Here's a rundown of most of the terms you'll see:

- Brut Nature, Brut Zero, Brut Sauvage—the least sweet.

- Extra Brut—still won't taste sweet.

- Brut—enough sweetness that you may or may not be able to taste it.

- Extra Dry, Extra Sec, Extra Secco—a touch of sweetness, which you'll mostly notice as a lingering sweetness after you've swallowed.

- Dry, Sec, Secco—slightly sweeter; think lightly sweetened iced tea.

- Demi-Sec—sweet, but not as sweet as, say, dessert wine. If you want to serve something at a wedding reception that actually tastes good with wedding cake, go for this style!

- Doux, Sweet, Dulce—very sweet. This used to be the most popular style of Champagne—in the 19th century in Russia, they liked it even sweeter! Now you rarely see it.

NOT the kind of wine to sip by itself while you veg out reading magazines. Its massive tannins grip your tongue and the insides of your cheeks and won't let go. Kind of reminds you of the man himself, still touring after almost four decades, still grappling with good and evil, sin and redemption—never quite as famous as he should be, but you get the sense he likes it that way.

These Gothic beauties can age for years and cost a fraction of what their high-end neighbors in Bordeaux do. **Clos La Coutale** is an easily obtained classic at $15–$17. Try that ambitious cassoulet recipe you've drooled over in French cookbooks for years, and crack open a bottle. With good old Nick on in the background, of course. **Château la Caminade** is a smaller estate, and their style is a little softer and fruitier (about $14). Although many estates in Cahors use Merlot in their blends to soften the tannic attack of the Malbec (also called Côt), the Merlot is a little more prominent in Château la Caminade's wines. A good Cahors with training wheels!

Music Festivals, or, Drowning Out the Stench of Patchouli and Weed.

Music festivals are always times when you see people consuming . . . other substances as well as alcohol, and that combined with the harsh summer sun can really do a number on you. So if you decide to brave one of these things, drink lots of water, stay away from weird drugs handed out by people you don't know, and have a nice refreshing beverage at a leisurely pace.

If you're stuck at a hokey jazz festival with your parents or other extended family, peel yourself off that sticky lawn chair and find yourself a beer. And don't forget to take the long way to the beer tents, because music festivals like this are great for people-watching: crazy beards, lady mullets, questionable tie-dye, it'll all be there. Then find a shady spot and have a few sips of a refreshing Belgian-style **witbier**. It's got all the hallmarks of a perfect summer beer: the ABV isn't too high (typically around 5 percent), it's tangy rather than hoppy, and the mouthwatering acidity feels thirst-quenching. Plus, the inclusion of wheat gives it a creamy texture and hazy appearance that will make you feel like you're floating away on a fluffy white cloud. **Hoegaarden** will get the job done, but see below for some more interesting suggestions.

At an outdoor camping festival like Bonnaroo you'll probably want beer in addition to lots of snacks, bug repellent, and sunscreen. This is the perfect time to explore the world of refreshing **fruit-based beers**, especially ones that come in a can! Often festivals like this don't allow glass, so cans are the way to go. This huge gathering of neo-hippies can get a little . . . fragrant, so if you need a break from the good vibes and sweaty humans, retreat to the camping area, and kick back in a lawn chair with an aromatic fruity beer.

KNOW YOUR STYLES

Witbier

REGION: Leuven and Hoegaarden, Belgium

DEFINING FLAVORS/AROMAS: Witbier's hallmark is its cloudy appearance when cold, hence the name, which comes from the word for "white." Belgian witbiers also often have coriander and orange peel added to the brew, giving a signature spicy twist to the creamy mouthfeel.

PERFECT FOR: A peppery arugula salad, fried calamari, or a hot afternoon

WHAT TO TRY: Hitachino Nest White Ale, a Japanese take on the witbier style, has a wonderfully plush, creamy mouthfeel, but finishes clean and tastes a bit like pineapple and white pepper. **Allagash White** is delicious, smooth, and refreshing, with just a hint of warmer spices, like nutmeg and clove.

For something fresh and sunny, try **A Hopwork Orange** from **Blue Mountain Brewery**, which comes in convenient cans and captures both the slightly bitter zest and juicy fruit of an orange. **21st Amendment Brewery Hell or High Watermelon** is a wheat beer brewed with real watermelon that's available from April through September. You get a big pop of watermelon flavor up front, and a crisp, dry finish—and it comes in cans as well! Who knows? Maybe these fun, juicy fruit flavors will be just the thing to get you into that "radiating positivity" spirit.

At those giant, crazy EDM shows, most people seem to be sucking down vodka and "popping Molly," wearing ridiculous outfits as though rave culture didn't do all this exact same stuff 20 years ago. No need to make your brain a guinea pig, too. Find a nice spot away from the madness (maybe in the parking lot, since you probably wouldn't be allowed in with an entire wine bottle unless you did some really artful concealing) and sip on an **organic rosé**. Provence's **Château Peyrassol Côtes de Provence Rosé** ($20–$22) is full of the tart flavors of cherries and raspberries, and is made from organically farmed grapes. Really impress all those crazy kids and add a little kombucha in a complementary flavor like cherry or cranberry.

If you're a fully developed adult, a festival like **Coachella** mostly serves as a reminder of how freaking old you are. Like, really old. Remind yourself that it's OK that you're years past being able to pull off a romper or look like anything but a crazy woman if you wear wilted flowers in your hair, and bring along a sophisticated sparkler that will have all those kids in flash tattoos jealous. ***Pét-nat***, the wine hipster abbreviation for ***pétillant naturel***, is a super-fun style of sparkling wine made all over France and Italy, but there's a big concentration of it in the Loire Valley. These babies undergo fermentation in the bottle just like Champagne (see pages 80–81), but unlike Champagne, there's just one

It's OK that you're years past being able to pull off a romper.

fermentation and no disgorgement, leaving you with exuberant bubbles, lots of fresh, yeasty tang, and usually a bit of sweetness.

Olivier Lemasson makes an adorably packaged rosé *pét-nat* called **Pow Blop Wizz** ($20), which is as fun to drink as it is to say—like sour watermelon candy, but fizzy. Pop Rocks for grown-ups—how great does that sound? **Eric Texier Rouletabulle** (about $23) is made in the Rhône Valley from the obscure Chasselas grape, and reminds me of Ting grapefruit soda, but even more sour and fizzy. Once you've had enough of the flash tattoos and flower headbands, head back to your hotel (because you're way too old for camping), pop open something bubbly and fun, and scroll through all the hilarious pictures you took during the day—you'll be enjoying yourself so much you won't miss your youth at all. OK, maybe you will a little bit.

Reading

Reading is the perfect activity to accompany with a beverage. At the very least, you're usually not moving, so there's little chance of spillage. And a nice glass of wine or beer allows you to fully immerse yourself in the fantasy life you've built with whatever magazine or book you're reading. Yes, tomorrow you'll go on the diet described in the pages of that thick, shiny fashion magazine, or actually finish the meaty classic you have proudly displayed on your nightstand, but today, well, these Goldfish crackers aren't going to eat themselves. And what better way to congratulate yourself for completing that serious classic or Really Important Book by a Female Author for your book club than a great glass of wine or beer?

Contemplate big ideas, or just the fall *Vogue*, with a glass of something just as thought provoking as your reading material. Whether or not you do said reading in the bathtub is up to you.

'Aspirational Magazines,

Newspapers may be dying a slow, painful death, but there is something so satisfying about digging into a big, glamorous magazine. Here's what to drink while losing yourself in the life you could have between those glossy pages.

Real Simple is bland, soothing, and wholesome, like the magazine version of oatmeal. Something about their recommendations for neutral beauty products and clothes that are just one notch of frump away from Chico's makes you feel like a real adult life is attainable. Crisp sheets, affordable throw pillows, a dozen ways to use baking soda right next to recommendations for $200 scarves—it's all there. You'll need something interesting to drink while trying to stay awake reading yet another recipe for kale and/or boneless pork tenderloin. If you like Pinot Noir, Italy's **Ruchè** is a delicious alternative. Ruchè has even more floral aromas than Pinot and, despite the fact that it's a red wine, can smell almost like peaches, too. It also lacks the aggressive tannins that many wines from Italy's Piedmont region have, so it's easy to sip on its own and it'll play nicely with almost any recipe you pull out of that weekly meal planning insert—it's balanced and not too assertive, just like all those variations on roast chicken. **Osél Ruchè** is less expensive than most Pinots at a similar quality level, retailing at about $12. **Crivelli**, another great producer, makes one that's only a few dollars more expensive.

Vogue. A big, rich Belgian dubbel is a great way to thumb your nose at teensy models. Just looking at these caramelly Belgian brown ales will make you feel like your thighs are expanding. Besides, Jeffrey Steingarten's column is worth the price of the magazine. The one where he buys ten different commercial soft-serve machines and tests them all in his apartment—classic. Never change, Jeffrey.

Belgian dubbels, **tripels**, and **quadrupels** are strong, rich, alcoholic beers meant to be sipped and savored—you can make one last even through the fatty fall *Vogue* (also useful as a door stop or weapon).

As you might expect, these traditional Belgian ales increase in strength along with their names. Dubbels are rich, brown, and mellow, and their ABV levels come in around 6.5–8 percent. Try **Westmalle** for a traditional, abbey-brewed take on this style. Tripels are higher in both carbonation and alcohol, and are more of a golden color. But don't let the delicate appearance fool you—these hover around 7–10 percent. Quadrupels are even stronger and richer, usually over 10 percent. (For an overview of Trappist ales, which include some of the most famous examples of these styles, see page 50.)

If it's hard to track down authentic Belgian offerings, there are plenty of American breweries trying their hands at these styles. From Colorado, **New Belgium Abbey** is an American take on the dubbel. Weighing in at 7 percent ABV, it's like a dessert in a glass, with flavors of bananas, chocolate, and cloves. And **Victory Golden Monkey** is a domestic Belgian-style tripel that packs an alcoholic wallop, so be careful while savoring its flavors of golden raisins and baking spices.

Nothing makes you feel like a smart foodie like *Gastronomica*. It's scholarly AND about food. There are poems about, like, snail farming and shit. It's amazing. Since it's published out of Berkeley, a **quirky red from California** is just the thing. California wine has gotten a bad rap for being homogenized and overly alcoholic, but they're not all that way. **Calder Wine Company**, a teeny tiny producer from Napa, is a great example of this renewal of California's pioneering wine spirit. Their **Charbono** is dark and rich, yet still light on its feet. Made from an obscure varietal that originated in the Savoie region in France, it somehow still yields a balanced wine in California's preternaturally sunny wine country. It tastes like ripe, yet sour blackberries. **Broc Cellars Carbonic Carignan** is another great example of a wine that's full of fruit and California sunshine, but not overdone. These also tend not to be the typical big, blowsy Cali reds, so they're a bit more food-friendly— if you're reading *Gastronomica*, chances are that's important to you. Cook something ambitious, crack open one of these quirky reds, and read all about heirloom runner beans.

There's nothing like reading *The Economist* to make you feel smart and informed. The Bordeaux trade has been largely controlled by brokerage firms in London for a couple of hundred years, so what better to drink with this classic, conservative mag than a **Right Bank Bordeaux**? Wines grown on the Right Bank of Bordeaux's Gironde River are a little softer than their more assertive, tannic, Cabernet-based counterparts grown on the Left Bank, because they're based mostly on the plummier, fruity Merlot. (See pages 108–109 for a deeper explanation of Bordeaux.) Try **Château Damase Bordeaux Supérieur** (about $15), full of soft plum and ripe cherry flavors, while you lie back in a leather chair and feel like an in-control grown-up.

KNOW YOUR GRAPES

Grüner Veltliner (GRU-ner velt-LEE-ner)

REGION: Grüner Veltliner is one of those grapes that is really only happy in its quirky little home country of Austria. The most famous growing region is the Wachau, but lovely wines are made in the Kamptal region as well.

DEFINING FLAVORS/AROMAS: Grüner is one of the grapes that masochists studying for wine exams dread because it is part of a category we refer to as "neutral whites." Lighter, less-ripe (i.e., less expensive) Grüners are kind of mildly citrusy, and that's about it. As they get richer and more expensive, you'll start to notice pear, melon, something softly herbaceous, like tarragon, and a signature peppery note. While it's not closely genetically related, Grüner Veltliner has a lot in common with another popular "neutral white": Pinot Grigio.

PERFECT FOR: That faint whiff of pepper and herb is what makes Grüner Veltliner perfect with vegetable-based dishes (greens like kale and arugula and pungent veggies like asparagus are especially good). It's also wonderful with sushi and other light seafood dishes.

WHAT TO TRY: **Steininger Kamptal**'s Grüner Veltliner will run you about $15, and reminds me of Granny Smith apples, slightly underripe peaches, and pea shoots, but in a good way. The Grüner from **Rudi Pichler** (about $30) will be a bit fuller-bodied, riper, and richer. Its flavors remind me of pears and fennel, with a touch of something almost honeyed, without being sweet.

Reading a magazine like **Nylon** for half an hour or so can lull you into the false sense that you can pull off things like blue eyebrows, or a crop top with a blazer over it for work, or asymmetrical bangs. If you were uncool enough that you first read about a fashion trend in a magazine that's three months out of date that you found at the gym, then you probably shouldn't attempt it. While you read, try something that's unexpected in a little more subtle way than designing brand-new eyebrows for yourself. Austria's **Grüner Veltliner** is a surprisingly versatile grape. Harvested not too ripe, it yields a fresh, tart little white; but let those grapes hang a little longer, and you get a richer, more layered, and more tropical fruity result, but with the same bright acidity that dances across your tongue.

Schloss Gobelsburg's late-harvest Grüner Veltliner is like the thinking person's dessert wine. It's sweet, to be sure, but it doesn't cloy, and its flavors are interesting and delicious—candied apricots, cucumber, a hint of melon—all underscored by nice, fresh acidity. All those 22-year-old models may be able to get away with wearing what is essentially a colorful bra out in public, but they're not quite cool and informed enough to seek out obscure dessert wine yet, so at least you have that.

Important Novels, You Pretend to Have, Read (or Can Barely, Remember . . .)

There are certain novels that everyone talks about, but that you suspect few have actually read, and fewer still understand. If you decide to finally tackle one of these intimidating classics, you might want something to drink while you read, or for when you give up and read the Wikipedia entry before your book club meeting.

Honestly, has anyone actually slogged through all of *Ulysses*? For finally getting through James Joyce's puzzle of a novel, with all the accompanying material you'll need to understand the myriad references to everything from early 1900s pop culture to the finer details of Homer's *Odyssey* that the entire structure of the book is based upon, you'll want something that also starts out strange, but sucks you in. A **beer brewed with a wild yeast**, like brettanomyces, is just the ticket.

Boulevard Saison-Brett is a great introduction to beers brewed in this style, which imparts an earthy, funky flavor and aroma. It starts out tasting wrong, like a barn that hasn't been cleaned out in way too long, but it kind of grows on you. You know how your first whiff of truly stinky cheese almost makes you shudder, but once you get past that initial near-revulsion, you can't get enough? It's kind of like that. There is something about these types of so-wrong-they're-right flavors and aromas that are more addictive than just blandly pleasant ones. At least that's my theory. What *Ulysses* and brett beers have in common is that they're better when you throw out the guidebook, stop trying to make it all make sense, and just let them wash over you.

For the depressing dystopia of Aldous Huxley's ***Brave New World***, try something that feels otherworldly and strange, like **orange wine**. Though it's a style of white wine that uses ancient methods, it's become newly hip. The simplest definition of orange wine is that it's made from white grapes, but in an old-school way that leaves the juice in contact with the skins longer and invites a little more air to the party. Normally in modern white-winemaking, the goal is to separate the juice from the skins as quickly as possible, and keep it from being exposed to air while it's being made. Both of these things make the wine taste fresh and fruity, and appear crystal clear. Orange wine, on the other hand, takes on a coppery, orange glow (hence the name) and has a much more robust, spicy flavor than your usual crisp white quaffer. The result is often something that feels like it's from another planet.

What's the Deal with Yeast?

Of all the elements that make wine and beer taste the way they do, yeast is probably the least noticed in relation to its importance and impact. Here's an overview of the role yeast plays in creating our favorite beverages.

WINE: SPONTANEOUS VS. CULTURED YEAST

In wine, the big debate is over using spontaneous yeast (sometimes called "ambient") or cultured yeast. Some people think wines fermented with the yeast found on the grapes and in their surrounding environment have more character, while others think that's a load of hogwash and that it's

better to use a cultured yeast so that you can be more assured that your wine will ferment all the way. There are delicious wines made both ways, so I don't think there's one right answer.

A great example of a style of wine that derives a lot of its character from cultured yeast strains is New Zealand Sauvignon Blanc. Those super-intense grapefruit and sharp citrus aromas are accentuated by using a strain of yeast that ferments at a very cool temperature. Cooler fermentations mean "cooler" flavors—think citrus rather than ripe apple or banana.

The same grape fermented with a different yeast strain, or an ambient yeast strain that just lives on the grape skins in the environment in which they're grown (say, in the Loire Valley), will have a very different character. It'll still be Sauvignon Blanc, but the volume on that intense grapefruit zest character will be turned down a little bit.

BEER: ALES VS. LAGERS

In the beer world, how yeast is used is what makes the most basic split at the top of the beer family tree: ales and lagers.

Ales are known as top-fermenting beers. So-called because the yeast cells rise to the top of the fermenting wort, they're brewed at a higher temperature and this brings out stronger, fruitier flavors in the finished beer.

Lagers are bottom-fermenting beers (because, you guessed it, the yeast settles at the bottom of the fermentation vessel). They're brewed at a cooler temperature, and just like with the

Sauvignon Blanc example, that cooler fermentation creates a beer with less of those rich, ripe fruit aromas and flavors, and more crisp, clean ones.

Think about the difference between a pilsner (in the lager group) and a hefeweizen (in the ale group). The pilsner's "crisper" character is mostly due to its being fermented at a cooler temperature, and those bolder, fruitier aromas and flavors in the hefeweizen are brought out by its being fermented at a warmer temperature.

BRETTANOMYCES

This little bugger is often considered a flaw in beer- and winemaking, but many styles of beer depend on it. It produces a huge variety of aromas and flavors. Some are in the earthy "barnyard" family: leather, hay, dirt, and, er, something less pleasant that the horses in said barn might produce, if you catch my drift. Others are in the "spicier" family, like cloves, smoke, and even a scent that might remind you of Band-Aids.

SPARKLING WINE

In sparkling wine, yeast by-products become very important. When sparkling wines like Champagne are aged *sur lie*, this means that they're aged with the dead yeast cells still in the bottle. This allows the wine to age longer (because the presence of yeast cells inhibits oxidation), and imparts that signature toasty, bready aroma and flavor. Wines like *pét-nat* (see page 172) and Bugey-Cerdon (see page 222), as well as bottle-conditioned beers, never go

....

Next time you take a sip of your favorite fermented beverage, remember all those hardworking yeast cells that sacrificed themselves for your enjoyment.

....

through the fancy disgorgement process that wines made in the Champagne style do, so a bit of sediment remains at the bottom of the bottle. The resulting bubbles are a little foamier and creamier than traditional Champagne, but also tend to disappear faster.

So just like how different types of bacteria can turn ordinary cows' milk into hundreds of different types of cheeses, yeast has a huge impact on the aroma, flavor, and even mouthfeel of beer and wine. Next time you take a sip of your favorite fermented beverage, remember all those hardworking yeast cells that sacrificed themselves for your enjoyment.

Scholium Project is a quirky California producer, and their wine **The Prince in His Caves** takes on a warm, cloudy amber color, despite being made from 100 percent Sauvignon Blanc. Just don't read *Brave New World*, *The Handmaid's Tale*, and *1984* all in one summer—no amount of wine, no matter how delicious, will help you recover from that. Trust me.

If you can even hope to participate in feverish discussions about Harper Lee's second novel, *Go Set a Watchman*, you'll have to go back and take a look at *To Kill a Mockingbird*. A book that appears on practically every "top novels" list calls for something classic, American, stalwart, and true. Much as I like to poke fun at Napa Cabernets, this style became popular for a reason—because when they're good, they're really, really good. I doubt Harper Lee would approve of the over-oaked, shoved-into-a-Wonderbra style that's popular these days—she'd want to kick it old school with something like a **classic California Cabernet**. Go back to a simpler time, when Atticus Finch was someone you could admire, and Cabernet wasn't so big and boozy-smelling, it made you think of bourbon. Older, classic California Cabernet is sort of halfway between a traditional Bordeaux (see pages 108–109) and the bigger, lusher style that's popular today. Try one from **Mayacamas** (around $80)—they're one of only a handful of California wineries that keeps a deep library of back vintages and occasionally sells them for prices that, while certainly not cheap, aren't quite at oil-baron-in-Dubai levels.

Go back to a simpler time, when Atticus Finch was someone you could admire, and Cabernet wasn't so big and boozy-smelling, it made you think of bourbon.

John Steinbeck's *The Grapes of Wrath* is definitely a slog—no judgment if you didn't get through it. And that ending that's supposed to be uplifting, well, kind of has the opposite effect if you read it at too impressionable an age. You'll want to sip something bittersweet, and the result of a lot of hardscrabble work. **Rivesaltes**, an obscure fortified red wine from the south of

France, tastes kind of shocking at first—like dried fruit and resin, and honestly not all that appealing—but it grows on you. The Rivesaltes from **Domaine Cazes** is great, and their 1976 release, aged for decades in glass demijohns, is mind-blowingly complex. As for what the demijohns do, who knows, but the wine is incredible. Dark, brooding, not exactly pleasant, but with all the gritty gravitas of Steinbeck. Or, I don't know, maybe just drink Night Train—or would that be better for *Cannery Row*?

Whether you actually read ***Pride and Prejudice*** or just enjoy watching the myriad film and miniseries adaptations, most of us identify with Elizabeth Bennet. We might be a little sarcastic or too quick to judge, but underneath we're good people worthy of our Mr. Darcy in the end. Try something that's a little tart, prickly, and even strange on the surface, but grows on you over time, like a **white from France's Jura region**. White wines from this area are often allowed to develop nutty, oxidative aromas similar to Sherry (see page 139). Those that really go in this direction are labeled *vin jaune* ("yellow wine"), but even the "regular" white wines from this region often have these characteristics. Tart and funky, Jura whites are made with Chardonnay and Savagnin grapes (sometimes blended, sometimes by themselves) and are wonderful partners with food, especially runny French cheeses, nuts, and oily fish. Try **Domaine de Montbourgeau l'Étoile Vin Jaune** for a Chardonnay you won't forget—like beeswax and honey, but without the sweetness. It's delicious when it's released and, like the classic plot of *Pride and Prejudice,* will stand the test of time as well.

Summer

ummer is not a time to drive yourself crazy with details. Summer is a time for ease and doing as little as possible, and it's a great time to explore alternative packaging, like wines that come in a bag-in-box or Tetra Pak. Does something you're going to guzzle at a barbecue with your friends right after you buy it, probably out of plastic cups, need to be bottled in heavy glass and closed with expensive cork? Haven't we ruined the planet enough?

And speaking of sustainability, all that wonderful, eye-wateringly expensive farmers' market produce needs to be washed down with something, doesn't it? You'll also want something to relieve that delightful combination of boredom and jealousy that comes with viewing your friend's vacation photos. We get it. The night markets in Vietnam are wonderful. The Taj Mahal was life changing. Some of us are broke, Suzy, and have only booze to amuse us all summer, so let's get drinking!

Embarrassing Yourself in the Great Outdoors,

Y ou wish you could be one of those people who is coordinated, never gets lost, and always has the right gear for hiking, swimming, and taking an impromptu Pilates class. Unfortunately, this isn't in the cards, but at least after making an ass of yourself on some nature adventure, you can soothe your bruised ego with the perfect beverage.

Summertime Reds

We think of summer as white and rosé weather, and for a good reason. They're refreshing, usually higher in acidity than their darker sisters, and served cold. But even in the summer, you'll have food like a grilled steak or a big juicy burger that cries out for red wine. Here are a few things to consider when choosing a red for the warmer months.

Chill out. It sounds strange, but chilling down your red wine can make it more summer-friendly. Making something colder brings out its acidity, so it'll make the red in question a bit more conducive to warm evenings on the deck. Beaujolais (see page 95) and Dolcetto (see page 35) are especially great after about 20–30 minutes in the fridge.

Go easy on tannins. While just bringing down the temperature can make a wine better for sweltering weather, there are certain reds that are just too heavy on tannin to be fun to drink when it's hot out. Tannin's main deal is that it dries out your mouth, and that's the last feeling you want in weather that already makes you thirsty. You'll probably want to steer clear of famously tannic wines like Cabernet Sauvignon (see page 243), Barolo (see page 59), Barbaresco, and Cahors (see page 169).

Consider fizz. You know what's great cold? Fizzy wine, even red fizzy wine! If you're noshing on pizza out on the back porch, try a fizzy red from the Naples area of Italy called Gragnano (**Grotta del Sole** makes a delicious one for less than $20). Thank me later.

Camping can be intimidating. There's so much equipment, and what if there are bears? While it might be true that extra precautions should be taken if you're on your period while camping, it's pretty mortifying when someone finds the bag of used tampons you thought you'd cleverly hidden away from a bear's radar in a back corner of the van with the other trash. What? Who wants to get tragically eaten? One thing that shouldn't be intimidating is the wine you bring to the great outdoors. What better to have with roasted wieners than a **nice, full-bodied red**? For a bigger crowd, the 3-liter bag-in-box **Vin Rouge**, a Grenache-based blend from quirky importer Jenny & François, is delicious and eco-friendly. For another lively red blend, try **Ad Libitum** from **La Grange Tiphaine**, a combo of Malbec, Gamay, and Cabernet Franc that usually goes for between $14 and $18. Try it a little on the cool side for real outdoor refreshment—and speaking of refreshing, any of the "Summertime Reds" listed on page 189 would work well, too.

A scenic boat ride seemed like such a good idea. Beautiful sunshine glittering off the water, a lovely breeze—bliss, right? But partway through you notice a herd of larger folks all congregating toward the front of the boat. Water starts to pool around your feet, soaking the gray carpeting. Luckily, despite the fact that the person steering this thing looks to be about 12 years old, he gets it to the dock just in time, with water sloshing around your ankles.

Sip it on the beach with your toes in the water—that's more your speed.

Dry your feet off, and have some brunch, for God's sake! You deserve it. This isn't the time for something fancy. The great thing about sparkling wine is that no matter how cheap it is, it still makes you feel like you're celebrating, and after a near-death experience, you deserve to celebrate a little! Now's the time for something festive and easy to acquire, like several **mimosas** made with cheap sparkling wine that the menu calls "Champagne," but is actually Cava that wholesales for $4 a bottle. No matter. You're alive.

The desk clerk at the hotel told you how easy **kayaking** would be. That any-one could do it. Oh, just a little paddling, she said. Just a gentle ride out on the water to see Puerto Rico's beautiful bioluminescence. You assure your mom it'll be fine. You've just started working out, and because you've managed to use the wimpy machines at your gym at the YMCA and get through about half a spin class, you think you can do anything now.

After you're almost decapitated by low-hanging mangrove branches in the dark, and barely make it back to the shore alive, nothing says comfort like a soft red that's not too heavy or tannic. **Grenache** (see page 168 for a profile of its Spanish alias, Garnacha) is a great choice, because it is a grape that is full-bodied and ripe, but produces wine that isn't too heavy or dry. Your mouth is probably already dry enough from, you know, fear and panic.

Though California isn't an area known for Grenache the way Spain and southern France are, Grenache made there tends to have an almost candied feel to it that is really appealing and comforting. **Tablas Creek** makes a wide range of wines on their sustainably farmed estate in Paso Robles, and their **Patelin de Tablas Rouge** is a soft and fruity Grenache-based blend, with just enough peppery bite to keep things interesting. Sip it on the beach with your toes in the water—that's more your speed.

Hiking is one of those things that seems easy, but after you do a few difficult treks, you realize why there is so much associated equipment. Soon, your feet are hurting, and you are dying to pee. After you finally relieve yourself near a tree and a few elderly budding naturalists walk by and examine the soaked leaves you just sullied, you'll need something really delicious to go along with the picnic you assembled at the dusty grocery store at the start of the trail. Blunt your embarrassment with a peppery, crisp **Grüner Veltliner** in a con-venient screwcap bottle.

Austria's **Paul D.** makes one that's actually a liter instead of 750 ml—$11 for basically a bottle plus an extra glass! A light Grüner Veltliner is refreshing and easy drinking, just what you want for a hike—plus you can consider it a little homage to the outdoorsy, hiking culture of its native Austria. Just don't overdo it, or you'll end up with the same problem all over again.

Tubing down a river seriously could not be easier, and yet you managed to fall out of the tube, and lose both your shirt and your sunglasses. Once you finally reach that little dock and your "adventure" is done, have a gently refreshing **kölsch**. Kölsch is a great style of beer for this situation—and honestly, many summer activities—because it strikes the perfect balance between being not too challenging, and not so boring you feel like you might as well be drinking water. It's low in alcohol, so it doesn't taste heavy; it has a very delicate hop flavor, so you don't get tired of drinking it; and it has a little more effervescence than some other styles, which keeps it feeling refreshing all afternoon. Some folks actually bring the beer tubing with them, but it's important to know your limits in life. If you're clumsy, just wait.

KNOW YOUR STYLES
Kölsch (KOL-sh)

REGION: Originated in Cologne, Germany, and the people of Cologne take this shit seriously. Almost every bar in the city serves this traditional beer, cold-conditioned (super-chilling beer right after it's brewed so that anything that might make it cloudy settles to the bottom of the tank and doesn't make it into the keg or bottle) to make it crystal clear. It's served in smaller, cylindrical glasses called *stanges*, because kölsch is so delicate that it loses its carbonation and head more quickly than other styles. Unless you put your coaster on top of your glass, waiters will keep serving you! It's a style of beer that's built for drinking many, many rounds.

DEFINING FLAVORS/AROMAS: Lightly hoppy and malty, crisp, light, effervescent, and refreshing!

PERFECT FOR: Summer picnic food—especially cold fried or roasted chicken, salads (think cold pasta salad), and of course, brats from the grill!

WHAT TO TRY: Kölsch tastes best when it's made nearby. With this style, freshness is key, so look for breweries that make one near you. Saint Louis–based brewery **Schlafly** makes an excellent kölsch, easy drinking, but with just enough flavor to keep things interesting—it kind of tastes the way fresh hay smells to me. If you want a taste of traditional German kölsch, **Gaffel** is grassy, crisp, and refreshing. On the East Coast, **Blue Mountain Brewery Kölsch 151** really emphasizes the clean, crisp aspect of this style. Unfold that lawn chair and chill out!

'Other People's, 'Vacations,

Something about our social media–heavy era, where everyone has their own "personal brand" (gag) can really make a person feel inadequate. And no situation is worse for this than when you're on a budget, or have a crazy work schedule and can't get away, and it seems like everyone, from your obnoxious random acquaintances from high school to your grandparents, is taking an exotic trip somewhere, while you rot away in obscurity. Here's what to drink while feeling bitter and pretending to be happy for other people.

Slide show. Oh my God, Grandma, we get it, you took a road trip in an RV to Vancouver. How many photos do we need of farmers' markets and rest stops? Older folks, bless them, always want to show you photos like it's an event, because they come from a time when photos WERE an event. They don't get that between Instagram and Facebook we're so saturated in people's goddamn pictures we're sick of it. You'll need something that will hold your interest over a long photo-sharing session, like a full-bodied red with a tannic grip. Try **Carignan** ("CARE-i-nyan"), a grape known for its flavors of just-ripe blackberries and blueberries. You mostly see it in blends from areas in southern France like Costières de Nîmes, but California's **Porter Creek** makes a single-varietal Carignan that tastes like sour, dark blueberry jam and is great with grilled meat.

Who are these people who manage to arrange their lives so that they can take months off at a time to **backpack through Europe or South America**? What the hell kind of jobs are these? I can barely use the restroom at work without someone calling for me like there's going to be some kind of wine-related emergency that can't wait two minutes, and these fuckers are just, what, taking a leave of absence? Without being replaced? It's really the only way to travel, they say, you have to really *sink into* a place. Have you read *Vagabonding*? As you look through dozens of their photos ("Oh, that guy with the waist-length blond dreadlocks? That's Sven! He was living at the hostel we stayed at in Brussels for the summer . . .") of coffee shops and them grinning on rented bikes, sip something that is a triumph of the exact kind of modern consumerism they claim to hate: a squeaky clean **New Zealand Sauvignon Blanc**. Try **Greywacke**, the relatively new project from the former winemaker for Cloudy Bay. It'll run you about $27, but you can afford it because you haven't quit your job.

Service vacations. Oh, you went to build a medical facility in Ethiopia? That's nice, I rested in a hammock on my deck and drank rosé wearing giant sunglasses. There's something just a little too altruistic about using your vacation time to volunteer. It's admirable, but sometimes smacks of someone who cares too much about what other people think. I mean, I'm part of the first generation in years whose standard of living will be worse than our parents'. I'm taking a fucking vacation, you know? Mentally travel to an iconic vacationers' paradise with a **fresh, juicy red from Provence**. One of my favorites is a little red blend called **Le Pigeoulet en Provence** from iconic importer Kermit Lynch (usually about $20). Its tart blackberry flavors and medium body are

> *Oh, you went to build a medical facility in Ethiopia? That's nice, I rested in a hammock on my deck and drank rosé wearing giant sunglasses.*

perfect with the olives and grilled lamb you're having in your fantasy stone cottage that you're traveling to in your mind's eye, while you listen to your friend go on and on about how *really* helping people and *seeing the world* just changed her *life*. We get it. You're better than us. **Château Puech Haut** makes a Provençal red that's a little less fruity, and has more of that earthy, resinous herb aroma that the locals call *garrigue*. Take that, smug do-gooders.

KNOW YOUR GRAPES

Sauvignon Blanc (so-vin-YAWN blonk)

REGION: France's Loire Valley and Bordeaux regions; New Zealand; California's Napa and Sonoma Valleys; and Chile

DEFINING FLAVORS/AROMAS: It's known as an "aromatic variety" for a reason. While its style will change based on where it's grown and how it's made, its basic personality stays the same: bright citrus and a whiff of something herbaceous and green, whether it's freshly mown grass or jalapeños.

PERFECT FOR: Salads, seafood, Mexican food, and tart, fresh goat cheeses (usually labeled chèvre)

WHAT TO TRY: For a light-bodied, minerally SB, try **Patient Cottat Le Grand Caillou** from the Loire Valley, which goes for less than $12 and is often very reasonable by the glass at restaurants, at least on the East Coast of the United States. **Dog Point**'s (about $22) is a classic New Zealand Sauvignon Blanc—it's all about the grapefruit! Zesty and lip smacking, it's great for hot summer days. The Napa Valley's **Spottswoode** makes a Sauvignon Blanc ($35–$40) that has more of a melon and lime fruit vibe, and would be great with a fancy lunch of chicken or lobster salad served over lettuce, like you're a sophisticated lady who lunches. Wear your best linen pants.

The street food is just amazing! While you're pretending not to be green with envy at your friend's exotic trip to Southeast Asia, why not explore the world of **Asian beers**? If you can't afford to fly halfway around the world to take Instagram photos of yourself near ancient temples and buying cute sarongs, you can at least get a nice buzz on while you read captions about the night markets, and about how the Thai food we get here in the United States is just NOTHING like the real thing. Try a **Singha** (pronounced "sing"), a light, malty Thai beer—it's inexpensive, so maybe it'll help you save up for your own trip to Asia to make other people jealous.

ʿSummer Trips,

Y ou're finally going somewhere! Now you get to post obnoxious photos of a glass of wine on a table at a sidewalk café that looks like 10,000 other similar photos and make all of *your* friends jealous. Vacations are, of course, wonderful (try to look up from Instagram and Snapchat once in a while and actually enjoy it, OK?), but they can present some drinking dilemmas. Drinking in an unfamiliar locale can mean either bringing your own, or shopping away from the warmth and comfort of your neighborhood wine store.

Here's how to make the most of that glorious string of days and nights when waking up at ass early o'clock for work is the last thing on your mind.

Road trip. Once you're done playing license plate bingo for the day, you're going to want something to drink out of those charming plastic cups in the hotel room (if you're really thinking ahead, bring your own plastic glasses— govino makes great ones that aren't depressingly ugly). If you don't want to pick through the scant options at the local convenience store wherever you've stopped each night (and in places like Elko, Nevada, the pickings are slim, my friends), try bringing a few **boxes of wine** along with you.

Wine that comes in bag-in-box or Tetra Pak format has gotten a bad rap, but there's way more out there than Franzia Chillable Red. Some of the best ones are **Yellow + Blue Malbec** (comes in a convenient 1-liter Tetra Pak) and **La Petite Frog Picpoul de Pinet**, a tart, snappy white from the south of France that comes in a generous 3-liter bag-in-box. The latter is great as a wine base for the white sangria on page 65 if you're making it for a crowd, too. Either way, a nice glass of wine at the end of the day will make you feel a little less grimy and road weary.

Ready for takeoff. One of the best feelings is wrapping up your last couple of tasks before you leave for vacation and turning on that out-of-office reply.

Think Inside the Box

People tend to shudder whenever bag-in-box wine is mentioned. Boxed wine reminds people of stuff like the "sweet blush" you may have had too much of in college. But the world has changed! There are plenty of good-quality boxed wines out there, so here are a few tips to get the most out of your box.

Keep it cool. Boxed wine will keep six to eight weeks after it's opened. Whites usually last longer than reds, but both will last quite a while if you keep them in the refrigerator.

Don't wait to open it. On the other hand, boxed wines don't last very long *before* opening. Try to buy your box right before you need it, and don't let it linger on your shelf for more than about eight months, otherwise you'll get a flat, tired-tasting wine, and no one wants that!

Tips for Boxed Reds: The trick when picking boxed reds is to stay away from styles that are traditionally heavily oaked. So if you're trolling Target and want to try one of the more mass-market brands like **Black Box**, go for a Syrah blend or a lighter grape like Pinot Noir rather than a Cabernet, which will most certainly be treated with oak chips, whose vanilla flavors can start to cloy after more than a few sips.

Tips for Boxed Whites: When looking for whites, Chardonnay can be tricky. Better to stick with Pinot Grigio, or an inexpensive white from France or Spain. The **Black Box Pinot Grigio** is actually pretty good, and **La Petite Frog** makes a great boxed version of the tart French white wine Picpoul de Pinet that is great for a crowd or in white sangria!

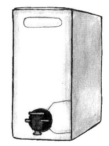

One of the worst is being trapped at the airport because your flight is delayed. You were SO CLOSE to finally being on vacation! If you're stuck at an airport bar, chances are you're not going to be spoiled for choice. If your preflight ritual needs to consist of something stronger than Coke Zero, Rolos, and fashion magazines that make you feel bad about yourself, fear not. A **crisp, citrusy white like Sauvignon Blanc** is almost always the best choice. Stay away from Chardonnay, or anything that could be sweet, like Riesling. Semisweet wines can be transcendent when done well, but when they're done badly, they're cloying and unpleasant and make your mouth feel kind of sticky. It's important to stay hydrated in the air, so if you cut your Sauv Blanc with a little soda water, just say it's for your health if anyone looks at you funny.

A theme park like Disney World can be a great place for a family vacation, but it can also be stressful and feel a little regressive. At the end of a long day of waiting in epic lines, soothing cranky kids, and spraying everyone in your family with sunscreen like you're shilling perfume at the mall, you'll need to feel like a grown-up again. Sneak down to the lobby of your hotel for a glass of something complex and red. It may be summer, but you'll be in air-conditioning, so who cares? **Pinot Noir** or **Nebbiolo** will allow you to swirl and sniff from a big glass, and that's really what this ritual is about. If you're able to bring your own, **Vajra Langhe Nebbiolo** (about $25 retail) is complex, smoky, and the furthest thing from a kid-friendly profile you're likely to find. Unlike Nebbiolo's more expensive big brother, Barolo, these wines tend to not have quite so much tannic power, so you can sip a glass by itself. By the time you're done, you'll be ready to face another day of too-bright sun and people dressed in costumes with giant foam heads. How did this become your life?!

Sure, **sunbathing at the beach** is supposed to be all about being blissed out in the sun and listening to the sound of crashing waves, but when you're a lifelong urbanite and lover of public transportation, you won't be able to stop yourself from people-watching. Wine-fueled giggling about all the characters you'll see is the perfect way to waste a lazy afternoon. Whether it's the guy in a ZZ Top beard and a neon pink Speedo doing strange calisthenic exercises, or the woman who seems to spend every afternoon riding back and forth along the same path in a four-wheeler, or the couple that seems to have forgotten that this isn't a nude beach (ack!), you never know what kind of quirkiness you'll find on a crowded beach.

As you watch the show, you'll need something refreshing, like a cool, crisp white wine. Spain's **Verdejo** will remind you of Sauvignon Blanc, but

it's usually a little more on the orange citrus side rather than grapefruit. And since you may or may not drop an ice cube into your mouthwatering white, this isn't the time to splurge on something expensive. **Palacio de Bornos** makes a Verdejo that's less than $10, tastes like tangerine sorbet, and stays that way even if it warms up a few degrees in the summer sun. Just make sure to check the beach's rules on alcohol and glass containers (a plastic cooler with a spigot is a good way around this), and don't forget the sunscreen.

Chill Out!

It's counterintuitive, but the fastest way to chill down a bottle of wine or beer isn't with a bucket of ice, or even putting it in the freezer—it's ice *and* water. To make wine or beer cold as fast as possible, fill a bucket (or your sink, if you've got a lot of beverages to cool down) with ice, and then enough water to make things good and sloshy. Spin the bottle(s) around frequently for faster chilling.

'Your Overpriced, 'Farmers' Market, 'Bounty'

Many classic food and wine pairings are for the kind of overly sauced, rich, usually French food most of us eat maybe once a year if we're lucky. These days, most of our Sunday night dinners are made with a different kind of luxury ingredient than *poulet de Bresse* or pâté: expensive, but worth-it (you tell yourself) produce from your local market, carried home on foot in a canvas bag. (Don't forget that bag or everyone will give you side-eye.)

Besides, what's the point of being a pretentious food hipster if you don't have something delicious to drink with your $15 arugula?

Where's the beef? Everyone is wetting their pants over grass-fed beef these days, and while it's delicious, it can be more difficult to cook and to pair with wine. For meat that's a little chewy, and not quite as don't-need-a-steak-knife soft as corn-fed beef, you want a wine that is soft, lush, and full of fruit. This is a great time for a big "fruit bomb" **Malbec**, because the juiciness of the wine will make up for the juiciness that the meat lacks. There are a ton of Malbecs out there,

What's the Deal with Vintage?

"**D**oes vintage matter?" is one of the most common questions I get about wine. I wish I had a more satisfying answer than "it depends," but . . . it depends.

How far north? In general, the farther away from the equator you get, the more vintage matters. So in cooler areas where you're closer to the edge of where you can successfully ripen grapes, little variations in weather matter more, so there are more differences between vintages. Places like Oregon's Willamette Valley, France's Burgundy, and the wine-growing regions of Germany are all places where there can be really big differences year to year.

Places like California's Napa Valley, where there is pretty much perfect grape-growing weather all the time, will still show variation year to year, but the differences will be less extreme.

How big is the operation? In general, the bigger and more commercial a winery is, the more effort they will put into producing a consistent product year in, year out. Smaller producers a) tend to not have the resources to employ all the tricks in the vineyard and winery to smooth out any bumps in the road they may have encountered that year, and b) usually don't want to anyway, and prefer to let the wine showcase whatever happened that year, for better or worse.

So, that $10 Malbec that's earned a near-permanent spot on the shelf at your local wineshop? When you see a new vintage pop up, you can be reasonably sure it'll taste almost the same as it did last year. A $60 white Burgundy from a winery you've never heard of? This is a good time to ask for help to make sure the style of the wine that particular year will line up with what you're in the mood to drink!

but one of my favorites is everywhere, and it's kind of a cliché for a reason: **Catena**—just the "regular" one that you see everywhere—retails for about $20 and is super consistent and delicious in pretty much every vintage. It's not incredibly interesting or flashy, but it's like that black skirt in your closet that you keep thinking of getting rid of, but it ends up saving your butt so many times when you can't think of what else to wear that you never will. All that lush, unctuous fruit will soften the chewy edges of your steak. Don't go crazy with sauces—a little salt and pepper are all you need.

Eat your greens. If you patronize a year-round farmers' market, you know how depressing those late fall and winter months can be. How many tough winter greens can one person eat?! And I'm sorry, I don't care what the food magazines say, beet greens are just not that delicious. For intensely "green" veggies like kale, turn to none other than every late 1990s sommelier's best friend: Grüner Veltliner. But this time, try a **sparkling Grüner Veltliner**. Look for **Steininger Sekt** (about $25) or **Bründlmayer Sekt Extra Brut**. It sounds weird, but trust me: Austria's cool climate is home to a surprising number of wineries that specialize in sparkling wine, and sparkling Grüner is a great way to punch up yet another recipe you found online for some healthy grain like farro and the ubiquitous kale, that tastes "just like risotto," and absolutely doesn't at all. You know what tastes like risotto? Delicious, short-grain white rice and an obscene amount of butter and some white wine. That tastes like risotto. But drink enough bubbly Grüner, and you'll manage to get through that pile of fiber you're telling your boyfriend is dinner. Go see an action movie with him this weekend—he'll get over it.

> *Sparkling Grüner is a great way to punch up yet another recipe you found online for some healthy grain like farro and the ubiquitous kale, that tastes "just like risotto," and absolutely doesn't at all.*

Ephemeral strawberries. Especially on the East Coast, the window for really great strawberries and raspberries seems like it's about two minutes long. Make the most of it by eating them with nothing but a cloud of freshly whipped, barely sweetened cream (bonus points for folding in a little vanilla extract and a spoonful or two of crème fraîche), and sipping on **Brachetto d'Acqui**, a truly underappreciated sweet, fizzy, light-colored red from northern Italy. Its heady fragrance and subtle sweetness perfectly mirror the flavors of fresh berries, and it's not so sweet that it will overwhelm your simple dessert. This is a style of wine that in Italy is often drunk with salty cured meats and cheeses, so if you're feeling adventurous, give that a whirl. **Il Falchetto**

KNOW YOUR STYLES

Brown Ale

REGION: This style originated in London in the late 17th century when it was a mild, sweet beer brewed with all brown malt. Now there are a few different styles of beer that fall under the brown ale umbrella, some are fuller-bodied with a stronger hop character, and some are more like the mild original.

DEFINING FLAVORS/AROMAS: Kind of like it sounds—brown ales encompass the "brown" end of the flavor and aroma spectrum. Some brown ales are fairly sweet, with brown sugar, nutmeg, and molasses as the dominant flavors. Others, like **Brooklyn Brewery Brown Ale**, have a little more hop character that acts as a balance to the nutty sweetness.

PERFECT FOR: Roasted veggies, roast pork, pork chops, some desserts if it's a sweeter style. I like **Samuel Smith Nut Brown Ale** with carrot cake or a gingery spice cake, personally.

WHAT TO TRY: **Newcastle Brown Ale** is a traditional English version of the style, while **Dogfish Head Indian Brown Ale** is a truly American mishmash of a brown ale, an IPA, and a little hint of the honeyed sweetness of a Scotch ale. It's dry-hopped, loaded with notes of ginger and brown sugar, and perfect with the aforementioned spice cake.

makes a wonderful one whose sweetness is balanced by the bubbles and just the right amount of acidity that is usually around $22.

Relishing roasting. Roasted root vegetables (because what else are you going to do with those knobby things, seriously?) take on wonderful caramelly flavors and aromas. Echo those nutty, browned flavors with a **brown ale**! This traditional style, with roots in British pub culture, will make a meal of vegetables feel a little more substantial. While the flavors are complementary, there's a nice contrast of textures, between the soft innards of your roasted veggies and the tingle of your beer's carbonation. Ah, fall.

Food and Beverage Pairing Basics

For the most part, analyzing wine and food pairing down to butt lint is kind of soul-sucking, and many people in the wine and beer industries pay very little attention to super-specific rules when it comes to their day-to-day drinking. There are a few guidelines that will help demystify things, though.

ACIDITY

What you're drinking should always be more tart than what you're eating. So if you're eating something like a salad with a tart vinaigrette, go with a light, tart style of wine with plenty of acidity on its own, like Sauvignon Blanc, otherwise your wine will taste kind of flat and bitter.

PROTEIN AND SAUCE

These days we eat foods from so many different world cuisines that those old rules about drinking only white wine with fish are all but irrelevant. A better way to think about it is this: The darker your cooking method gets your protein, the fuller-bodied and darker you can go with wine and beer. Likewise, the heavier and more complex your sauce, the heavier your wine or beer can be.

You would want to serve something like poached chicken with an equally delicate beverage, like kölsch (see page 192) or Chablis (see page 53). Take that same little bird, season it heavily, and grill it until it shows charred black grill marks? Now you're ready for a brown ale (see page 203) or a lighter red like Pinot Noir (see page 101).

DON'T FUEL THE FIRE

For spicy food, a big, alcoholic red is just going to dump gasoline on the blaze. Instead, go for beer or a crisp, lighter white, especially one with a little residual sugar. It'll balance out that spiciness.

With beer and spicy food, you have a bit more wiggle room. Because beer is generally lower in alcohol than wine, and it's cold and carbonated, you've got several built-in qualities that will tame spiciness already. But if you want to balance that spiciness, go for a lighter beer just like you would with wine— think lagers, or maybe an amber ale. If you really want to feel the burn, an IPA will accentuate the sharp flavors of whatever chilies or spices are in the dish.

TAME THAT TANNIN

When you've got a wine that's heavy on tannin—say, a young Barolo or a current-release Cabernet Sauvignon from California or Washington State— and you want to taste more of the fruit the wine has to offer, eat something high in protein, salt, and/or fat.

Tannins want to bind to protein, so to keep them from binding to the protein in your mouth and making you feel like you swallowed a pair of those big chalkboard erasers from your elementary school days, eat either something that will blunt the effects of tannin, like fat or salt, or something that has a lot of protein that the tannins can bind to instead, like a big juicy steak.

AND WHEN IN DOUBT

There's always Champagne. It goes with everything—seriously.

Weddings

Weddings are often more about getting through than grand, celebratory occasions that require the perfect Champagne. No one can afford to serve that to a crowd anyway, so here are wines and beers to keep your sanity as you or someone you used to like (before they became a bridezilla) rides that crazy wedding train.

'Your Best Friend's, 'Wedding

Helping a close friend get married can feel akin to deploying a complicated military operation. The consequences of getting things wrong, especially when family is involved, can feel about as severe.

Shopping for a bachelorette party. Why are there so many ridiculous parties leading up to what is, essentially, just another big party? Weddings now just seem like an excuse to make your friends do a lot of pointless errands, the most pointless of all being going to five stores to create little party favor bags for the guests at the bachelorette party. No one wants penis-shaped pasta, and we can all provide our own breath mints and hair ties, like we have at every other party of our adult lives. After an evening of party-favor-and-mimosa-bar-planning torture, you'll need something refreshing that reminds you you're an interesting adult with taste. Try a **saison**, a style of Belgian farmhouse ale that's experiencing something of a renaissance in the United States. These are tart, refreshing, not too high in alcohol, and flavored with an interesting variety of additives from fruit to peppercorns. Sip one in the bathtub while listening to *This American Life* podcasts and trying to forget you ever purchased anything phallic at a party store.

A sweltering outdoor reception. Weddings and other catered events always have a dismal array of choices, so here's how to navigate bad wine lists. When in

KNOW YOUR STYLES

Saison (say-ZON)

REGION: Belgium (originally created as a summertime refreshment for Belgian farmers)

DEFINING FLAVORS/AROMAS: Tart, fruity flavors that are the perfect antidote to the hoppy, high-gravity monsters American craft breweries seem to love turning out by the dozen these days

PERFECT FOR: Mexican food, bloomy-rind cheese, seafood

WHAT TO TRY: **Saison Dupont** is a very traditional saison that's made in Belgium and is a bit more heavily spiced than some of the American versions I've tried. **Ommegang Hennepin** feels a little thicker than some more traditional styles, and features delicious flavors of orange peel, coriander, and a nice yeasty, bready note. **Goose Island Sofie**, aged in oak barrels with citrus peel, is a lighter, more refreshing saison. Beers like this are often described as "session" ales by beer geeks, which just means that you can have a few before you start to feel like you've been run over by a train.

doubt, stick to white, and stay away from Chardonnay and Riesling. Some of the greatest wines in the world are made from these grapes, but the bad ones are really terrible. **Pinot Grigio** and **Sauvignon Blanc**, on the other hand, tend to be bearable even when they're pumped out, factory-style, from over-cropped grapes, cultured yeast, and giant stainless steel tanks. No one tries to doctor them with oak chips like they do Chardonnay. Reds at an event like this will also tend to be given the fake-oak treatment, but worse than that, they're usually too warm, which amplifies their offensive flavors and aromas. If you must, stick with the **Pinot Noir** and ask for an ice cube in it. Sounds like sacrilege, but it'll make it taste better. But seriously, stick to the white. Who wants to drink red wine or whiskey when your clothes are sticking to your body like cling wrap because you're so sweaty?

Bridesmaids' dress fitting. Why is the sizing for formalwear so out of whack with sizing for the rest of the insane lady-clothing universe? As if stuffing yourself into a strapless, pastel concoction didn't make you feel huge enough, it has to be five sizes bigger than the size you usually wear. People complain about size inflation as if sizing has any meaning other than relative and emotional. It's meaningless! So why go all retro with the sizing during an emotionally fraught event like a wedding? Size-of-ass-related panic calls for desperate measures: Pilates, and, to reward yourself, a **white wine spritzer**.

Take a pint glass and the whimsically colored straw of your choice, and fill the glass with ice. Fill halfway with something inexpensive, dry, and not oaky or creamy—Sauvignon Blanc or an Italian white like Verdicchio will do nicely. Take the fancy juice of your choice—mango or one of those mixed juices that includes peach both work well with Sauvignon Blanc—and add a few splashes. Fill the glass the rest of the way with seltzer water or sparkling mineral water. Sip, enjoy, and feel the toning and lengthening start to kick in. Maybe you can cut off the bow on that dress without anyone noticing.

Never-ending toasts. Sure, sparkling wine is the traditional choice for toasting a new couple, but it has a way of going to your head, so the fizz from a nice **wheat beer** might be a better choice. **Hoegaarden** will do in a pinch, but if the bar's really got it together, try **Bell's Oberon**, with its mildly malty flavor and orange citrus notes. Now if only you could get the groom's uncle away from the microphone . . .

The morning after. It's the morning after an awkward, wedding merriment—induced hookup, and you've woken up facedown, drooling, with your mascara flaking into the hotel pillow cushion. This situation calls for a slightly classier hair of the dog.

This situation calls for a slightly classier hair of the dog.

Most people, when they think of France and bubbles, think of Champagne, but almost every other wine region makes a sparkling wine, and one of the best values is sparkling Chenin Blanc from the Loire Valley. There are several styles, but look for **dry sparkling Vouvray**. Don't be fooled by its bad reputation. It may be a style of wine (well, actually a region) that makes many people shudder when they hear it—a lot of anonymous, semisweet, not very good Vouvray made its way into the United States in the 1970s, and the name has come to be associated with that—but the region is home to a wide variety of delightful styles using its signature grape, Chenin Blanc. The best thing about Vouvray's bad rep is that it's kept the prices low. Dry versions will remind you more of Champagne—for about one-third to half of the price! (Because you'll need your extra money for all

---

KNOW YOUR STYLES

Vouvray (voov-RAY)

REGION: Vouvray, in France's Loire Valley

GRAPE: Chenin Blanc

DEFINING FLAVORS/AROMAS: It's agreed upon that Chenin Blanc is a grape naturally high in acidity, but when it comes to what aromas define it, there's more healthy debate. Sometimes it smells like wet wool, other times chamomile tea, sometimes like those slightly musty candles you find in cathedrals, and still others like gasoline, or the leather in a new car. All of this is rather subtle, so don't worry that you'll feel like you're sucking on a gas hose. As fanciful as wine descriptions get, usually the wine in question still tastes mostly like, well, wine.

PERFECT FOR: Drier, crisper Chenins are delicious with the fresh goat cheeses the Loire Valley is also famous for. Sweeter ones are great with more pungent cheeses, or just on their own. A friend of mine calls them "afternoon wines," as though any of us has time to lie in a hammock, sip demi-sec Vouvray, and read a trashy novel. Sounds fabulous though, doesn't it?

WHAT TO TRY: Domaine Champalou is a great producer that's imported by Kermit Lynch, a famous importer, so it's available all over the country. Their sparkling Vouvray is dry, yet packed with flavors of fresh, crunchy pears and marzipan—not that it's sweet, it just manages to call to mind that creamy, unroasted almond flavor and aroma. The Vouvray by **Christophe Thorigny**, a small producer that I love, is carried by an importer called Wine Traditions and found mostly on the East Coast.

The Loire Valley is home to dozens of great, small producers like this, though, so ask your local wine shop for a crisp, dry sparkling Chenin, and see what they come up with!

the fucking twine to tie around Mason jars, and the organic floral hairpiece you're supposed to make and pay for yourself, to "reflect each bridesmaid's personality." Ugh.)

Fruitier than Champagne, but not sweet, and a little more sophisticated than Prosecco, dry Vouvray is the perfect thing to have stashed in the mini-fridge the night before and drink out of a plastic cup from the bathroom while you nurse your sore feet and try to find something to wear that doesn't scream "walk of shame."

Your Proposal

N ow that we don't have as much rigid etiquette to keep us on the straight and narrow, all that choice can leave you floundering for how to pop the question. Whether you're going to celebrate your upcoming nuptials, or drown your sorrows because the answer was no, you'll probably want something to drink. . . .

Popping the question in Bali or some other **exotic location** seems like the best of all possible worlds, because it's a special moment, but one not witnessed by a restaurant full of people you may know, or in a freaking stadium. Try to avoid Instagramming this, OK? The proposee could say no, after all. These days it seems like proposals and engagements are so well rehearsed and orchestrated that everyone knows what the end result will be. Where is everyone's sense of adventure? Wait until you're relaxed on the beach, sharing a **Corona** or similar anonymous, mass-market beer like what you'd get at a cheesy resort, and pop the question. No crazy-expensive bottle of Champagne, no choreographed dance routine, just the two of you. Perfect.

Chances are that you're thinking of proposing **in a restaurant**. You're probably also thinking about sticking the ring into a dish of crème brûlée, or one of those hideous molten chocolate cakes that are like the last remnant of the early 1990s that just refuses to die. Don't do that. First of all, it's too expected, and secondly, she's going to break a tooth! Diamonds are hard, remember? And after you've shelled out for a ring (actually, why are we all still doing this? Wouldn't you rather have a cubic zirconia and just be able to drink more Champagne over the course of your lifetime?), do you really want to add a trip to the dentist on top of that? Instead of the whole dessert thing, pop the question at the beginning of the meal. Find

a restaurant that has great seafood, and ask if you can nestle the ring in the dish of ice that holds a bunch of fresh, delicious oysters. Wash them down with a crisp, refreshing **Muscadet**, a tart style of wine from France's Loire Valley. This style is all about light body, a dry finish, and clean, citrus aromas and flavors that often remind me of cutting into a fresh lemon. Muscadet ("moo-ska-DAY") is great with seafood, especially anything served raw and/or chilled, like oysters. **Les Bêtes Curieuses** makes a great one, fruity, light, and with such fresh, lively acidity that it almost tastes carbonated (but it's not).

If you don't see Muscadet on the menu, other wines to look for are Chablis, a crisp Chardonnay from northern France, and Sancerre, a lean, citrusy Sauvignon Blanc from France's Loire Valley. Now that you've gotten the proposal out of the way, you can spend the rest of the meal celebrating, i.e., getting handsy under the tablecloth. Plus, if the answer is no, then you don't have to shell out for the rest of the meal!

More than grand, romantic moments and experiences, someone who makes **ordinary moments** better and more fun, not more tedious and annoying, is what you really need in a life partner. Sure, fancy restaurants and vacations are great, but most of your relationship—hell, most of your life—is going to be made up of grocery shopping, replacing lightbulbs, and reminding your significant other to stop canceling that dentist appointment over and over again and freaking go already! So what better way to reflect that than to propose in the middle of the frozen foods aisle, or in the parking lot at Target? You'll still want something to toast your engagement, so bring a few fun, bright-pink cans of the **Francis Ford Coppola Winery Sofia Mini Blanc de Blancs** to clink together. They even come with straws! Is it the most complex sparkler ever made? No, but it's fruity and fizzy, and . . . I mean, pink cans! Come on!

The longtime-coming proposal. When you've already been cohabitating for years, whether because it just didn't occur to you to get married, or because it wasn't legal in your state until now, you've probably already exchanged romantic gifts and declarations of love. But just because you've been together long enough that you've seen it all, from a bad night with the stomach flu to skid-marked underwear in the laundry basket, doesn't mean you can't pop the question in style. Think back to **a style that was popular when you first met, and propose over something inspired by that**. If you met in the 1990s during the heyday of big, rich Cali Chardonnay, pop a bottle of **Kistler** (about $80), and toast your golden years with a glass of this rich, golden wine. It's oaked, for sure, but it's no Kendall-Jackson. (And if you didn't meet in the '90s, read "Wine Through the Decades" to find which style might apply to you.) Best wishes!

Wine Through the Decades

1960s

In the 1960s if you had a hot date, you'd likely order a bottle of **Mateus** or **Lancers**. These off-dry, slightly fizzy rosés were created in the 1940s in Portugal mostly for the export market, and they were wildly popular. Unfortunately, they were also kind of blandly sweet and one-note, and are now the wine equivalent of orange corduroy bell-bottoms.

1970s AND 1980s

In 1975 **Sutter Home** accidentally invented White Zinfandel. In their attempt to make a dry rosé out of Zinfandel grapes, they ended up with a winemaking problem called a stuck fermentation. This happens when the yeast that is happily fermenting sugar into alcohol starts to die, often because there is too much alcohol present and it starts to kill the yeast before all the sugar is gone. At a loss as to what to do with this partially fermented pink wine, they decided to sell it, and it became incredibly popular. Throughout the late 1970s and into the 1980s and early 1990s, White Zinfandel was so popular that folks in the wine business would joke that their "paychecks were pink" because White Zin accounted for such a big part of their sales.

1990s

In addition to the Cali Chard mentioned on page 214, soft, fruity, but still mostly dry styles of red wine like Merlot were all the rage during the 1990s. Merlot has softer tannins and ripens a bit earlier than Cabernet Sauvignon, so it was the perfect candidate to plant like crazy in fertile, sunny California, and pump out by the gallon. With its soft, plummy fruit flavors and not-too-grippy tannins, this style of red was served by the glass at countless restaurants and kind of helped ease America into "real" wine.

2000s

The early aughts were all about what I call "expense account Cabernets." Vines in the Napa Valley that had been planted after the region's last bout with phylloxera (insects that feed on the roots of grape vines, eventually destroying them) were maturing, and California wine was increasing in popularity. This was the era of crazy prices for wines like **Screaming Eagle** and **Harlan**, before the crash of 2008 came and reordered everything. Now the cool status symbol to flash is a trendy bottle of rosé. I couldn't be happier about this.

Spawning

Ah, babies. Whether you've got a tiny person inside you sucking away your life force, your friends are starting to multiply like creepy suburban rabbits, or you're just annoyed by them on airplanes, children are a fact of life. At least babies are cute, and you can dress them in adorable, themed onesies and try to eat their squishy little feet.

Since babies are all about new beginnings, many of the wines and beers suggested here are best drunk young, to highlight their fresh flavors and youthful vigor. What better way to toast a new life than with a delicious, brand-new beverage?

Baby Showers,

Whether you're having a kid yourself or just attending someone else's baby shower, beverages will be involved. The guest of honor may not be able to drink (don't worry: I still have a virgin cocktail for you), but in order to get through all those ridiculous games, not to mention pretend to be enthralled by the ritual opening of yet another set of burp cloths, everyone else will need one or four.

It's my party and . . . At your own baby shower, you want to offer something delicious that you can also drink, right? So now's the time to try a fun gourmet mocktail, and if people think it's cheesy or lame, well, too bad, you're pregnant! A **Sweet and Spicy Ginger Sparkler** will make you feel fancy, whether you're gestating or just stuck being the designated driver for your degenerate friends once in a while. Pregnancy can result in a range of tummy troubles (understandable—there's a lot going on in there!), so a refreshing drink with the soothing presence of ginger is perfect. Ginger adds an interesting kick to drinks without being too spicy-hot.

Susan from human resources. It's one thing if you're close to your coworkers, but if you just work down the hall from someone, celebrating the birth of their child and talking about nipple cream and dirty diapers seems kind of . . . well, weird, doesn't it? For something festive that will help create a feeling of camaraderie where none really exists and calls to mind fertility and new beginnings, try a **rosé Vinho Verde**.

Aside from Port, Vinho Verde is Portugal's most famous wine export. Bottled young, the style earned its name ("green wine") because it's the first

SWEET AND SPICY GINGER SPARKLER

Ginger Simple Syrup:

This will make more than you need.

4 ounces roughly chopped ginger

1 cup sugar

1 cup water

Bring all ingredients to a boil in a small saucepan and let simmer for a few minutes. Let the mixture steep for 30 minutes to 1 hour, then strain and refrigerate. This will keep for a month in the fridge, and you'll be surprised how many other uses you find for it!

For the Mocktail (serves 1):

1 ounce Ginger Simple Syrup

Juice of ¼ lemon

1 ounce peach juice

4 ounces club soda

1 slice candied ginger

In a Champagne flute (if you want to feel festive) or just in a wineglass, combine the syrup, lemon juice, and peach juice. Stir a bit, and top with the club soda. Make a slit in your slice of candied ginger, and perch it on the side of the glass. If you have fancy cocktail glasses, now is the time to break them out! This mocktail looks great in one of those old-fashioned coupes that are horrible for serving actual Champagne, but look really cool and retro. For a non-virgin version, use Cava or Prosecco in place of the club soda.

tart, fresh wine of the season—so fresh it's almost still green, get it? And the name's not just a metaphor: The whites often have a pale, greenish tint to them, reminiscent of that cucumber water you get at fancy spas, and many are packaged in green-tinted bottles to accentuate this. These wines are light and refreshing, and usually have a little fizz. (Historically, the fizz came from the fact that they were bottled so early that the wine retained a bit of fizziness from the fermentation process. Today, most Vinho Verdes are injected with CO_2 to mimic this. No matter how it gets there, that little prickle is a freaking delight.) The rosé versions are a little fruitier, without being overly sweet like a White Zinfandel, and great with the types of fruit salads, finger foods, and light desserts served at showers. (Why such wussy food at these things? The guest of honor is gestating a new person—she should get a steak or something, for Pete's sake!)

For rosé versions, **Conde Villar** and **Broadbent** are good names to look for (see box for full descriptions); however, as delicious and gulpable as Vinho Verde is, the styles of different wineries are more alike than different. Kind of like baby shower games.

Long-ago frenemy. You were maybe sort of friends once, in college, but you still get that "Huh?" feeling when the invitation to her baby shower arrives. When you look back on things, you really weren't that close. You spent most of your time at Campus Women's Organization meetings yelling at each other about politics. You may or may not have made out with a guy you kind of knew she liked, but you convinced yourself it was OK because she never specifically told you. (It really wasn't OK.)

To avoid dredging up old grievances, you'll want something innocuous and crowd-pleasing. Bring a nice, fruity **Sauvignon Blanc** from the United States. **Honig** makes a great one that tastes like Meyer lemons and fresh pineapple, but isn't so tart that you can't have a glass by itself. Plus the bottle looks pretty and appropriately gift-y. **Beckman** is another good producer known mostly for reds, but their Sauvignon Blanc is juicy and has more of the sweet grapefruit flavors you find in Ocean Spray pink grapefruit juice than in real, tart grapefruits. A wine like this is refreshing and pleasantly tart, but not over the top. After sipping and playing nice for several hours, you can privately gloat about how annoying she still is in the car with the friend you dragged with you on the way back.

BFF. A good strategy for baby showers is to bring two bottles of the delicious rosé sparkler **Bugey-Cerdon:**

KNOW YOUR STYLES

Vinho Verde (VEE-noh VAIR-day)

REGION: Northern Portugal's Minho province

GRAPE: For white Vinho Verde, it's usually a blend of obscure, mostly white grapes like Loureiro, Rajadura (Treixadura), Avesso, Pedernã (Arinto), and—although it is typically bottled separately—Alvarinho (which you may recognize when spelled the Spanish way: Albariño). For rosé and red Vinho Verde, equally lesser-known red grapes— Espadeiro or Padeiro, anyone?—are blended with other native varieties.

DEFINING FLAVORS/AROMAS: Vinho Verdes are usually light and crisp, with flavors and aromas such as fresh lemon, green melon, and golden apple for the whites; fresh, ripe strawberries for the rosés; and slightly underripe blackberries for the tart and tannic reds. They're also low in alcohol (most hover around 8 to 11 percent).

PERFECT FOR: Solo sipping and fresh summery dishes like gazpacho and fruit salad

WHAT TO TRY: Broadbent is a well-known importer and bottler in Portugal and Spain. Although it's most famous for its Port and Madeiras, its white and rosé Vinho Verdes are rock solid and widely available.

Conde Villar isn't as famous, but both the white and the rosé Vinho Verdes are especially easy to drink. Imagine you're at a pool party on a scorching hot day, with people doing drugs in designer swimsuits in some creepy bedroom down the hall, but you're just chilling on a deck chair ineffectively flirting with someone and sipping from a chic yet unbreakable plastic tumbler. This is what you'd want in that tumbler. Much nicer than gray-market prescription drugs. The rosé is also nice because it's on the fruitier side without being cloying, which makes it great for new wine drinkers. You know, to ease them over to the dark side gently.

---

one for guests or a hostess gift, and one as an insurance policy for yourself against whatever terrible crap is being served. At usually well under 10 percent ABV, you can almost get away with downing most of the bottle yourself, and to get through another round of Baby Bingo, you might have to. Bugey-Cerdon is made from a process even more old-school than the Champagne method: *méthode ancestrale,* where the wine is partially fermented in tanks, and then bottled along with the yeast and residual sugar. It can sometimes make the wine a little cloudy, and gives the bubbles an especially foamy, delicate texture. **Patrick Bottex** from Kermit Lynch Imports is a classic: frothy, semisweet, and delicious, like foamy strawberries. Yum! Seriously, this stuff is delightful—don't just save it for baby showers!

Father-to-be. Moms-to-be are generally the center of attention at baby showers, and deservedly so. But the expectant dad is special, too—and more and more, men are part of baby showers. Why shouldn't they be? Having kids is a big deal for guys, too! More importantly, men can still drink while the

---

KNOW YOUR STYLES
Bugey-Cerdon (boo-jee ser-DON)

REGION: Just west of Savoie in France lies Bugey, an obscure little wine region in the Jura Mountains. They grow and make all kinds of wines in this area, from Burgundy's Chardonnay to Jura's Poulsard to their own native grapes, but they are best known for their pink, semisweet sparkling wine made in and around the commune of Cerdon.

GRAPE: Gamay and Poulsard (Poulsard is a geeky red grape—if you like red Burgundy and you see this on some hipster wine list in Brooklyn, give it a shot!)

DEFINING FLAVORS/AROMAS: Fresh, ripe strawberries, blackberries, and plums; roses; and on the palate, a touch of sweetness

PERFECT FOR: A big fat sandwich piled high with cheese and charcuterie for the ultimate sweet/salty picnic pairing, or by itself as a light afternoon quaffer

WHAT TO TRY: **Patrick Bottex** is a classic producer imported to the United States by Kermit Lynch. Because Kermit is such a famous importer, it's pretty widely available.

Renardat-Fache is another great producer. Their Bugey-Cerdon is a touch more red wine–like than Bottex, and just as delicious.

mother is gestating, although a lot of guys are such sweethearts that they abstain along with their partners. If foregoing wine and beer when you don't even HAVE to isn't love, what is?! So whether the dad-to-be will crack one open at the shower, or save it until he can share one with mom, consider bringing a six-pack of a beer that will remind him of his manly virility at a ritual that tends to be all about the ladies. A **doppelbock** is a big, strapping beer (they range from 7 to over 10 percent ABV) with flavors of toasted nuts, a rich, malty mouthfeel, and bubbles that almost feel creamy. Those goats you see on the label are a symbol of male fertility, so consider it a subtle pat on the back for the dad and his . . . contribution to the family.

Bell's Consecrator Doppelbock looks almost ruby red in the glass, and tastes like really dark English toffee. **Spaten Optimator** is a classic version of this style and its flavors also call to mind foods from the sweet end of the spectrum, but rather than toffee, there's a spiced note to the maltiness here, kind of like Dr Pepper without so much fizz. Or maybe speculoos cookies? Either way, it's great with hearty food like braised pork shoulder.

'Learning the Ropes,

Motherhood isn't all ladies in tasteful high-waisted dresses with cooing Gerber babies in soft focus in a field. Why are those commercials always shot in some mythical meadow? Jesus Christ, who has time to go out to the country with a toddler, a newborn, and a full-time job?! Parents are people, too, and they need to let loose once in a while! You may not be out partying all night, but you'll still want to incorporate some fun, and of course, delicious beverages, into your new life.

Having people over (because you can't leave your house). When you feel like you haven't had contact with the outside world for months, just hosting folks from that distant planet called Earth can feel amazing. You can ask them what movies are out! Have an adult conversation with someone other than your equally sleep-deprived spouse! Plus, hosting a (very quiet) girls' night at your place is cheaper than hiring a babysitter. Make it worth your friends' while by having some nice **Spanish rosé** on hand. Provence may be the gold standard when it comes to rosé, but if you want tasty and cheap, Spain is your best bet. Open a bottle—some even come in screwcap for newbie parents too exhausted to work a corkscrew—and ply your friends with rosé-friendly snacks like smoked salmon and prosciutto with melon while you show them dozens of baby photos and share the dramatic tale of how you finally learned to breastfeed. We know, baby feet are cute, but after the tenth or so time you see them, well . . . While there are a few rosés out there that are known for their aging ability, in general, the current vintage is best. Just like a lot of baby behavior, it becomes less cute as it ages.

Clua is kind of an obscure producer, but if you live on the East Coast, you should be able to find it. Their Rosado (what the Spanish and Portuguese call rosé) is a little more expensive than most—it tends to hover between $16 and $20—but it's got this tart, lip-smacking cranberry quality that makes it a little too easy to drink. **Martínez Lacuesta** is a producer from Spain's Rioja region, and both their white and their rosé come in screwcap, are right around $10 (and you can often find them for less), and are perfect for parties. They're also great for white and rosé sangria. **Muga** is another Rioja producer, and their Rosado is

It's tart, sassy, and perfect for swilling while grazing on finger foods and watching reruns of Sex and the City, or some awful movie about male strippers.

widely available. It's tart, sassy, and perfect for swilling while grazing on finger foods and watching reruns of *Sex and the City*, or some awful movie about male strippers.

Assembling baby furniture. It's a sad fact of modern life that most affordable furniture requires at least some assembly after it's purchased, baby furniture included. This is a cruel task to foist upon new parents. One minute, you're daydreaming about making your own organic baby food. The next minute, the kid is actually born, and you're eating cold Chinese takeout from three days ago while trying to assemble a playpen with so many parts it looks like it could, if assembled another way, be a replica of that particle accelerator in Switzerland. Sipping a delicious **coffee-inflected stout**, like **Founders Breakfast Stout** or **Keegan Ales' Joe Mama's Milk**, will keep you awake and mellow—even in the face of those maddening IKEA blob men. (Note: Beer brewed with coffee tastes best when it's at its freshest, so be sure to check the date on the bottle if there is one, or buy from a store that seems like it has good turnover.)

These types of stouts also tend to have a rich, creamy mouthfeel, so in addition to the stimulating effects of caffeine, they're great to pair with baked goods or desserts. Coffee stout with vanilla-bean-flecked ice cream or chocolate chip cookies is a comforting and stimulating treat while working on a project that never seems to end.

Sleep deprivation and anxiety. So you're going to need chocolate. That much is obvious. But first, rant alert: big, full-bodied dry reds like Cabernet Sauvignon from the Napa Valley do **not** go with chocolate. No matter how many hokey signs California Cabernet producers put up on Valentine's Day, the actual combination in your pie hole is disgusting. What does go with chocolate are wines with those same bold-red flavors, but with the sweetness to balance the chocolate instead of making it taste bitter.

Banyuls, a delicious, sweet fortified red from the south of France, is cheaper than Port, doesn't have to age, and will go wonderfully with the Dove dark chocolate squares you're stress-eating from the bag as you stay up all night thinking about the million ways in which you could accidentally kill or crush your offspring. Or ruin his life by saying the wrong thing/sending him to the wrong preschool/causing him to jump off a bridge because you didn't have just the right reaction when he came out to you. Banyuls won't keep you from accidentally destroying the life of a future Simon Doonan, and keep him from flipping out and becoming a Mormon insurance salesman, feeling repressed and miserable forever, but its deep, ripe berry flavors and satisfyingly rich mouthfeel will definitely take the edge off your nerves.

Cooking for the kids. When you have kids, cooking becomes less an expression of self, or a way to fulfill your 2 a.m. craving for grilled cheese with Fritos pressed in between the cheese layers (what?), and more of a daily grind. Nutritious dinners, bake-sale cupcakes, picky young appetites—it's exhausting! Anyway, whether you're sneaking vegetables into pasta sauce or baking cookies for the annual school fund-raiser, you might want something to sip while you stir. If you're a busy parent, you probably don't have time to keep track of a complicated matrix of what wines in your collection are ready to pop, so you'll want a **sexy, full-bodied red that's ready to go right now**. Drink it out of your biggest glass. It'll make you feel fancy and important even if you have spit-up on your shoulder.

Keplinger Kingpin Rows Syrah is about as big and sexy as they get. Like a really expensive piece of lamb with perfect grill marks and some kind of fancy blackberry compote, in a glass. With no dishes afterward. From California, small producer **Relic** makes an unctuous, satisfying blend of Grenache, Syrah, and Mourvèdre called **Ritual** that is delicious right when it's released. These grapes are traditional blending partners for a reason— Grenache brings that rich, ripe, almost jammy mouthfeel, while Syrah adds some dark, meaty base notes, and Mourvèdre brings a little funk. For a deep, dark Rioja with plenty of spice and vanilla from oak barrels, try **Muga Selección Especial**. It is probably better with a few years of age, but it's pretty darn scrumptious upon release, too. Just don't tell any of the big,

KNOW YOUR STYLES

Banyuls (ban-YULES)

REGION: Languedoc-Roussillon, France

GRAPE: Grenache, sometimes blended with small amounts of Carignan

DEFINING FLAVORS/AROMAS: Banyuls is like Port's younger French cousin who's way more fun at parties. It's made the same way as Port, in that spirits are added to full-bodied red wine before the fermentation has finished gobbling up all the sugar, resulting in a higher-alcohol wine that retains natural sweetness from the grapes. But unlike vintage Port, Banyuls can be enjoyed right off the store shelf, no long aging required. It tastes like roasted strawberries and blackberries, and smells like toasted nuts, jam, and coffee.

PERFECT FOR: Chocolate! Banyuls is wonderful with chocolate desserts, but it really shines as an accompaniment to that fancy box of artisanal chocolates you impulse-bought. It's complex, but not so complex that it won't allow you to enjoy all that expensive ganache.

WHAT TO TRY: Banyuls is wonderful because it gives you that "fancy red dessert wine" feel without breaking the bank. **Domaine La Tour Vieille Banyuls "Rimage"** retails for about $25 and is on the fruitier side—fresher, sweet berries and berry jam rather than roasted fruit. It's great with desserts or by itself as an after-dinner sipper.

M. Chapoutier, the famous Châteauneuf-du-Pape producer, also makes a Banyuls that's similarly priced to La Tour Vieille's. Although not quite as widely available, it's worth hunting down. Their Banyuls shows off more of those roasty, toasty coffee and mocha notes and is great for super-dark chocolate. Or Dove squares. Sometimes those inspirational phrases on the wrappers seem a little preachy, don't you think? I have a lot going on, Dove, maybe I don't have time to dance like nobody's watching, or "breathe" or whatever.

important critics or you might have your fancy glasses confiscated by the wine police and be forced to drink out of the bejeweled plastic "pimp cup" you kept from ridiculous college parties. Or something.

Your first night out. When you haven't been out in what seems like decades and the chance *finally* presents itself, the urge to *really* let loose can be strong. Unfortunately, after gestating and breastfeeding for however many months,

What's the Deal with Hangovers?

We've all been there. You were a little overenthusiastic the night before, and have woken up with a headache, the shakes, and possibly even diarrhea. Gross.

WHY YOU FEEL LIKE CRAP

What causes all these unpleasant symptoms? Well, at the end of the day, alcohol is a toxic substance, and your body treats it like one.

- **Dehydration.** When you drink, your brain slows down and has trouble secreting the antidiuretic hormone (ADH). This is why once you "break the seal," you have to pee every five seconds. All those bathroom visits cause the dehydration that is a major component to hangover nastiness.

- **Toxins.** As your body metabolizes alcohol, it also produces a toxic chemical called acetaldehyde, which is responsible for some of the shaky, flu-like symptoms you feel the morning after one too many.

- **Inflammation.** There is some evidence that metabolizing alcohol triggers inflammatory responses in your body, so that when you have a hangover, it's almost like you're having an allergic reaction to something.

HOW TO FIX IT

Well, there are all kinds of wacky hangover cures out there, but here are some common sense tips that actually work.

- **Hydrate, eat, and take it slow.** When drinking, you want to slow down the absorption of alcohol as much as possible. Eat foods with plenty of fat and protein, and sip your wine or beer slowly. And of course, have water in between drinks.

- **Get moving.** Once you actually have a hangover, the only thing that really helps is time, but the other thing that makes you feel better is forcing yourself to do the things your body least wants to do at that moment. Get up, take a shower, eat something nutritious, drink water, and get outside. A moderate workout can really shake you out of that sticky, headachy feeling, but even a short walk outside helps.

- **Pull yourself together.** Put on clothes you really like. Yes, also counterintuitive, but if you look put-together, you'll feel better faster than you will if you spend the day in sweats.

THE VACATION APPROACH

People often say, in this ridiculous, conspiratorial whisper, that there is something special about the wine in Europe, because they can drink all night and never get hangovers. *There are fewer sulfites in European wine,* they say. *They put more in when they're sent here!*

That is a load of horse manure. You didn't suffer after drinking copious amounts of wine on vacation in France because you were drinking while eating high-fat, protein-rich foods like pâtés and cheeses, and you were probably drinking at a slower, more leisurely pace over several courses while sipping plenty of mineral water in between. Also, pours in restaurants and bars tend to be a bit smaller in Europe. Then you got enough sleep, woke up the next morning, got out into the sunshine, and had a nice brisk walk to a café before your morning coffee.

Of course you felt great! So the trick is to try to mimic that while at home. Wings and spiced nuts don't have the same continental *je ne sais quoi* as pâté, but to keep you from going from zero to drunky in five minutes, they'll do the trick.

your tolerance will not be what it once was. Don't go all out and start ordering cocktails, or, worse, shots. You'll be the much-older version of "that girl," who could always be found at parties in college crying, blind drunk, in the bathroom by 11 p.m. Ease into your evening with the new crop of **"session" ales and IPAs**, which have a nice hit of hoppy flavor, but a bit less alcohol (typically between 4 and 5 percent ABV) than the high-octane IPAs that tend to flood the craft beer market.

Long Trail Summer Ale (4.3 percent ABV) will remind you of mowing the lawn, but in a good way—it has this fresh, grassy aroma and flavor to it that's mellow and refreshing at the same time. Other flavors include green tea, tarragon, and just a hint of grapefruit juice. It's great for a prelude to a night out, or an afternoon in a hammock with a magazine. **Founders**, out of Michigan, makes a great session IPA, called **All-Day IPA** (4.7 percent). A nice pop of hop flavor underscored by a little maltiness makes it easy to sip all evening, and it comes in cans, too! And if you're a die-hard hop fan, **Stone Go To IPA** has almost all of the resiny, fruity, stanky hop character of their flagship beers, at a much more reasonable 4.5 percent ABV.

Work

All those personal finance books that make you feel like you'll never be able to retire always say to "pay yourself first." Really what they mean is, "Hey, dummy, don't buy $400 boots if you haven't put money into your savings account," but "pay yourself first" sounds a little more dramatic and glamorous. This concept, though, applies to beer and wine as well. Investing in your future enjoyment is always a good idea. Not only are you worth it, but consciously spending money on beverages you like will help you spend less in the long run. Set a budget for what you enjoy, instead of telling yourself you won't buy any at all and will put that money in your retirement fund like a real grown-up, thus leaving your-self open to unwise impulse spending.

Anyway, enough lecturing. You'll need to earn a pay-check to even think about all this budgeting, so let's dive into the world of work. Except, don't drink AT work. Unless you're an extra on a show like *Mad Men* trying to get into character (how did people regularly drink warm Scotch from someone's desk drawer at 10 a.m., on an empty stomach, back in the day? Doesn't it make you feel queasy just thinking about it?). Or a waiter about to work brunch on Mother's Day. Anyone doing that deserves a glass of the world's finest Champagne and a foot rub. Here are some beers and wines to consume while dealing with work functions or recovering from a tough day at the office.

Your "Just for Now" Job,

Those sort of "in between" jobs can be really depressing. So while you may be toiling away in a gray cubicle, never seeing the sun, or emptying bus pans in a coffee shop, you can always treat yourself to something delicious at the end of the day.

Coffee shop barista. Working at a quirky neighborhood coffee shop has its ups and downs. While you may get to blast whatever music you want, and certainly don't have to wear anything dry-clean only, you also may have to deal with crazy people who demand to pay the prices the place charged in, say, 1978, or mop up gastrointestinal explosions in the bathroom. (Here's a

tip: If you're having tummy troubles, maybe a coffee shop isn't the
best place to hang out. Coffee will
tend to, you know, move things
along, which may not be what
you want, especially in public,
and especially if a kid making
minimum wage will have to clean

it up.) Anyway, while you're mopping the floors after all the crazy regulars
have left, send a coworker to a bar across the street for a growler of something
roasty, toasty, and cozy, like a **wood-aged ale**. It'll be the closest noncaffein-
ated thing to a latte's soothing warmth, but won't keep you up all night. And if
there is no bar, well, you can always slip a few bottles behind the jugs of half-
and-half. Hopefully no one will notice.

Dogfish Head Palo Santo Marron is a delicious American brown ale
aged in wood to give it warm, vanilla flavors. It even has an espresso-colored
head and rich coffee notes. But it's a different kind of buzz: This one, like
many American takes on traditional beer styles, packs a punch (12 percent),
so be careful! **Schlafly Oak Aged Barleywine** is another classic take on
wood-aged beer, with notes of vanilla, caramel, and dark fruit, and a full, rich
mouthfeel. If you have a few leftover pastries to munch on with your yummy
beer, so much the better. Mopping is good exercise, right?

Temping your life away. Temping can be really demoralizing. You're never
truly part of the team, so it can be hard to get friendly with your coworkers.
And temps are often paired with difficult employees who can't hang on to full-
time assistants, like, say, a professor who uses low talking as a sort of weird
power move, and sends emails with a strange color-coding system that is
impossible to discern. Why is this particular phrase lavender? Does it mean:
"This is important," or, "Relax, see, this is written in a soothing color"? Your
supervisor may take out her psychological issues on you by going through
your desk drawers every time you leave to go to the bathroom (your coworkers

What's the Deal with Wood?

Whether you're talking about wine or beer or even cocktails these days, there's a lot of hubbub about things being "wood aged," or aged in French oak, yada yada yada. So what does wood actually do for wine and beer?

Aging. Wood ages wine and beer in a specific way. Because it's a porous material, there is a slow, steady exchange of air that is tough to recreate with any other material. That air exchange allows for slow, controlled aging. This tends to give wine and beer that "smooth" character—the tannin and acidity isn't as sharp, and the fruit flavors are more mellow.

Adds tannin. Just like the stems and seeds of grapes contain tannin, so does wood. Wood aging imparts tannin to wine and beer, providing that mouth-drying sensation that gives beverages structure and makes them better partners to foods high in fat, protein, and salt. The newer the barrel, the more tannin it will impart.

Adds aroma and flavor. Wood also adds aromas and flavors to wine and beer. Again, how strong these elements are is a function of how new the barrel is; a barrel that's been used over and over won't impart much aroma or flavor at all. But there are all kinds of aromatic compounds in wood, and these leach slowly into the beer or wine. A newer barrel will add stuff like vanilla, nutmeg, cedar, even coconut or dill.

French or American? These are the two main types of oak that are used for aging wine and beer. French oak has a tighter grain, so less air gets in and out, and there's less room for the liquid to soak into the wood and extract its flavor and tannin. The aromas that French oak imparts tend more toward the spice rack part of the spectrum—think nutmeg and a subtle whiff of vanilla. American oak has a looser grain, and its vanilla aroma is much more overt. American oak can also impart aromas and flavors like dill and coconut, and its mark tends to be a bit heavier. If you want to know what American oak smells like, stick your nose in a glass of bourbon—it gets most of its character from American oak! In fact, some

American brewers are aging their ales in bourbon barrels, so in addition to a bit of vanilla character from the wood itself, the beer also picks up that spicy, spirity flavor of bourbon.

Oak chips and other oak substitutes are often used in cheap wine because they are much, much less expensive than barrels. An American oak barrel costs about $500, and a new French oak barrel can cost as much as $2,000. Unfortunately, small pieces of low-quality wood impart flavors in a much less subtle way than barrels do, and when you're just soaking wine in wood chips in a stainless steel tank, you're not getting the benefits of that slow air exchange we talked about earlier. The result is a wine that has an oak flavor and aroma that tends to tromp all over everything else in the wine. To all the wineries using oak chips and staves badly, I say, if you can't do something right, maybe don't do it at all!

at least have the decency to let you know), apparently thinking that *maybe this time* she'll find something other than a box of tampons and a bag of stale pretzels. Cheer yourself with something that feels luxurious, but won't bankrupt you. Try a **Coteaux du Layon** ("co-toh doo LAY-on") from France's Loire Valley. It's a late-harvest Chenin Blanc that falls somewhere between a dry white and a dessert wine. **Domaine des Baumard** makes a delicious one (about $25) that tastes like apricots and honey that have been plugged into an electrical outlet and zinged to life with bracing acidity. Splurge on some fancy, runny cheese and stop thinking about all those emails!

A job from Craigslist *seemed* like a good idea. Craigslist is good for some things. Occasionally finding roommates, trolling Missed Connections for someone who might be your one true love, or obtaining IKEA furniture that's already been assembled by someone more competent than you. But finding an office job is probably not the best use of the Wild West of the Internet (or is that 4chan?). Should you decide to take the plunge, you may find yourself in a strange "office" that feels like a total sham, creating those weird ads you hear when you're on hold at the bank, or doing telemarketing for some charity whose mission you don't really understand. *Sure, I can work a sound booth,* you think. *No problem!* At the end of a long, dreary day, treat yourself to a **nice white Burgundy**. A rich, but not too oaky and buttery, Chardonnay is the perfect counterpoint to something hearty, like roast chicken with mustard butter—or, hell, just one of those rotisserie chickens from the grocery store.

Vincent Girardin's entry-level white Burgundy will run you about $20, but will fool a lot of people into thinking it's more expensive. Unlike the joke of a company you're working for, this wine is from a real place you can read about, and you probably need something authentic in your life. Soak up those chicken juices with some crusty bread, and forget all about your stupid job.

Everyone wants to fuck the hostess. You'll learn a lot of important life lessons being a coat check girl. One is that if you bring a tote bag full of singles to the bank, the teller will look at you funny, and, by some perverse stroke of misfortune, you'll always get the same prim woman who wears beige twin sets and pearls and speaks with a clipped British accent. You'll also learn that trying on rich people's furs in the coat closet with your favorite waiter friends is a great way to spice up an otherwise boring evening. And you'll learn that no matter what you look like, and whether or not your pencil skirts are from the clearance rack at H&M, something about standing at that podium makes you seem much more attractive than you really are, and this can be turned into cash by smiling nicely at older men. "Everyone wants to fuck the hostess," a bartender will tell you knowingly, as though he's imparting some kind of cosmic wisdom.

At the end of your shift, change out of those horrible heels and shuffle over to the nearest dive bar, and order something that is also mediocre, but elevated by its station, as your post-shift drink: **Yuengling**. This lager's not the greatest thing ever, but you're sitting down, and that's enough. On the West Coast, your beer with working-class roots has gone a little more upmarket: **Anchor Steam Beer**. Brewed from a special strain of lager yeast bred to ferment at higher temperatures, it was created in the late 19th century to compensate for the lack of refrigeration available to brewers. It's a truly American style that Anchor has trademarked—anyone else making beer in this style has to call it

California Common. You may not be a hardscrabble rail worker, but you can at least drink like one.

'Work Functions'

With many work functions, you need to walk a fine line between having fun so as to seem like a team player and not an antisocial weirdo, and not having TOO much fun and being pulled into HR the next morning. Here are some beverages to choose, and ways to deal.

Office holiday party. Firstly, for any work function, try to actually follow that rule where you drink a big glass of water between every drink. This serves the double function of keeping you from getting too tipsy, and making it so you spend so much time in the restroom you won't have time to end up in the coat closet making out with someone inappropriate. Even if the sparkling

wine available is **cheap Prosecco** or, worse, cheap domestic variations (the expensive ones like Iron Horse are good, but the cheap ones are really, really bad here in the United States), just drink it. It'll make you feel festive, and it's often a bit lower in alcohol than the other wines that are on offer. Just don't suck down gin and tonics all night and end up dancing on a table in a Santa hat. Remember: Water! Professionalism!

Team-building exercises. After a day of zip lining and catching Rita from human resources in a trust circle, you'll need something really strong, like a **double IPA**. Double IPAs capture the essence of the American craft-brewing scene in the late 1990s and early 2000s—bigger is better! At much higher ABVs (8–10 percent) and crazy-high hop levels (IBUs can push 90), these are often a deep honey color, super bitter, and not for the faint of heart. **Flying Dog Double Dog** is a rich, red, and hoppy example of this style with a strong emphasis on citrus. If you've been stuck in an anonymous hotel during a staff retreat, it is the perfect thing to sneak up to your room. And since you'll be in a snarky frame of mind already after so much forced small talk, the illustrations by Ralph Steadman, a frequent collaborator of Hunter S. Thompson, will refresh you before you've even popped a bottle open. For a classic take on the double IPA, **Russian River Brewing Company Pliny the Elder** is considered to be the first of this style, and its flavors tend more toward the pine and sweet malt end of the spectrum. Whichever version you choose, you've definitely earned it. Just don't go too crazy, because tomorrow there will be a hike, and a sexual harassment seminar.

KNOW YOUR STYLES

Prosecco (pro-SEC-co)

REGION: Italy's Veneto and Friuli-Venezia Giulia regions

GRAPE: The grape used to make Prosecco used to just be called Prosecco, but now it goes by the name Glera.

DEFINING FLAVORS/AROMAS: With aromas of pears, golden apples, and fresh almonds, and with big, festive bubbles and varying levels of fruitiness, from crisp Meyer lemon to ripe, juicy pear, Prosecco is one of the most fun styles of sparkling wine around.

PERFECT FOR: A stand-alone drink, something to sip with party munchies, and great with prosciutto and melon

WHAT TO TRY: **Adami**'s vintage-dated Proseccos are fabulous and usually around $25 (they make a few different Proseccos, though, and they're all delicious), and **Casabianca** makes a fun, fruity Prosecco that is right around $10—perfect to stock up on for a party or use for sparkling cocktails.

Dinner with your boss. If your boss has invited you to dinner at his house (seems so 1950s, doesn't it? And how will you resist going through his medicine cabinets like the creeper you are?!), bring something made from a grape everyone knows, but from a place they wouldn't expect, like a **Pinot Noir from northern Italy**. Producer **G. D. Vajra** is known for Barolo, but their **Langhe Rosso**

It's kind of how you want to appear to your boss: interesting, but not too weird.

PN Q497 (about $27) has all the bright, friendly fruit of a Pinot Noir from California, but is just a touch more earthy and tart. There are a few producers in this part of Italy that make Pinot Noir, but this is one of my favorites. Pinot also has the advantage of pairing well with a wide variety of foods, so if your boss wants to serve it, it'll almost certainly shine. It's kind of how you want to appear to your boss: interesting, but not too weird.

An important presentation. You've spent several days tearing your hair out over that big presentation for today's meeting. Once you get home afterward, peeling off those binding clothes will feel especially fantastic. A luxurious, yet refreshing wine will make you feel good as new once you're in your comfy pants. You know, the perfectly broken-in sweatpants you wouldn't be caught dead in? Yeah, those. Pour a glass of **Viognier** ("vee-own-YAY"), a full-bodied, aromatic white variety that's perfect for sipping by itself because it lacks the sharp acidity that many other popular whites have.

Penner-Ash, a wonderful Oregon winery known for its Pinot Noir, makes an elegant Viognier (about $35) that smells of orange blossoms and tastes like ripe, juicy pears. **E. Guigal Condrieu** ($45–50) is a good example of a more traditional Viognier—those floral and fruity aromas are there, but they're not in your face. You've earned an evening in soft comfy pants, and a wine that's just as soft and luxurious!

For a happy hour with your coworkers at a TGI McCrappy's type outfit, ordering the freshest beer is your safest bet, and the best way to get the freshest brew is to just ask for **the most popular beer on tap**. Why, you

KNOW YOUR STYLES

Châteauneuf-du-Pape (sha-toh-noof doo POP)

REGION: France's Rhône Valley is home to a few villages famous for the wines made in the surrounding land, and Châteauneuf-du-Pape is the most famous.

GRAPE: There are 13 grapes allowed in this region, and most producers make wines that are a blend of some, but not all of them. The main grape in most blends is Grenache, while the other grapes, like Syrah, Carignan, and Mourvèdre, are supporting players. Like Bordeaux (see pages 108–109), this is a region where each producer has their own style.

DEFINING FLAVORS/AROMAS: Like most wines famous for their power and complexity, Châteauneuf-du-Pape combines fruity, "pretty" aromas with more earthy, masculine ones—think roasted strawberries and cherry jam, but combined with smoky aromas, like roasted meat, resinous herbs, and that oddly appealing smell asphalt gives off on a hot summer day. Maybe I just like that smell because it reminds me of lazy summer afternoons at the pool.

PERFECT FOR: Grilled or roasted lamb or sausages, and dishes involving lots of rosemary, garlic, and olives

WHAT TO TRY: Domaine du Vieux Télégraphe (about $75) is a classic, old-school style that is heavy on those smoky, earthy aromas and definitely calls for a big piece of grilled lamb. **Clos du Mont-Olivet**'s Châteauneuf is less expensive at $35–$40, has a bit more of that strawberry fruit, and is a little lighter in body.

ask? Because freshness is way more important to beer than most people realize, and ordering something where the keg is changed frequently and there's stuff moving through those tap lines at all times is the easiest way to ensure that you don't end up choking down something skunked or tainted with nasty bacteria that grows in dirty or infrequently used lines. It's bad enough you have to pretend to care about looking at everyone's photos of their kids and their vacation to some bland resort in Mexico—you don't need a mouthful of skunk, either.

Entertaining clients. It's not 1998 anymore, so ordering a big, expensive Napa Cabernet will seem about as dated as giant cuff links. Instead, a bold **Châteauneuf-du-Pape** will give everyone that "big red" feeling in an impressive, old-fashioned bottle, but without all the extra oak. Just don't accidentally make any politically charged comments. They might be secret Republicans. Try **Château de Beaucastel** if you see it on the list. It's a big, rich classic, tasting of ripe strawberries and expensive leather—hey, you're on an expense account, right?

‘Career Milestones›

For a new job, or just finally getting an office of your own, you'll want to celebrate with something that really says you've arrived. And of course, getting canned or getting passed over for that promotion you thought was in the bag definitely merits a drink or three.

Your first job. Celebrate being a real grown-up with a real job by buying a **mixed case of wine** (a case is 12 bottles), a little something for every occasion. Well, at least wait until you get your first paycheck. The key here is to NOT do this someplace with a terrible wine selection like Trader Joe's. You can find gems occasionally at TJ's, but it's not worth the crapshoot. This is the time to stop in at your favorite wineshop, tell them what you like, and have them make recommendations. Try a few new things, and a few tried and true favorites. There is nothing like knowing you have enough different wines on hand for any occasion that might arise.

Your friend's promotion. You're happy for her, you really are, but goddammit, she's the one who should be buying you wine, amiright? Something to remind you that success is just around the corner for you, too.

But you know, a little friendly rivalry never hurt anyone. Sure, get it out of your system and rant to your mom for a bit about how she doesn't deserve that fat paycheck and what about meeeeee, but then you need to get it together, girl, and let her success inspire you to get your own big promotion. Try a beer that's been steeped in rivalry for centuries—Germany's **altbier**. This unique style is brewed at a higher temperature like a traditional ale to bring out slightly fruity flavors, but conditioned at cooler temps to keep

> *Get it together, girl, and let her success inspire you to get your own big promotion. Try a beer that's been steeped in rivalry for centuries—Germany's altbier.*

the finish nice and crisp. It's the hometown pride of Düsseldorf, a city that has been locked into a rivalry with the nearby Cologne and their signature kölsch (see page 192) for years. While kölsch is all about crisp refreshment, altbier is darker in color, is fuller in body, and has more malt and caramel flavors. Decide for yourself if Düsseldorf's alt deserves the top spot as you sip on a classic example of this style like **Füchschen Alt**. With a big emphasis on toasty, bready notes to the malt character, it's perfect for some grilled sausages with mustard (something this part of Germany is also known for) and planning your next big move.

First management job. One of the many reasons *30 Rock* was so popular was that it expressed perfectly what it's like to be in charge of a group of people while also feeling completely inadequate at actually making them do anything. Instead of the badass boss lady you thought you'd be (see pages 97–98), you feel like you're at the helm of a derelict pirate ship, and the crew might make you walk the plank at any moment. Get in touch with your inner badass with a big, bold **Napa Cabernet**—dense and rich, like blueberry compote, and dark as ink in the glass, these wines just scream "impressive."

KNOW YOUR GRAPES

Cabernet Sauvignon (cab-er-NAY soh-vin-YAWN)

REGION: Bordeaux, France; Napa Valley, California; Argentina; Chile; and Washington State, just to name a few!

DEFINING FLAVORS/AROMAS: Dark, ripe blackberries, blueberries, plums, and currants; tobacco leaf; sometimes a hint of cocoa powder

PERFECT FOR: Steak, baby! Really, though, any red meat will work here, especially grilled. And if you're a weirdo vegetarian, try a grilled mushroom with some truffle oil.

WHAT TO TRY: **Honig**'s Cabernet Sauvignon is an American classic. Aged in American oak, it's the perfect marriage of bold, ripe fruit and spicy, vanilla-y oak flavors. A wine that is rich and mouthfilling, but doesn't feel cloying, it usually retails for around $45.

The Cabernet Sauvignon from **Catena** shows that Argentina can do more than just Malbec! And it usually sells for around $20 or less.

Château Calon-Ségur is a classic Cabernet-based blend from Cabernet Sauvignon's ancestral home, Bordeaux, and a bit of a splurge at around $150 depending on vintage and source. If you want to know what a classic Bordeaux is "supposed" to taste like, this is a good place to start! Traditional Bordeaux has many of the same fruit flavors as New World Cabernets and Cabernet-based blends, but with the volume turned down just a little. So, the fruit flavors are a bit fainter, and they're complicated by these kinds of dusty, musty aromas that remind me of a used bookstore. Classic Bordeaux will make you feel sophisticated in an old-school way, and start wondering if your next workplace should have a designated library!

Try **O'Shaughnessy Howell Mountain** and practice yelling at people on the phone. It's OK, no one's watching.

Getting fired can feel like a breakup. You keep going over and over in your mind what you could have done differently, and all those stages of grief that you're supposed to go through one by one—they tend to come all at once.

KNOW YOUR STYLES

Port

REGION: The Duoro Valley in northern Portugal

GRAPE: Touriga Nacional is the most prized Port grape, but it's a little hard to grow. Ninety-nine percent of Port is made from a blend of grapes, and there are more than 100 grape varieties grown in this region. The most widely planted is Touriga Franca, and the five most common Port grapes are: Tinta Barroca, Tinta Cão, Tinta Roriz (Tempranillo), Touriga Franca, and Touriga Nacional.

DEFINING FLAVORS/AROMAS: When it's young, ruby Port can smell, well, grapey. As it ages, it takes on aromas like violets, smoke, and expensive face powder. Tawny's longer barrel aging gives it more nutty, caramelized aromas and flavors.

PERFECT FOR: After-dinner sipping, preferably around a fire. And some kind of plaid robe, like an older English gentleman. Or something. Blue cheese like Stilton and other strong cheeses are classic matches for Port. Dark chocolate is great as well.

WHAT TO TRY: Port is one of those styles of wine where a lot of old British guys have OPINIONS, let me tell you. It's also a region where single-vintage wines are made only every few years, so every time the quality control body in Portugal declares a vintage, there are millions of articles about how good this latest vintage is going to be in 25 years, how Port just isn't the same as it was when I was a young lad at an all-boys school in England and we were all drinking it down in the headmaster's cellar wearing nothing but our ascots, etc., etc. There are also several different styles of Port, so here are a few to try that will give you a feel for the range so you can decide what you like:

Tawny Port: Graham's 10 Year Old Tawny (about $30) tastes like flan and orange blossoms. It's like dessert in a glass—no need for cake with this one!

Late Bottled Vintage: Quinta do Noval Late Bottled Vintage Port is around $25 and is a luscious combination of jammy fruit with a little bit of nutty aroma.

Vintage: Warre's Vintage Port 2011 goes for about $80, but it's worth it. Damn, she's an elegant lady. This is a wine that will age for decades, and it's full of beautiful aromas of violets, roses, ripe blackberries, and plums, with this lovely powdery quality that reminds me of old-fashioned, expensive perfume.

A **sour ale** is aggressively tart and funky—probably kind of how you feel right now. **Cuvée des Jacobins** from **Bockor** is a traditional Flemish sour red ale. Fermented from natural yeast and aged in oak barrels, it's got funky, spicy, earthy flavors in spades. For a domestic take on the sour style, **New Belgium La Folie** is made in a very similar way to Bockor's, but brings brighter, fresh fruit flavor to the party. There's a little malty sweetness, and lots of flavors of green apples and tart cherries. There's no time to wallow—let the assertive acidity in these beers spur you on to your next move. Just don't write any cover letters drunk, OK?

A room of one's own. Finally having your own, real office, complete with an assistant, is definitely something to celebrate. This is a "treat yo'self!" moment for sure, and what better way to treat yourself than chocolate and fancy dessert wine? Try an expensive **vintage Port**—the one from classic producer **Warre's** is elegant and full-bodied, and will age for decades—and the best dark chocolate you can afford. Close the door and put your feet up on your desk, Elaine Benes–style. Cigar optional.

Glossary

Or, what are all those nerds talking about?

Here's a small collection of useful wine and beer words to know. Some are technical terms, and some are more, should we say, nuanced (and sometimes kind of douche-y sounding, to be honest) terms that you will see sprinkled through reviews and descriptions. This is by no means a definitive glossary of wine and beer terms. For that get a book like *The Oxford Companion to Wine* by Jancis Robinson or *The Oxford Companion to Beer* by Garrett Oliver. This is more of a little cheat sheet for words you might see on labels or in reviews, or hear people throw around and wonder what the hell they're talking about. Now you'll know!

ABV refers to alcohol by volume, i.e., how boozy is what you're drinking? For wine, the range is generally 9–15 percent, and for beer, about 4–10 percent or more for some really hefty craft beers. Watch out for these, because a 12-ounce serving of one of these super-alcoholic beers can make it time for bed a little earlier than you might want! Alcohol is the main thing that drives how full or light bodied a wine or beer will be. Higher alcohol in wine and beer can also leave an impression of sweetness on your palate.

Aeration, i.e., the biggest scam in the wine industry since Robert Parker's 100-point scale turned everyone into myopic idiots, scanning shelf talkers for a number that made them feel better about their penis and/or station in life. There are a million gadgets and gizmos that will force a bit of air into your wine, usually by pouring it through something that agitates it. Aeration almost always changes how you perceive a wine, but you won't necessarily enjoy that change. If you want to mess around with aerating your wine, try a sip pre-aeration, and then try a little bit that's been put through the aerator. Then decide which way to drink it—you might be surprised at how often you prefer the wine as is!

Ales are beers produced with top-fermenting yeast (so-called because it stays at the top of the liquid as it does its work) that ferments at a warmer temperature. This produces fruitier, stronger flavors.

Balance is a murky, yet important concept in wine and beer. It means that all of the elements are harmonious, and no one sticks out more than another like a crazy long sleeve on only one side of a dress from some crazy Japanese designer.

Body. The full- or light-bodied quality of a wine or beer is closely related to, but not exactly the same as, how much alcohol it contains. Alcohol contributes more to the body (meaning texture) of wine and beer than the flavor. The more alcohol a beverage has, the thicker it will feel on your tongue. In wine, if the alcohol is out of balance or higher than usual for a given style, it can come across as a faint sweetness.

Bottle conditioning. When a beer undergoes bottle conditioning, it's experiencing a second fermentation in the bottle, much like Champagne. This gives the bubbles a livelier feel, and also often leaves sediment on the bottom of the bottle—those yeast cells have to go somewhere. Bottle-conditioned beers, just like Champagne, are good candidates for aging because adding live yeast to the bottle staves off oxidation.

Brett. When a wine is called "bretty," it has been infected by a secondary fermentation by the wild yeast brettanomyces. While there are several traditional beer styles where brettanomyces is the primary yeast used for fermentation, in wine the presence of brett is often, but not always, a flaw. Brett produces a few different aroma compounds—some, like the one that smells like a Band-Aid (seriously!) or a dentist's office, are not desirable at all. Others, like the ones that produce that kind of earthy, barnyard-y aroma, can add character to a wine in small quantities. Brett is a tenacious little bugger— if you have it in your beer or wine equipment and don't want it there, it is very, very difficult to eradicate.

Cooked. When a wine is cooked, it's been exposed to a great deal of heat. Heat-damaged wine is also referred to as "maderized," but most people don't drink Madeira anymore (although they should! See page 115), so that's not a very useful description. Heat-damaged wine will have aromas that remind you of prunes, or cooked fruit, and if you taste them, will taste very bright and fruity for about half a second, and then taste like nothing. Madeira is a style of wine that has been cooked on purpose, so smelling one just to get the aroma in your brain isn't a bad idea.

Dry and off-dry. When it comes to wine, dryness refers to the presence or absence of sugar. A wine is dry when there is no residual sugar, or so little, like 2–3 grams per liter, that it's below the threshold of human perception. Off-dry is kind of a broad category, and it refers to wines that fall in between dry and super-sweet dessert wines. That old bogeyman White Zinfandel is a perfect example of an off-dry wine.

Dry hopping refers to adding hops to the beer after the brewing process has been completed. Since the hops aren't boiled with the wort, they don't release their magical, bitterness-producing oils, so all you get is the hop flavor and aroma—it's a way to add a second layer of hop goodness to hoppy styles like IPAs and APAs.

Earthy refers to flavors and aromas that aren't fruit, flowers, or green herbs/vegetables. So, if a wine or beer's aromas or flavors remind you of a damp forest floor, or mushrooms, or a barnyard, those are earthy flavors and aromas. Sometimes a wine is downright funky, and can remind you of a dog in need of a bath, etc.,—some wine critics try to make this sound nicer by calling these concepts *animale*, as though putting a French accent on it makes it nicer. Ha!

Esters. Chemically, esters are the combination of an acid + an alcohol. This family of compounds creates many of the fruit flavors and aromas we experience in wine and beer.

Finish refers to whatever lingers in your mouth after you've swallowed. People could just say "aftertaste," but *finish* sounds nicer. In general, flavors that linger longer are signs of a complex, higher-quality wine.

Fortified. When a wine is fortified, it's been doused with some kind of neutral spirit, usually brandy. This acts as a preservative, but its other function is that it usually stops the fermentation in its tracks. This allows some of the sweetness to stay in the wine. Sweet and boozy—what's not to love? Most fortified wines hover between 18 and 20 percent ABV, while regular table wine is usually between 10 and 15 percent.

Gravity. Refers to the relative density of the product you're measuring compared to water. It's a term used in the fermentation process, mostly by brewers, although it can be applied to wine as well, and it's used as a way to talk about what the alcohol content will be in the finished product. There are a couple of different scales for gravity, or specific gravity, but the beer industry mostly uses the Plato scale, which is measured in degrees. Especially with European beers, you might see them referred to as a "10 degree beer" or a "12 degree beer," and these descriptions refer to their strength on the Plato scale.

Hops or *Humulus lupulus* are the female flowers of the hop plant. They provide a pleasing bitter bite to beer, as well as a whole host of aromas and flavors ranging from tangy citrus to pine resin. Hops also have antibacterial properties, so back in the day they kept beer from spoiling when we didn't have access to proper refrigeration.

IBU stands for International Bittering Units, and it's shorthand for describing just how bitter a beer is, with 0 being not bitter at all, and 100 being almost undrinkable. Theoretically the scale goes past 100, but there aren't many beers like this around.

Lacing is the white film that clings to the side of the glass as you drink your beer. The more lacing you get, the better and stronger the quality of foam there is in the beer. More stable foam means a better drinking experience. Why? Foam contributes to the creamy mouthfeel of a beer, and it also acts as a little protective hat, keeping the beer from going flat in your glass.

Lagers are beers that are produced with what is referred to as bottom-fermenting yeast (so-called because it ferments at the bottom of the tank). This type of yeast ferments at a cooler temperature, and produces crisp, clean flavors.

People talk about **"legs"** in wine, as though they were tea leaves. The legs, or tears, that wine leaves on the side of the glass just tell you how full-bodied the wine is. The thicker and slower moving the tears are, the fuller and richer the wine will feel on your palate. But soap residue and hard water can keep legs from forming, so not seeing them doesn't necessarily mean there's anything wrong with the wine you're drinking.

Malt. While hops provide the bitterness in beer, malt provides heft, sweetness, and roasted flavors. Just as you need sugar from grape juice to ferment into alcohol to make wine, you need sugar to ferment to make beer, and that's where malt comes in. Malt comes from barley—in order to have sugar to ferment, barley is sprouted and allowed to germinate, releasing the sugar within. This sprouting process is then halted, and the malt is then toasted to varying degrees of darkness. Lighter malts are used to make pilsners and pale ales, and darker malts are used to make porters and stouts.

Meritage (pronounced like "heritage") is an American term for a wine blend that is modeled after the classic blends made in France's Bordeaux region. It's a way of signifying on the label not just the grapes you've used (usually some combination of Cabernet Sauvignon, Merlot, Petit Verdot, Cabernet Franc, and/or Malbec), but that you are emulating the style of the great red blends of Bordeaux. White Meritage blends are made from Sauvignon Blanc, Sémillon, and/or Muscadelle.

Mouthfeel. While body refers to how much "stuff" like alcohol and dry extract is actually in the wine, mouthfeel refers to the overall impression a wine or beer creates when you drink it. So elements like tannin, the character of the bubbles if there are any, and overall texture also contribute to mouthfeel. A beer like Guinness, for example, will have a creamy mouthfeel because of the character of the bubbles and head—that nitrogen canister or tap creates bubbles that feel creamy rather than, say, the prickly bubbles you get in Champagne. A low-alcohol Riesling, on the other hand, has light body and high acidity that will make it feel like it's racing across your tongue.

Phenols are, broadly, a class of aromatic chemical compounds that are similar in structure to the chemical structure of alcohol, which is why the word also ends in -*ol*. They occur naturally in many of the plants used to make wine and beer, like grapes, wood barrels, and hops. More phenols, and the related family of compounds, polyphenols, are created by the fermentation process. A good example of a phenolic compound whose aroma might be familiar to you is that clove-y aroma in a traditionally made hefeweizen, which comes from 4-vinyl guaiacol.

Racy is a term you see in wine descriptions fairly frequently, and it usually refers to a wine that is so light, tart, and delicate, that it "races" across your tongue.

Smooth is one of those descriptions that means something different to every person who uses it. Basically, a wine or beer tastes smooth to you if whatever element you perceive as harsher than others is less apparent. If you are sensitive to tannin and a wine is lower in tannin or the tannin is balanced out by other elements, the wine is "smooth" to you.

Structure is another one of these vague-sounding terms that wine and beer industry people throw around often, and it can be tough to pin down exactly what the hell they're talking about. Think about the concept of structure like this: There are sort of "hard," astringent qualities in wine and beer, and "softer," immediately pleasing qualities. Soft qualities include things like alcohol (remember, this is what creates body and fullness in beer and wine), sweetness, and "ripe" fruit flavors like tropical fruit, ripe berries, jam, juicy apples, etc. A good wine or beer needs to have a balance between those soft qualities and the "harder," astringent qualities. These hard qualities provide a counterpoint to alcohol, sweetness, and fruit flavors. These elements are referred to as structure. These are qualities like acidity, tannin, and bitterness. Structural elements are the skeleton, and alcohol, fruit, and sweetness are the flesh, if you will. The more you try to pick out these qualities as you're tasting wine and beer, the more you'll come to appreciate the way they interact with each other, and how these interactions affect the overall impression of the beverage.

Tannins are a class of compounds found in the stems and seeds of grapes and in oak barrels, and their one true desire in life is to bind to proteins. They're what make you feel like you're chewing on felt and your tongue is drying out. If you've ever steeped tea for too long and gotten that weird, puckery feeling, you're experiencing tannin. Tannin, along with acidity, are the two main things that give wine its "structure."

Terroir is another hard-to-define concept. Basically, it's how the combination of soil and climate affects wine. So when people say they can taste terroir, that isn't literally true, it's just a shorter way of saying, "This wine tastes very typical of how the weather and soil in this region affect the grapes commonly grown here."

Online Resources

Building a relationship with a wineshop or beer store in your area is the best way to find beverages you'll love at good prices—the more the staff knows you, the better their recommendations will be. However, sometimes you might be looking for something specific (something you read about here, per chance?), and maybe "your" store can't get it for you. Or, maybe you live in an area where the stores stink, or there just aren't any. Don't fret, because in some states, you can order wine and beer online and have them shipped to you!

Every site you order from will have different shipping policies. The laws regarding shipping alcohol across state lines are kind of in flux right now in terms of how they're enforced and interpreted. My best advice is to call or email the store you're interested in working with and speak to or email with a person. For instance, it's also usually more economical to buy wine in cases. Some stores will hold your orders until you have enough to ship a full case to help you save on shipping, but you need to ask if they'll do that. Another thing to ask about is if they will hold off shipping your wine during weather that's too hot or too cold for shipping. Again, do your homework and communicate with the store. A store that will just blindly ship an order to southern Virginia during a heat wave in August is a store that isn't paying attention. If you're a true wine or beer hobbyist, then you're willing to devote time to finding great deals from possibly sketchy stores and instructing them on how to ship your orders. If you're a normal person who just wants nice wine or beer, you want to work with a store that takes care of you so you don't have to worry about it.

What I don't recommend is getting fixated on a particular wine or beer that you had on vacation or in a restaurant, Googling the name of it, and placing an order with the first store that pops up without checking them out first. You have no idea how the beverages in that store in Indianapolis have been stored or what kind of operation it is. A better option is to treat the store you buy online from like you would your neighborhood shop: Find one that does a good job and has a good reputation, place a small-stakes order or two, and see how it goes. Then, if you're looking for something specific, ask "your" store. If they don't carry it they might be able to special order it, find you something very similar, or help you find a reputable store that does carry what you're looking for. Wine and beer stores are more than just clearing houses—the good ones should be itching to do more for you, whether you've ordered online or in person.

Wine

Here are a few sites that have solid reputations.

winelibrary.com, based in New Jersey—they've got a little bit of everything, and are a big operation with reliable shipping. Their emails are a bit . . . aggressive, but you can always unsubscribe.

klwines.com, based in San Francisco, has a large selection somewhat slanted toward European imports, and nice detailed descriptions of most of their wines that are not just copies of reviews or descriptions from the winery, which is what you find on most wine stores' websites. Whenever you see descriptions that seem like they're written by an actual staff member, it's a good sign—it means that the staff is actually curating the selections and the store isn't just some anonymous clearing house.

chambersstwines.com, based in New York, is the ultimate hipster wine merchant. If you want to geek out and order some weird, oxidized white wine that no one's ever heard of, this is the place for you. The brick and mortar store is loads of fun to browse, too.

Beer

I really don't recommend shipping beer unless you're in dire straits. First, beer is heavy—mostly packaged in individual glass bottles—so it's going to cost a lot to ship. And while wine is definitely susceptible to damage from extreme heat or cold, beer is a little more delicate. Beer also generally has a shorter shelf life than wine, and there are more styles of beer that just taste better when they're consumed as close to the date they're brewed as possible. While many beers still don't have any kind of drink-by or freshness dating, more and more do, and when you're ordering online, you can't see that. That being said, here are two reliable resources for ordering beer online:

craftshack.com has a wide selection and a really easy-to-navigate website. I also trust the freshness of their products a little bit more because they have a whole section devoted to beer that's near its drink-by date, which means they're making an effort to sell the freshest beer possible.

The Beer Temple (**craftbeertemple.com**) in Chicago is a great place to shop if you're new to beer. There is all kinds of information about the brewing process, not to mention a couple hundred videos—some are interviews with brewers, others focus on specific topics, like blind-tasting a lineup of Belgian-style lambics. The Beer Temple is great because while there is lots of information for folks at every stage of their beer-appreciation journey, the selection is not dumbed down. They've got all kinds of quirky shit and the navigation menu for the online catalog was clearly put together by someone smart, who knows beer inside and out. You wouldn't think this would be a selling point, but a lot of sites I've looked at are really tough to navigate, and look like they were designed by a ten-year-old boy who's into monster truck rallies. Enough with the weird neon and dark backgrounds, kids, this isn't your MySpace page circa 2002.

Acknowledgments

There are a lot of people who helped make what started as some silly articles I wrote on a whim into an actual book, but here are just a few: Kate McKean and Sam O'Brien, for showing the ropes to a total newbie idiot like me and convincing me I could write a whole big, scary book; Doug House, for his support and the use of his lovely, peaceful lake house; Lynn and Pierce McMartin, for encouraging me to follow my dreams, no matter how weird and circuitous my route; Ricky—thank you for always making me coffee; my Sparkle Sisters, for being the best friends anyone could ever hope for; and Bob Flood—without you, I'd still be answering the phone and emptying bus pans. Thank you.

Index

A

Abbey ales, 50
Academy Awards, 156–157
accidental nudity, 133
acetaldehyde, 228
acidity, 204
Ad Libitum, 189–190
Aecht Schlenkerla Rauchbier Märzen, 136
aftertaste, 5
aging, signs of, 85–88
aging wine, 82
A Hopwork Orange, 172
Ah-So, 29
airport bars, 196–198
Albariño, 133
Alentejo region, 114
ales, 38, 40, 46–47, 49–50, 69–70, 88, 118–119,
    177–178, 182–183, 203, 229, 238, 243, 245
Allagash Confluence, 118
Allagash White, 171
Allegrini Ripasso Valpolicella, 98
all–Pinot Noir rosé Champagne, 167
altbier, 242
Amarone, 98
amber ales, 46–47, 204
American craft beers, 79, 86, 88, 99
American IPAs, 69–70
American pale ales, 38, 40
Anchor Brewing Christmas Ale, 143
Anchor Porter, 126
Anchor Steam Beer, 236–237
Anderson Valley Blood Orange Gose, 125
Anderson Valley Brewing Company Boont
    Amber Ale, 47
antidiuretic hormone (ADH), 228
anti-inflammatory diet, 121
Anton Bauer, 166
appearance, 3
apps, 6
Arnaud de Villeneuve, 72
Arneis, 16
aromas, 4, 27, 28, 234
aromatized wines, 40–41
Asian beers, 195
Atlas Brew Works Rowdy Rye, 110–111
Auslese, 18
Austrian rosé, 166

Austrian wine labels, 19–20
awards shows, 156–159
Ayinger Bräu-Weisse, 45

B

baby furniture, 225
baby showers, 218–223
bachelorette parties, 208
back-to-school party, 142
Banyuls, 225–226, 227
Barbaresco, 15
Barbecue Fritos, 136
Barbera, 16
Barolo, 15, 58, 59
Barolo Chinato, 32, 33
Bartholomew Broadbent, 115
Basel Cellars Estate Claret, 94
baths, 68–69
Battlestar Galactica, 159–160
beach vacations, 198–199
Beaujolais, 94, 95, 116–117, 154
beauty rituals, 72–74
Beckman, 220
beef, 105, 200–201
beer
    buying, 6–9, 143, 254–255
    chilling, 199
    freshness of, 239–240
    glasses, 24–26
    tasting, 2–6
Beerenauslese, 18
Belgian ales, 49–51, 118, 177–178
Belgian Chalice, 25
Bellavista, 49
Bell's Amber Ale, 47
Bell's Consecrator Doppelbock, 223
Bell's Oberon, 210
Bell's Special Double Cream Stout, 123
Bell's Winter White Ale, 112
Berliner Weisse, 163
beverage directors, 9
binge-watching, 159–163
birthdays, 78–84
Black IPA, 133–134
Black Velvet, 155–156
blanc de blancs, 14, 81
blanc de noirs, 14

blonde ales, 118
Blue Mountain Brewery, 92, 172, 192
Boal, 116
boating, 190–191
Bodegas Carrau, 100
Bonnaroo, 171
Boozy Peach, 157
Bordeaux, 11–12, 82, 107–110, 178
boss, 145–146, 239
Boulevard Saison-Brett, 181
Bourgogne, 54
boxed wine, 196–197
Brachetto d'Acqui, 202
Brandborg, 123
Brauerei Heller-Trum, 136
Brave New World, 181
breakups, 32–35
brettanomyces, 180–181, 183
Broadbent, 220, 221
Broc Cellars Carbonic Carignan, 178
Brooklyn Brewery Black Chocolate Stout, 40
Brooklyn Lager, 88
Brouilly, 94
Brouwerij Boon Geuze Mariage Parfait, 68
Brouwerij Huyghe Delirium Noël, 143
Brovia, 59
brown ales, 203, 204
brunch, 67–68, 141
Bründlmayer Sekt Brut Rosé, 33–34
Bründlmayer Sekt Extra Brut, 202
Brunello di Montalcino, 105
Brut Nature/Brut Zero/Brut Sauvage, 15, 169
Buffy the Vampire Slayer, 160–161
Bugey-Cerdon, 183, 220–222
Burgundy, 12–13, 34, 53–56, 235–236
buttery Chardonnay, 87

C

Cabernet blends, 93–94, 108–109
Cabernet Sauvignon, 108–109, 184, 215, 225, 243
Cahors, 169–170
Calder Wine Company Charbono, 178
California Cabernet, 184
camping, 189–190
Cantine del Taburno, 44
Cappelletti, 41
career milestones, 241–245
Carema, 52
Carignan, 74, 178, 193
Cariñena, 17
Carod, 43
Casabianca, 141
Cascadian Dark Ale, 133–134

Castello dei Rampolla, 135
Catena, 201, 243
Cava, 42, 110, 111, 134, 156
cellaring, 29
Chablis, 53, 204, 213
Chamisal, 48
Champagne, 32–33, 42, 48–49, 78, 80–81,
        106–107, 110, 134–135, 205
Champagne glasses, 23
Champagne labels, 13–15
Champteloup, 95
Chardonnay, 16, 48, 85–86, 87, 116, 209, 213, 214
Charleston Sercial, 115
Château Calon-Ségur, 243
Château Damase Bordeaux, Supérieur, 178
Château de Beaucastel, 241
Château de Ségriès, 146–147
Château Doisy Daëne, 84
Château d'Yquem, 84
Château Fonbadet, 109
Château Guiraud, 84
Château la Caminade, 170
Château Larose-Trintaudon Haut-Médoc Cru
        Bourgeois, 109
Châteauneuf-du-Pape, 240–241
Château Peyrassol Côtes de Provence Rosé, 172
Château Puech Haut, 194
Château Recougne Bordeaux Supérieur, 109
Château Thivin, 94
Chenin Blanc, 123–124, 210–211, 235
Chianti, 15–16, 135
childhood fantasies, 97–101
Chimay, 49
Chipotle Ale, 99
chocolate, 33, 225–226, 227
chocolate stouts, 40
Chrysalis Vineyards, 125
Ciacci, 105
Cinco de Mayo, 125–126
Clairette de Die, 43
classic folk music, 167–168
class reunions, 89–92
Cleto Chiarli e Figli Lambrusco di Sorbara
        Vecchia Modena Premium, 90
Clos, 15
Clos La Coutale, 170
Cloudy Bay, 160
Clua, 224
clubbing, 64
Coachella, 172–173
Cocchi, 33
Cocchi Vermouth di Torino, 41
coffee-inflected stout, 225

coffee shop barista, 57, 232–233
college graduation, 93–97
color, 3
Conde Villar, 220, 221
cooking for kids, 226–227
corks, 28
corkscrews, 27, 29
cork taint, 60
Costières de Nîmes, 193
Coteaux du Layon, 235
Country Music Awards, 157
coworkers, 58–59, 145–146, 239–240
craft brews, 79, 86, 88, 99, 127, 238
Craigslist, 235–236
Crémant de Bourgogne, 143
Crianza, 17
Crispin, 142
Crivelli, 66, 176–177
crushes, 57–61
cultured yeast, 182
cuvée, 14
Cuvée des Jacobins, 245

D

Damilano, 33
Dashe Cellars, 75, 113
dating, online, 36–42
decanters, 26–27
dehydration, 228
Deschutes Brewery Fresh Squeezed IPA, 70, 92
Deschutes Brewery Hop Trip, 119
diacetyl, 87
Diesel, 92
dieting, 121–124
Di Lenardo Pinot Grigio, 97
dinner parties, 145–148
dinner with boss, 145–146, 239
Dogfish Head 60 Minute IPA, 79
Dogfish Head Palo Santo Marron, 233
Dolcetto, 16, 35
Domaine de la Chapelle des Bois, 117
Domaine Cazes, 185
Domaine de la Fruitière, 116
Domaine de Montbourgeau l'Étoile Vin Jaune, 185
Domaine des Baumard, 235
Domaine des Malandes Chablis, 53
Domaine Jean-Michel et Laurent Pillot Mercurey, 101
Domaine Jérôme Chézeaux, 53
Domaine Labbé Abymes, 35
Domaine La Tour Vieille, 227

Domaine Louis Michel & Fils, 53
Domaine Sigalas, 106
Domaine Vacheron Rouge, 100
Domaine Weinbach, 72, 155
Domaine Weinbach Cuvée Theo, 100
doppelbock, 223
dosage, 15
double IPAs, 238
Drake's 1500, 40
dry hopping, 39
dubbels, 177–178

E

The Economist, 178
EDM shows, 172
Edmund Fitzgerald Porter, 127
Efestē Final Final, 93
E. Guigal Condrieu, 239
Eiswein, 18–19
Elk Cove, 74
English ales, 88
entertaining, 129–149, 240–241
Eric Bordelet, 142
Eric Texier Rouletabulle, 173
estrogen overload, 130–131
Etichetta Bianca, 52
Eurovision Awards, 158
Evesham Wood, 101
exes, 43–44, 51–52, 56
Extra Special Bitter (ESB), 56

F

Falanghina, 44
family occasions, 46–51
family reunions, 46
farmers' markets, 200–203
Faugères Montfalette, 135–136
fermentation, 87, 182–183
Ferrando, 52
Fiano, 36, 37
Finca Valldosera, 111
finish, 5
Fiore, 135
firings, 243, 245
first job, 241
five-year reunions, 89–90
Flying Dog Double Dog, 238
folk music, 167–168
Fonseca 20 Year Old Tawny, 118
food pairings, 200–205
fortified wines, 120–121, 139
Founders All-Day IPA, 229
Founders Breakfast Stout, 225

4-Hour Body diet, 123
40-year reunions, 91
Fowles, 153
France, wine regions of, 10–13
Franciacorta, 49
Francis Ford Coppola Winery Sofia Mini
    Champagnes, 214
French 75, 157
French wine labels, 10–13
Friendsgiving, 114
fruit aromas, 4
fruit-based beers, 171–172
Füchschen Alt, 242
Fuller's, 56

G

game day, 146–147
Garnacha, 17, 167–168
Gastronomica, 178
G. D. Vajra, 239
German wine labels, 18–19
Gewürztraminer, 99–100, 123
gift giving, 104–111
Ginger Fizz, 158
girls' nights, 63–68
Giuggiolo, 132
glassware, 3, 20–26
gose, 124–125
graduations, 93–97
Graham's 10 Year Old Tawny, 118, 244
Grammys, 157–158
Grand Cru, 13–14
Gran Reserva, 17
The Grapes of Wrath, 184–185
gray hair, 85
Great Divide Fresh Hop, 119
Greco di Tufo, 37
greens, 202
Grenache, 137, 191
Greywacke, 194
Grignolino, 65–66, 113–114
grisette, 148
Grosses Gewächs, 19
Grüner Veltliner, 20, 179–180, 191, 202
Guy Larmandier Blanc de Blancs, 81

H

Hacienda López de Haro, 160
Halloween, 116–121
hangovers, 228–229
happy hour, 239–240
hard ciders, 142
heat damage, 60

Hedges House of Independent Producers Merlot,
    43–44
hefeweizen, 45–46
high-school reconnections, 58, 61
hiking, 191
Hitachino Nest White Ale, 171
Hoegaarden, 171, 210
holiday beers, 143
holiday-card party, 143
holiday parties, 237
holidays, 103–127
Honig, 220, 243
hops, 39, 118–119
hostess, 236–237
house parties, 66–67
Huber, 69

I

IKEA, 137
Il Falchetto, 48, 202–203
India Pale Ales (IPAs), 69–70, 229, 238
indie rock, 166
inflammation, 228
International Bittering Units (IBUs), 39
Italian whites, 36, 37, 38
Italian wine labels, 15–16

J

Jacquère, 35
Jaillance, 43
jazz festivals, 170–171
Jean-Marc Lafont Domaine de Bel Air Brouilly,
    95
Jean-Marc Lafont Domaine de Bel Air
    Chiroubles, 117
Jean-Paul Brun, 94, 154
Jean Vesselle Cuvée Friandise, 167
J. Mourat, 124
Joe Mama's Milk, 225
Joh. Jos. Prüm, 85
Joseph Carr, 43
junk food, 134–136
Jura region, 185

K

Kabinett, 18, 85, 160
kayaking, 191
Keegan Ales, 225
Kellerei Kaltern, 61, 71, 97, 131
Keplinger Kingpin Rows, 226
Kir Royales, 143
Kistler, 214
Klemens Weber, 113, 154

Knauss Wurttemberg Riesling Sekt Zero, 154
kölsch, 192, 204
Krug Grande Cuvée, 107

L

labels, wine, 10–20
lactic acid, 87
Ladies Who Shoot Their Lunch, 153
La Femme Nikita, 160
lagers, 86, 88, 182–183, 204
La Grande Dame, 14
La Grange Tiphaine, 189–190
Lagrein, 130–131
La Grive Bleue, 101
lambic, 67–68
Lambrusco, 89–90
La Mondianese, 114
Langhe Rosso PN Q497, 239
Langlois Père et Fils, 143
La Spinetta, 35
law degree, 93–94
Left Bank Bordeaux, 108
Leipziger Gose, 125
Leo Hillinger Secco, 33, 167
Le Pigeoulet en Provence, 194
Les Frères Couillaud Le Souchais, 116
Lindemans, 67–68
Locked Up Abroad, 162
Long Trail Summer Ale, 92, 229
Louis/Dressner Selections, 154
Lovisolo, 34
Lustau, 138
Luther, 162–163

M

Made by G, 57
Madeira, 114–116, 120
magazines, 176–180
Maine Beer Company Mean Old Tom, 127
Maison P-U-R La Bulle, 57–58
Malbec, 169–170, 200–201
Malmsey, 116
Mango Madness, 158–159
Manincor, 61, 71
Manincor Kalteresee Keil Schiava, 148
Martínez Lacuesta, 224
Mas d'Alezon, 135–136
Match.com, 41–42
M. Chapoutier, 227
Merlot, 43–44, 215
méthode ancestrale, 221–222
Michelada, 126
milestones, 77–84, 93–97, 241–245

mimosas, 190
mocktails, 218
Mollydooker The Boxer, 153
Montalcino, 15
Montepulciano, 15
Moscato d'Asti, 34, 35
Mourvèdre, 135
movie night, 152–156
moving, 133–134, 141
Muga, 224–225
Muga Selección Especial, 226–227
mulled wine, 131
Müller-Thurgau, 71
Muri-Gries, 71, 131
Murphy's Irish Stout, 127
Muscadet, 213
Muscat, 71–72
Musella Amarone della Valpolicella, 98
music, 165–173
music festivals, 170–173

N

Nals Margreid Punggl, 97
Napa Cabernet, 242–243
Nebbiolo, 15, 34, 59, 198
New Belgium Abbey, 177
New Belgium Fat Tire, 46
New Belgium La Folie, 245
new home, 136–141
new parents, 223–229
New Year's resolution diet, 121–124
nights out, 64, 227–229
NM, 15
Nonick Imperial Pint, 25
North American grapes, 125
Northern Hemisphere Harvest Wet Hop, 119
notetaking, 5–6
novels, 180–185
Nylon, 178–180

O

oak, 234–235
Oddero Barolo Normale, 59
office parties, 237
OkCupid, 36, 38
Olivier Lemasson, 173
one-night stands, 42–46
online dating, 36–42
online shopping, 71
orange wine, 181, 184
Orval, 51
Oscars, 156–157
Osél Ruchè, 176

O'Shaughnessy Howell Mountain, 243
oxidation, 60, 162

P

Palacio de Bornos, 199
Paleo diet, 123
parents·
    gifts for, 105
    new, 223–229
    of significant other, 47–49
    sleeping over at, 49, 51
Patelin de Tablas Rouge, 191
Patrick Bottex, 222
Paul D., 191
Pecchenino Dogliani San Luigi, 35
Pecorino, 36, 37
Penner-Ash, 239
Peroni, 90
pétillant naturel, 172–173, 183
Ph.D.s, 94
Piedmont region, 15–16
Pierre Gimonnet "Special Club de Collection,"
    106–107
Pierre Péters Cuvée Spéciale Les Chétillons,
    81
pilsner, 140, 141, 167
Pilsner glasses, 25
Pinot Bianco, 61
Pinot Grigio, 91, 96–97, 209
Pinot Gris, 73–74, 96
Pinot Noir, 18, 83, 100, 101, 176–177, 198, 204,
    209, 239
plastic glasses, 24
Ponzi, 74
Pop-Tarts, 135
Port, 118, 120, 135, 244, 245
Porter Creek, 193
porters, 126, 127
Portugal, 114
potato chips, 134–135
Pow Blop Wizz, 173
Prà Amarone della Valpolicella, 98
Premier (1ᵉʳ) Cru, 13–14
presentations, 239
Presidents Day, 125
pretzels, 135–136
Pride and Prejudice, 185
Prince in His Caves, 184
Priorat, 17, 145–146, 147
promotions, 242
proposals, 212–214
Prosecco, 42, 141, 238
Provence, 194

Puerto Fino, 138
pumpkin ales, 112
punk music, 166–167

Q

quadrupels, 177–178

R

Radler, 92
Rare Wine Company, 115
Rauchbier, 136
raw food diet, 123–124
reading, 175–185
reality TV, 64–65
Real Simple, 176–177
Recuerdo, 73
red Burgundy, 12–13, 53–56
reduction, 28, 162
Relic Ritual, 226
remodeling, 138
Renardat-Fache, 222
Reserva, 17
restaurants
    wine lists, 8–9
    wine tasting at, 60
retirement, 83
Ribera del Duero, 17
Ridge, 74, 75
Riesling, 18–20, 68–69, 70–71, 85, 113, 154–155,
    160–161, 209
Right Bank Bordeaux, 108, 178
Rioja, 16–17, 160, 161
Rita, 163
Rivesaltes, 184–185
R. López de Heredia, 160
RM, 14–15
road trips, 196
roasted vegetables, 203
Robert Stemmler, 83
Rogue, 99
roommates, 130–134
Rosado, 224–225
rosé, 95, 146–147, 166, 172, 215, 224–225
rosé spritzer, 58–59
rosé Vinho Verde, 218–220, 221
Rosso di Montalcino, 105
Rovero, 66
Rozès, 135
ruby Port, 244
Ruchè, 176–177
Russian River Brewing Company Pliny the
    Elder, 238
rye-based beer, 110–111

S

saison, 208, 209
Samuel Adams Boston Lager, 79
Samuel Smith Nut Brown Ale, 88, 203
Samuel Smith Oatmeal Stout, 123
Sancerre, 100, 213
Sangiovese, 15, 105, 132
Santa Barbara, 64
Sauternes, 83–84
Sauvignon Blanc, 91, 121, 159–160, 182, 184, 194,
    195, 197–198, 209, 213, 220
Schiava, 148
Schlafly ESB, 56
Schlafly Oak Aged Barleywine, 233
Schloss Gobelsburg, 69, 180
Scholium Project, 184
screwcaps, 28
seasonal beers, 112–113
secret single behavior, 68–71
sediment, 26–27
sekt, 19
Sercial, 116
service vacations, 194
session ales, 209, 229
70th birthday, 83–84
shandies, 91, 92
Sherry, 120, 138, 139, 162
Shiraz, 152–153
Siduri, 83
Sierra Nevada, 40, 119
Singha, 195
slide shows, 193–194
Sly Fox Grisette, 148
Smaragd, 20
Smuttynose Hayseed, 148
snow days, 131
snowstorms, 134–136
social media stalking, 51–56
Sol'Acantalys, 147
sommeliers, 9
sour ales, 243, 245
Southern Tier Iniquity, 134
Southern Tier 2xRye, 110
Spanish rosé, 224–225
Spanish wine labels, 16–17
sparkling cocktails, 141, 156–159
sparkling Gamay, 57–58
sparkling rosé, 33–34
sparkling wine, 48–49, 110, 141, 142, 149, 154,
    169, 172–173, 183, 202, 210–212, 237
sparkling wineglasses, 23
Spätburgunder, 18
Spaten Optimator, 223

Spätlese, 18
spicy foods, 204
Spiegelau IPA glass, 26
spontaneous yeast, 182
Steininger Sekt, 202
Stelvin closures, 28
stemless wineglasses, 24
Stillwater Artisanal, 99
Stillwater Classique, 88
Stone Go To IPA, 229
Stone Smoked Porter, 136
Stony Hill Chardonnay, 85–86
stores, 6–8
Storybook Mountain, 75
stouts, 123, 126, 127, 225
strawberries, 202–203
summer, 187–205
summer trips, 196–199
summertime reds, 189–190
Sunday dinner, 132
Sweet and Spicy Ginger Sparkler, 218, 219
swirling, 3
Syrah, 152–153, 162–163, 226–227

T

Tablas Creek, 191
Tannat, 100
tannins, 4–5, 26, 189, 204–205, 234, 252
tasting, 2–6
Tavel, 146–147
tawny Port, 118, 244
team-building exercises, 237–238
Tegernseerhof, 166
temp jobs, 233, 235
ten-year reunions, 90
Terredora di Paolo, 44
Tête de cuvée, 14
Thanksgiving, 111–116
theme parks, 198
theme parties, 141–144
3 Sheeps Brewing Roll Out the Barrel, 118
30th birthday, 79, 82–83
Tinder, 38
Tinto de Verano, 67
toasts, 210
To Kill a Mockingbird, 184
Toro, 17
Torrontés, 73
toxins, 228
Trappist ales, 49, 50
tripels, 177–178
Trocken, 19
Trockenbeerenauslese, 18

Tröegs, 45
Tröegs Nugget Nectar, 46
Trumer Pils, 167
tubing, 192
Tulip glasses, 25
Tuscany, 15
TV watching, 64–65, 151–163
20-year reunions, 91
21st Amendment Brewery Back in Black, 134
21st Amendment Brewery Hell or High
     Watermelon, 172
21st birthday, 78
27th birthday, 78–79

U

Uinta Punk'n Harvest Pumpkin Ale, 112
Ulysses, 180–181

V

Vacuum Readymade, 99
Vajra Langhe Nebbiolo, 198
Valdicava, 105
Valentine's Day, 126
Valpolicella Ripasso, 98
varicose veins, 88
Verdejo, 198–199
Verdelho, 116
Verdicchio, 36, 37, 64
vermouth, 73, 120
vernal equinox, 124–125
Victory Golden Monkey, 177–178
Victory Helles Lager, 86
Victory Kirsch Gose, 125
Victory Prima Pils, 167
Vietti, 35, 59
Vigneto Saetti Lambrusco Salamino di Santa
     Croce, 90
Villa Jolanda, 141
Viña Taboexa, 133
Vincent Girardin, 236
Vin Doux Naturel, 120
Vinho Verde, 218–220, 221
Vin Rouge, 189
vintage, 201
Viognier, 239
Vogue, 177–178
Vouvray, 210–212

W

Wachau, 20
waiter's key, 27
Warre's Vintage Port, 245
weather emergencies, 134–136

weddings, 207–215
wedding-themed party, 143
Weil diet, 121
Westmalle, 177
wet-hopped ales, 118–119
white Beaujolais, 154
white Burgundy, 34, 235–236
white Port, 135
white sangria, 64–65
white wine spritzer, 117, 210
White Zinfandel, 75, 215
wild yeast beers, 180–181, 183
wine
    aging, 82
    buying, 6–9, 144, 254
    chilling, 199
    food pairings, 200–205
    glasses, 3, 20–24
    mixed cases of, 241
    preservation, 29
    through the decades, 215
wine coolers, 153
wine fridge, 140
wine labels, 10–20
wine regions, 10–20, 54–55, 108–109
wine tasting, 2–6
witbier, 171
wood-aged ales, 233
wood aging, 234–235
work, 231–245
work crush, 58–59
work functions, 237–241

X

Xavier Clua, 137

Y

yeast, 182–183
Yorkshire Stingo, 88
Young's Double Chocolate Stout, 40
Yuengling, 236–237

Z

Zin Gris, 75
Zind-Humbrecht, 99–100
Zinfandel, 74–75, 113